RADICAL PHILOSOPHY

2.19
Series 2 / Summer 2025

Law's search for biological truth
Flora Renz 3

Reproductive subsumption
Elena Baglioni 9

Phenomenology of necessary illusion
Robert Lucas Scott 25

On the bourgeois concept of real abstraction
F.T.C. Manning 42

Smash the feminist family
An interview with Sophie Lewis 54

Breaking out of the circle
Francesco Anselmetti 66

REVIEWS

Christoph Schuringa, *A Social History of Analytic Philosophy*
Adam Knowles 79

Victoria Browne, *Pregnancy Without Birth: A Feminist Philosophy of Miscarriage*
Sophie A. Jones 84

Walter Benjamin, *On Goethe*
Christopher Law 87

Robert Linhart, *The Sugar and The Hunger*
Jacob Seagrave 90

Michael Hardt, *The Subversive Seventies*
Trey Taylor 94

David Gordon Scott, ed., *Abolitionist Voices*
David Gordon Scott and Emma Bell, eds., *Envisioning Abolition*
Isabella Gregory 98

Andrés Saenz de Sicilia, *Subsumption in Kant, Hegel and Marx*
Christopher Geary 101

Melyana Kay Lamb, *Philosophical History of Police Power*
Oscar Talbot 104

Mohammad Reza Naderi, *Badiou, Infinity, and Subjectivity*
Joe Stapleton 108

Paulin Jidenu Hountondji, 1942–2024
Zeyad el Nabolsy 111

Editorial collective
Brenna Bhandar
Victoria Browne
Maria Chehonadskih
David Cunningham
Isabell Dahms
Marie Louise Krogh
Lucie Mercier
Robert Nichols
Hannah Proctor
Rahul Rao
Martina Tazzioli
Chris Wilbert

Engineers

CC BY-NC-ND
RP, Summer 2025

ISSN 0300-211X
ISBN 978-1-914099-08-3

Law's search for biological truth
For Women Scotland and the UK Supreme Court
Flora Renz

On 16 April 2025, the UK Supreme Court handed down its judgment in the *For Women Scotland* case (hereafter FWS),[1] a decision that has attracted widespread political and media attention as it sets out to legally define what it means to be a woman for the purposes of the *Equality Act 2010*. To make sense of the FWS decision, it is worth briefly considering the legal background and terrain in which it is situated.

The case concerns three specific pieces of law, namely the *Gender Recognition Act 2004*, the *Equality Act 2010*, and the *Gender Representation on Public Boards (Scotland) Act 2018*. The *Gender Recognition Act 2004* (GRA 2004) was introduced in response to a finding against the UK at the European Court of Human Rights.[2] The *GRA 2004* allows a person to change their legal sex marker on their birth certificate as long as they are over 18, have two medical reports attesting to a diagnosis of 'gender dysphoria', have lived in their 'new' gender for two years prior to applying and swear to remain in that gender for the rest of their life.[3] Meanwhile, the *Equality Act 2010 (EA 2010)* is the main piece of anti-discrimination law in this country (although it does not apply in Northern Ireland) and unified the previous disparate legal frameworks in this area. It covers discrimination and harassment in employment and service provision contexts for the protected characteristics of age, disability, gender reassignment, marriage/civil partnership, pregnancy/maternity, race, religion/belief, sex and sexual orientation. Notably, the framing of 'gender reassignment' is much broader than the *GRA 2004* and covers anyone who is proposing to undergo, is undergoing or has undergone any changes to their gender, including non-medical measures like a change of name.[4] As such it protects both those who have changed their legal sex and those who have not; and lower-tier Tribunals have also included non-binary and gender-fluid people within this.[5]

Importantly for the purpose of the FWS decision, the *EA 2010* does not prevent the creation or maintaining of single-sex spaces or services, which of course *de facto* discriminate as they exclude the 'opposite' sex and therefore would in principle amount to sex discrimination under s.11 of the *EA 2010*. S.27 of the *EA 2010* sets out that the creation of single-sex spaces is permissible where such 'limited provision is a proportionate means of achieving a legitimate aim.' Such spaces can also exclude anyone with the protected characteristic of gender reassignment, i.e. all trans and non-binary people, again, where this is deemed to be a proportionate means of achieving a legitimate aim.[6] However, this provision has been interpreted to only apply to those spaces that cannot effectively run otherwise, with domestic violence services being the classic example of this.[7] Finally, the *Gender Representation on Public Boards (Scotland) Act 2018* only applies to Scotland and is intended to ensure that at least 50% of members of a public board are women and essentially allows for a very limited form of positive discrimination to achieve this outcome. From its inception, the *Public Boards Act 2018* included trans women within its definition of women, by referring to the protected characteristic of gender reassignment in the *EA 2010*.

The group For Women Scotland Ltd sought to challenge this trans inclusive approach through an initial judicial review. The Inner House of the Court of Session agreed with their argument and held that the Scottish government needed to modify the definition of 'woman' in the *Public Boards Act 2018* as the current approach was outside their legislative competence subject to the authority of the Westminster government.[8] The Scottish government consequently produced guidance in 2022 stating that the amended definition of 'woman' in the *Public Boards Act 2018* did not include trans women unless they had gone through the *GRA 2004* to amend their birth certificate, as at this point they were simply women for almost all legal purposes, including for the definition of 'sex' in the *EA 2010*.

This led to a second judicial review by For Women Scotland Ltd who argued that the *EA 2010* definition of 'sex' was not affected by someone going through the *GRA 2004* process. They further argued that the *GRA 2004* had a very narrow purpose, including allowing trans people to marry, and had been largely superseded by subsequent legislation, including the *EA 2010*. This petition was dismissed by Lady Haldane in the Outer House in December 2022.[9] Lady Haldane held that the *GRA 2004* was clear in changing a person's sex for all purposes with a few exceptions listed specifically, e.g. peerages and trusts, and that this therefore was in line with the amended *Public Boards Act 2018* definition of who counts as a woman.[10] Lady Haldane's decision was confirmed by the Inner House on appeal.[11] For Women Scotland Ltd then appealed this to the Supreme Court where a panel of five judges found unanimously in their favour.

The judgment by Lord Hodge, Lady Rose and Lady Simler, with Lord Reed and Lord Lloyd-Jones concurring, held that the definition of 'woman' and 'man' in all sections of the *EA 2010* is intended to refer to 'biological sex'.[12] Further, they held that this is not affected by the *GRA 2004* and that it is therefore immaterial if a person has changed their legal sex, as for the purpose of the *EA 2010* provision on the protected characteristic of 'sex' they remain the sex they were assigned at birth. The judgment argues that any other interpretation would lead to incoherence across different sections of the *EA 2010*, including the sections on 'sex', 'pregnancy'[13] and 'sexual orientation' and that therefore the Inner House decision was incorrect in saying that the words 'woman' and 'man' can have variable meanings across different parts of the *EA 2010*. Therefore, the *Public Boards Act 2018* should only cover those who were assigned female at birth within its use of 'woman'.

The judgment, however, goes further than just determining the specific issue of the *Public Boards Act 2018*, and additionally notes that while this interpretation of 'sex' does not *require* single-sex spaces to exclude trans people whose sex assigned at birth does not match that of the group the spaces are intended for, failing to do so may amount to indirect discrimination on the grounds of sex as it may lead to people self-excluding from these spaces. Beyond that it may even be possible for service providers to also exclude trans people who are of the 'right' sex for that group if their appearance has been sufficiently changed so that they may be perceived as the 'opposite sex'.[14] Both of these arguments have been reiterated and to some extent expanded by the new draft guidance on the *EA 2010* produced by the Equality and Human Rights Commission, currently under consultation.[15] The judgment has already attracted a high volume of attention for a number of reasons and in what follows I turn to three of these in detail, specifically the question of trans inclusion, the appeal to a presumed biological 'truth' about sex, and finally the attempt to define who legally is a lesbian.

Whither trans inclusion?

The first and perhaps most well-discussed issue raised by the judgment is its relationship to principles of non-discrimination, and wider principles of trans inclusion, established over the last two decades. From a legal perspective, the relevance of legal sex or gender has been gradually decreasing over this time period, partially because legislation is now increasingly written in gender-neutral terms rather than using the masculine default of old,[16] but also because there are now far fewer instances where a person's legal sex still matters in law.[17] At the same time, more and more institutions are recognising genders beyond the female/male binary in a range of contexts, while legally the presumption had become that trans people should generally be included in spaces that match their gender whether changed through the *GRA 2004* or self-certified, with only some narrow exceptions in areas like sports and prisons that had always been exempted from the workings of the *GRA 2004* and spaces explicitly covered by the *EA 2010* definition of single-sex spaces. The FWS case in many ways reverses this trend, by saying that while trans exclusion is not mandatory, it may well be legally necessary in most single-sex contexts.

This seems to limit the purpose of the non-discrimination provision regarding 'gender reassignment' very sharply, by reducing its application primarily to not treating someone as the sex they were assigned at birth precisely because they are trans – for instance, excluding a trans man from a women's domestic violence service because he is no longer recognised as a woman – and to obvious acts of harassment against trans people such as the use of slurs in the workplace. It also raises the question of what the purpose of the *GRA 2004* is if its effects can be disregarded in almost all contexts. As others have pointed out, this will likely lead to a new case at the European Court of Human Rights regarding the UK's potential non-compliance with the European Convention on Human Rights in the fairly immediate future.[18]

Beyond these precise legal questions, there is a real risk that the FWS decision will be seen by some as *carte blanche* to exclude trans people from public life, particularly when it is seen as possible to legitimately exclude this group from both male *and* female spaces, including bathrooms. The suggestion by the chair of the Equality and Human Rights Commission, Baroness Kishwer Falkner, that trans people should instead request 'third spaces' clearly highlights this problem.[19] Given that disabled people (who are legally entitled to accessible bathrooms under the *EA 2010*) still find themselves routinely without adequate bathroom provision, it seems very plainly unworkable that a group who has no such legal entitlement should rely on this as a solution to being excluded from existing public spaces. This is especially non-feasible in a time of austerity when most public services, including the NHS, face severe financial constraints that make it utterly unlikely that they would have the resources to offer third spaces, such as separate hospital wards for trans people. It also opens the door to potentially malicious litigation against any single-sex spaces potentially deemed not trans exclusionary enough, with domestic and sexual violence services being perhaps most at risk given that they are predominantly single-sex but tend to be trans inclusive.

'True' sex

Beyond these immediate practical issues, the judgment also has a troubling relationship to claims of biological truth. Overall, the judgment states that it interprets sex to mean biological sex as determined at birth, compared to the 'certificated sex' of trans people who have applied to change their birth certificate under the *GRA 2004*.[20] It further argues that using this approach will create greater consistency in law by continuously distinguishing between trans and cis people regardless of whether someone has changed their birth certificate. This of course dramatically overstates how straightforward biological sex is, including the fact that it is made up of many different characteristics, such as hormone levels as well as primary and secondary sexual characteristics, not all of which are easily observable. It also ignores the existence of intersex people who may not have, for example, neatly aligned secondary sexual characteristics, hormone levels and karyotype. What the court is actually referring to here by 'biological sex' is really the sex that was recorded at someone's birth on their birth certificate and which for most, but not all, people at that point will generally align with the factors we associate with sex. Why changes through medical procedures that are loosely grouped under the umbrella of 'gender affirmation' are somehow not biological, despite affecting biological factors like primary and secondary sexual characteristics and hormone levels, is never addressed in the judgment. As such, it seems the law presumes that the idea of biology as recorded on an initial birth certificate offers some greater claim to biological truth than anything else, including how a person is perceived. It is notable here that the British Medical Association promptly passed a motion describing the judgment as 'scientifically illiterate' precisely because of its limited reading of the state of biological and scientific knowledge on sex and gender.[21]

The Supreme Court rightly acknowledges the fact that in daily life we rarely ask for someone's birth certificate before assuming their sex or gender, but rather tend to make an assessment based on someone's external appearance. This poses a particular challenge for the FWS case because the *EA 2010*, amongst other things, covers discrimination based on perception, i.e. it does not matter legally whether you are actually Muslim if you are experiencing discrimination because your employer simply assumes that you are. This also applies to the protected characteristic of sex. The Supreme Court on this point notes that some trans people may indeed be falling into the category of 'man' or 'woman' even if that does not align with their sex as assigned at birth, simply because they are perceived as such and experience discrimination in line with this. This means that a trans man, regardless of whether he has changed his legal sex to also be male, who is treated worse by his employer based on the perception that he is a man, has the same legal protections in this instance as someone who was assigned male at birth even though the former is not 'biologically' a man according to the judgment.[22]

This reasoning by the Supreme Court has two effects: a) it immediately highlights how little coherence is actually created by defining 'man' and 'woman' in the *EA 2010* solely through biology at birth, given that the very idea of discrimination by perception promptly undermines the consistency of this rationale; and b) it creates different legal standards for those trans people who pass as a sex other than the one they were assigned at birth. While point a) undermines the internal logic of the judgment, point b) is also deeply problematic given that it is thoroughly documented that visual or aesthetic norms of sex/gender in the West essentialise notions of white masculinity and femininity that predominantly exclude those from ethnic minorities and many people with disabilities, as well as being heavily mediated by class. In countries that have attempted to ban trans people from bathrooms that do not align with their sex assigned at birth, there is at the very least anecdotal evidence that those whose bathroom access is subsequently most policed are in fact non-white cis women.[23] Embedding the idea in law that there is a 'correct' way to present as a certain sex, then, further embeds heavily racialised and ableist norms and assumptions.

Legal lesbians

A further instance where this incoherent and fundamentally inaccurate notion of biological 'truth' can be seen is in regard to the Supreme Court's choice to not just define what 'sex' means for the purpose of the *EA 2010*, but also to define 'sexual orientation'. The Supreme Court, in an attempt to elaborate on why 'man' and 'woman' should be defined through the sex someone is assigned at birth, defines lesbians as people assigned female at birth who are attracted to people assigned female at birth.[24] In practice, this means for the purpose of the *EA 2010* that a cis woman dating a trans woman is now in a heterosexual relationship, while a cis woman dating a trans man is now in a lesbian relationship. This erases both the more complex dimensions of sexual orientation – after all, a significant portion of lesbians have at some point dated men – and the way people define their own sexual orientation. Many people assigned female at birth who date trans women would understandably see themselves as lesbians, while a woman dating a trans man might see herself as heterosexual and may well be perceived by others as such. In contrast, the implication of the Supreme Court's ruling is that people are not able to define their own sexual orientation in relation to clubs and associations governed by the relevant *EA 2010* provisions. For example, a cis woman dating a trans woman would be prevented from joining a lesbian swimming group.

This again seems to presume that original birth certificates carry some kind of ultimate legal and biological truth that then shapes the entirety of a person's life, down to their sexual orientation. This kind of biological essentialism for sexual orientation, just like the idea of there being a 'gay gene' and that people's sexual orientation is therefore fixed at birth, is both exclusionary and at its worst feeds into highly concerning ideas of not being heterosexual as some type of genetic defect. It also suggests that one can 'legally' be a true lesbian only in the way that aligns with the FWS definition, which entirely ignores that in almost all settings sexual orientation is something a person determines for themselves.[25]

Legislating everyday life

Using the examples above, the judgment is evidently problematic in its immediate legal context. However, it's also hard not to read this judgment in a wider context where political discourse seems to be shifting towards at best seeing only 'true' minorities as deserving of rights and protections. The FWS case was about the issue of identifying 'true' biological women who can be subject to limited positive discrimination measures, but in the process also seeks to define 'true' trans people, i.e. those who pass and therefore may have some slightly better protections, and 'true' lesbians and gay men, i.e. those who experience sexual attraction only to people assigned the same sex as them at birth. This turn to a supposedly stable, permanent biological truth to determine group membership for at least three of the protected characteristics in the *EA 2010* could have potentially far-reaching consequences for the remaining protected characteristics in the longer term.

For instance, Wes Streeting, in his role as Health Secretary, recently stated that he believed that mental health conditions are 'over-diagnosed' and this was leading to too many people claiming disability-related benefits.[26] Other parliamentarians have similarly stated that mental health conditions and some other related disabilities are either not real or at a minimum over-diagnosed. Consequently, the proposed changes to welfare legislation would make it disproportionately harder for those with mental health conditions and less 'severe' impairments to claim disability benefits. Overall, the supposed consensus seems to be that protections and rights for minority groups have in some way gone too far and that we should at a minimum limit these to only a few 'true' cases.

The challenge of course is that neither law nor biology is rarely that straightforward. Even by using a heavily abstracted and simplified definition of biological sex, the FWS case immediately creates a series of inconsistencies. It also significantly overstates the relevance of legal status and documents in everyday life. If birth certificates are now the sole arbiter of someone's ability to access men-only or women-only spaces, how is this meant to work on a day-to-day basis? Unless everyone now becomes legally required to carry a birth certificate with them at all times, this is hardly a practical way to determine who should use which bathroom or changing room. It also entirely denies the reality that those who are disproportionately going to be challenged in these spaces are those who do not meet stereotypical norms of what it means to look like a man or a woman, regardless of the sex they were assigned at birth. The notion that anti-discrimination principles demand that in most circumstances we should ignore that trans people are in fact a different gender to the one they were assigned at birth was always going to be a difficult one to sustain. It is therefore perhaps unsurprising that the Supreme Court sought additional legitimacy for its rationale in claims of biological truth. However, this has meant further tying minority status to forms of biological essentialism that ignore both the complexity of biology, and the crucial role of the material and social world that law operates within.

Flora Renz is a Senior Lecturer in Law at Kent Law School and Co-Director of the Centre for Sexuality, Race and Gender Justice. Her monograph Gender Recognition and the Law: Troubling Transgender Peoples' Engagement with Legal Regulation *was published by Routledge in 2024.*

Notes

1. *For Women Scotland Ltd (Appellant) v The Scottish Ministers (Respondent)* [2025] UKSC/2024/0042, hereafter 'FWS'.
2. *Christine Goodwin v. United Kingdom and I v. United Kingdom Grand Chamber Judgements of July 11*, [2002] (application nos. 28957/95 and 25680/94).
3. Ss.1-3 of the *Gender Recognition Act 2004*.
4. S.7 of the *Equality Act 2010*.
5. *Taylor v Jaguar Land Rover Ltd* [2020] ET 1304471/2018.
6. See s.740 of the *EA 2010*, Explanatory Notes, 'gender reassignment: paragraph 28'.
7. Flora Renz, 'Gender-based Violence Without a Legal Gender: Imagining Single-sex Services in Conditions of Decertification', *Feminist Legal Studies* 31:1 (2023), 43–66.
8. *For Women Scotland Ltd v Lord Advocate* [2022] CSIH 4; 2022 SC 150.
9. 13 December 2022 ([2022] CSOH 90; 2023 SC 61.
10. Ibid., para 45–47.
11. [2023] CSIH 37; 2023 SLT 1216.
12. Ibid., n.1, para 265.
13. Notably here the Supreme Court argued that by accepting that trans people change sex, and reading the terms 'man' and 'woman' in a trans inclusive manner, protections on the basis of pregnancy would not apply to pregnant trans men as the pregnancy provisions talk about 'women'. This is despite the fact that these provisions have to date clearly been interpreted in a trans inclusive manner, including by the government. For instance, the Health and Safety Executive's guidance on pregnant workers to date still states that it also applies to trans men and non-binary people who are pregnant: https://www.hse.gov.uk/mothers/employer/index.htm.
14. Ibid., para 221.
15. Equality and Human Rights Commission, 'Code of practice for services, public functions and associations: consultation 2025', https://www.equalityhumanrights.com/equality/equality-act-2010/codes-practice/code-practice-services-public-functions-and-associations.
16. Emily Graham, 'Exploring the Textual Alchemy of Legal Gender: Experimental Statutes and the Message in the Medium', *Feminists@ law* 10:2 (2020).
17. For some examples, see Davina Cooper and Robyn Emerton, 'Pulling the Thread of Decertification: What Challenges are Raised by the Proposal to Reform Legal Gender Status?'. *Feminists@ law* 10:2 (2020).
18. Crash Wigley, 'For Women Scotland: A Case of Significant Silences. UK Constitutional Law Association', 6 May 2025, https://ukconstitutionallaw.org/2025/05/06/crash-wigley-for-women-scotland-a-case-of-significant-silences/.
19. PA News Agency, 'Equalities boss outlines changes on toilets, changing rooms and women's sport. The National', 17 April 2025, https://www.thenational.scot/news/national/25097138.equalities-boss-outlines-changes-toilets-changing-rooms-womens-sport/.
20. n.1, para 7.
21. Millie Cooke, 'Doctors Condemn Supreme Court Ruling on Trans Women as "Scientifically Illiterate"', 29 April 2025, .https://www.independent.co.uk/news/uk/politics/trans-gender-supreme-court-ruling-bma-doctors-b2741304.html.
22. n.1, para 250.
23. Heath Fogg Davis, 'Why the "Transgender" Bathroom Controversy Should Make Us Rethink Sex-Segregated Public Bathrooms', *Politics, Groups, and Identities* 6:2 (2018), 199–216.
24. n.1, para 205–209.
25. See also the discussion of the sexual orientation issue here: Robert Mullins, 'For Women Scotland: Fastening the "Biological" Straightjacket', UK Constitutional Law Association, 22 May 2025, .https://ukconstitutionallaw.org/2025/05/22/robert-mullins-for-women-scotland-fastening-the-biological-straitjacket/.
26. Joshua Nevett, 'Mental Health Conditions are Overdiagnosed, Streeting Says', *BBC News*, 16 March 2025, https://www.bbc.co.uk/news/articles/cd7ejvr3y0zo.

Reproductive subsumption
Notes on the making of reproductive labour in capitalism

Elena Baglioni

> And to hell with hibiscus, frangipani, and bougainvillea.
> Martinican poetry will be cannibal or it will not be.
> Suzanne Cesaire, *Tropiques* n.4, 1942

How do we trace internal fractures of the working class? What histories do they have? How to *explain* the manifold production of difference within 'classes of labour'? A few decades ago, Diane Elson was asking a question, the answer to which points in a useful direction: why does labour take the *form* it does in capitalism? And what are the political consequences? In posing this puzzle, Elson's goal was to recast the centrality of labour within Marx's value theory, as a theory of the specific way labour is transformed in capitalism.[1] In this article, I draw from Elson's analysis to think about how workers are differently formed in capitalism by focusing on how capitalism changes the relation between production and social reproduction and with what consequences for labour. The analysis allows us to understand the fragmentation between productive and reproductive labour as processes intrinsic to class-making. I therefore ask: how is labour formed – reconstructed – as reproductive labour in capitalism? I suggest that a fruitful answer to this question may reside in an augmented analysis of the subsumption of labour. Responding to the needs to develop gendered global histories[2] and overall histories that chart the development of capitalism 'beyond the immediate process of production',[3] I extend the analysis of labour subsumption beyond the productive sphere to include the sphere of reproduction.[4]

The sphere of reproduction is intended here as involving all labour that is devoted to the reproduction of life, human and extra-human, in capitalism, the labour of social reproduction. In one of the early, comprehensive definitions, the labour of social reproduction includes 'various kinds of work – mental, manual, and emotional – aimed at providing the historically and socially, as well as biologically, defined care necessary to maintain existing life and to reproduce the next generation. And the organisation of social reproduction refers to the varying institutions within which this work is performed, the varying strategies for accomplishing these tasks, and the varying ideologies that both shape and are shaped by them'.[5] Since the 1960s and 70s Marxist feminists have demonstrated that reproductive labour is a fundamental ingredient of capitalism, it is essential for the regeneration and renewal of daily and generational labour power, which is the only source of new value in capitalism.[6] This work invariably involves the reproduction of ecosystems, i.e. the 'conditions of the natural world which make life, society and production possible'.[7] Thus, my analysis benefits from decades of social reproduction scholarship to ask what can be gained historically by viewing the historical development of capitalism from the vantage point of social reproduction. As it has been argued, the making of these life-making workers ought to be at the heart of 'global labour' as 'an international multiverse of class forces'.[8]

Why 'subsumption'? The subsumption of labour represents a powerful analytical framework, with great untapped potential. Echoing Elson's fundamental question above, for Andrés Saenz de Sicilia 'subsumption' provides a recipe for understanding how in capitalism individuals are *formed* as workers.[9] Within the 'classic' analysis of labour subsumption, individuals become workers as the labour process becomes subsumed – enveloped, dominated – by the valorisation process. The work done in fields, workshops, ships and households first 'simply' intensifies and then drastically changes as capital comes to regulate fully the labour process. For Patrick Murray, different forms of subsumption 'point to the diverse ways that capital, understood as a specific – and explosive – social form of wealth, revolutionises society, its goods and services and the way they are produced'.[10] In taking these remarks most seriously, I assume that capital's explosiveness and 'epoch-making power'[11] must exceed the labour process, and I propose to extend subsumption accordingly. Indeed, the classic analysis of labour subsumption remains essentially an analysis of capitalist *production*, as the pedestal of the valorisation process. This analysis therefore omits that part of labour working elsewhere other than immediate production. Specifically, it overlooks all that work *separated* from, and *subordinated* to, production and instead devoted to the reproduction of the working class. I suggest this labour encounters a different form of subsumption – reproductive subsumption – and call to study its historical trajectories in concrete settings. In other words, reproductive subsumption – or the subsumption of reproductive labour – designates the historical reconstruction of how some part of labour is divorced and subordinated to production and reconstituted as reproductive labour due to the material contradictions inherent to the valorisation process. Hence, reproductive subsumption is a process specific to capitalism, emanating from its internal material limits.

Calling for a history of reproductive labour as a process of capitalist subsumption allows us to do several things. Retaining the category of subsumption highlights the simultaneously differential and intertwined incorporation of productive and reproductive labour in capitalism and their mutual and contradictory relationship. First, this allows us to recover a rich sense of capitalism, neither reducible to stereotypical forms of exploitation nor the relationships involved in the immediate process of production.[12] Such a rich perspective takes subsumption to capitalism as occurring 'when the reproduction of any class, social category or formation, became impossible outside capitalist commodity relations, even *if reproduction is not constituted exclusively by them*'.[13] Second, as a category, subsumption represents a powerful tool to investigate concrete settings in their dialectical relationship with capital's compulsions. Accordingly, subsumption 'marks the *interface* between capital as a system and capital as history',[14] thus allowing us to 'strike a balance between theory and history'.[15] The analysis of reproductive subsumption starts theoretically from detecting the reproductive function in capitalism as necessary for supplying labour power and sustaining life more generally. Reproductive subsumption then becomes a historical charting of how this function is secured through the construction of workers partially, or sometimes and in some places entirely, dedicated to this life-making work. In the movement from theory to history – from work to workers – this process of class-making vehiculates, catalyses, refashions, imports, adapts (and creates) available forms and systems of oppression, like gender, race, religion and sexuality (to name a few), to produce a canvas rich with all the contingency and jumble of history, a 'concrete universality' where 'distinct experiences of oppression are in fact internally related, discrete but interconnected parts of a totalising system'.[16]

When investigating processes of subsumption, a third point thus crops up: violence. Like subsumption in general, reproductive subsumption is invariably a violent process. Threaded to the sheer violence of the primitive accumulation of capitalism, reproductive subsumption unearths the forms of oppression and coercion serving the subordination, naturalisation and even annihilation of reproductive labour to gain a greater understanding of its ubiquitous as well as specific manifestations. It therefore digs into how reproductive workers are at once different and the same. One of the greatest works charting the long reproductive subsumption in Europe is Silvia Federici's *Caliban and the Witch*. Here we discover the subordination of reproductive to productive labour through the violent gendering machine and the primitive accumulation of capital 'as a primitive *accumulation of differences and divisions within the working class*'.[17] While the labour of reproduction is immediately associated with the gendering of individuals, its relationship to processes of racialisation is less rehearsed. Yet, as

Gargi Bhattacharyya shows, threaded to gender, racialisation is a most powerful 'differentiating force' of the working class and one entangled with social reproduction in determining different 'scales of humanness'.[18] In her understanding of racial capitalism, 'reproductive labour is the input that enables workers to be highly differentiated and differently constituted as workers, sometimes workers and non-workers'.[19] Hence the need to reconstruct the manifold ways in which reproductive work becomes a marker of difference in different places and times, i.e. the specifically capitalist form of these differentiating forces as they yield a variegated and segmented global working class.

The reflections proposed in this article are far from catching or explaining all sources of fracture in the working class. Rather, by calling for historical inquiries into the constitution of reproductive labour, I wish to emphasise one element within the totality, conscious 'that any category we use to cut the continuum of the material world can only capture a partial knowledge, a particular aspect seen from a certain vantage point'.[20] The hope is that an augmented understanding of subsumption can provide fertile ground to approach complex unfolding debates, including the rich debate on the character of primitive accumulation[21] or the structural/contingent role of gender and race within capitalism.[22]

The rest of this article develops as follows. The next section sketches the classic analysis of the subsumption of labour and some of its most notable developments. I turn to construct the category of reproductive subsumption in section three, gradually moving from the abstract to the concrete level. I analyse some key contradictions of reproductive subsumption in section four and move to consider gender and race as key forms of violence in section five.

The 'classic' analysis of the subsumption of labour and beyond

Saenz de Sicilia captures the ground rules of subsumption as a nuanced, open and materialist framework for analysing capitalism in its logical and historical development.[23] By tracing the genealogy of the concept from Kant to Hegel, and then Marx, Saenz de Sicilia reconstructs subsumption as a logical category displaying in my opinion a four-fold character: it is a *relation* that is intrinsically *violent*, and it is a *process* constituting that relation, which is inherently *developmental*, i.e. open-ended and contingent. First, as a *relation*, subsumption indicates a hierarchy, a subordination of a 'particular' to a 'general'. Second, a qualification: this relation is violent. Subsumption 'always involves a kind of imposition or violence, as a particular "content" is determined by a "form" that remains in some sense abstract or indifferent to its specific qualities and so violates its singular identity'.[24] Third, as a *process*, subsumption actively expresses the formation of that relation as a reciprocal movement where the particular and the general co-determine each other. Fourth, rather than circular, this process is inevitably *developmental*: 'the subsumption of the particular under the universal is no longer an infinitely self-same act realised within an unchanging totality, but rather takes on a fundamentally different character depending on the stage of the development of that totality, whilst at the same time driving that development onwards'.[25]

These elements characterise Marx's analysis of labour subsumption as an analysis of how individuals become workers subsumed to capital as a dominant social form and how this process is inherently violent, internally contradictory, characterised by struggle, contingency, and thus open-ended. The fundamentals of this analysis are in the 'Results of the Immediate Process of Production'.[26] Here Marx distinguishes mainly between the *formal* and *real* subsumption of labour delineating a process of development of capitalist relations of production that move from the former to the latter.[27] A rough summary goes as follows.

Within the *formal* subsumption of labour, capital seizes the labour process – subsumes it – 'as it finds it, that is to say, it takes over an *existing labour process*, developed by different and more archaic modes of production'.[28] In this scenario, the labour process does not change its functioning and organisation and remains '"technologically" continuous with earlier modes of labour'.[29] Subsuming here means that labour becomes imbricated and subject to capitalist extraction of surplus value within capital's compulsion to produce as much surplus value as possible. Capital extraction is here *absolute*: surplus labour is obtained through labour intensification, by lengthening the working day. This happens 'either when the producer is self-employing or when the immediate producers are forced to deliver surplus labour to others', and 'A man who was formerly an independent peasant now finds himself a factor in a production process and dependant on the capitalist directing it, and his own livelihood depends on a contract which he as a commodity owner (viz. the owner of labour-power) has previously concluded with the capitalist as the owner of money'.[30]

Instead, the *real* subsumption of labour implies a drastic change in the form of the labour process: a 'complete revolution takes place in the mode of production, in the productivity of the workers and in the relations between workers and capitalists'.[31] In its most classic tale, this happens when capital directly penetrates and technologically transforms the production process, so that the productivity of labour increases without increasing the working day. Typically, this also happens when the scale of production increases, workers no longer work in isolation from one another, and capital reaps the benefits of economies of scale, cooperation, etc. This form of subsumption is typically developed by *relative* surplus value extraction.

Subsequent elaborations of the category of subsumption extend this analysis in important directions. A well-known elaboration is Antonio Negri's expansion of 'real subsumption', often reverberating in and out of his writing as 'total subsumption'.[32] For Negri, subsumption is an incremental process of capitalist development as a gradual annihilation of the 'outside' of capital. That is, subsumption is capital proceeding like a colonising force from the shopfloor outward through to society – 'from manufacture to big industry to social factory' – spatially conquering the whole of the world market and capturing every form of social exchange and production.[33] Once *society* is 'really subsumed' there is no outside of capital left, production, circulation and consumption collapse into each other, nature is reproduced as capitalist nature, and reproduction is capitalist reproduction.[34] Thus, within real/total subsumption we gain a flavour of the all-encompassing nature of capitalist development in time and space, yet much is lost along the way. First, differential trajectories of subsumption acquire a rather 'stageist' flavour where the bulk of the global South seems merely late down the line rather than another (larger) face of a Western present.[35] Second, and as a consequence of this narrow view, 'the planetary proletariat' as 'the value-creating labor of billions of people' is lost.[36]

A less-known development of subsumption comes from feminist agrarian political economy. Here, Veronika Bennholdt-Thomsen transcended the inside/outside capitalism logic by looking at those who *seemed* to be not subsumed, the Third World 'marginal mass'.[37] This included all workers who 'work under any conditions' and who 'only struggle to survive': the urban poor garbage collectors; shoe-shiner boys; housemaids; prostitutes; small peasants; the mass of migrant-day labourers; 'the primitive artisans'.[38] Essentially, all the working mass 'in charge of its own reproduction' and 'responsible for its necessary subsistence work' and therefore very cheap to capital. Rather than excluded, Bennholdt-Thomsen saw these workers as in a position of *marginal subsumption* to capital, 'not outside the capitalist system but in fact very much within it', their work still valorised by capital.[39] Marginal subsumption, therefore, indicates the 'specific socio-economic position of this vast majority of producers within the capitalist mode of production, their specific relations to capital, and the mechanisms by which their social position is reproduced'.[40] That is, although subsistence occupies most of the work/time/energy of the 'marginal masses', these masses are adversely incorporated rather than expelled from capitalist relations of production.

In their classic formulations, both the formal and real subsumption of labour consider how labour is subsumed in capitalism within the terrain of the labour process, i.e. the process of capitalist production, itself always mediated by exchange and circulation. This is because it is in the labour process that labour produces value for capital directly, whether this is exchanged for wages or any other phenomenal and disguised form that the extraction of surplus from labour occurs.[41] Yet, this focus excludes all that labour subsumed differently or *elsewhere* along the circuit of capital. Similarly, while notions of total subsumption crucially raise the totalising nature of capital relations, they can obscure important 'details', including how commodities and labour are reproduced differently in capitalism. Among the masses of workers who are not immediately included in the capitalist labour process, one finds multitudes disproportionally working to reproduce labour power and the very conditions for life, yet they are disappearing from the analysis. How to retrieve them? Or, as Leopoldina Fortunati once asked, 'How can we write a *workers' history of reproduction*?'.[42]

I argue that the classic analysis of the subsumption of labour takes for granted that part of (the) labour (force) subsumed differently from the other: this part of labour encounters a form of *reproductive subsumption*, i.e. it is subsumed differently, as reproductive labour, a portion of labour separated from production and necessarily spent to regenerate life. This separation is structural: there is no formal or real subsumption of labour without the reproductive subsumption of part of (the) labour (force) that is not deployed to produce value for capital *directly*, but instead labours to reproduce the labour force and nature (the environment). Labour power lives in bodies, whose physical materiality requires, precisely, labour, i.e. 'the universal condition of life itself'.[43] Because labour needs to be reproduced, replenished and renewed, reproductive subsumption is therefore the means through which formal and real subsumption can occur. Like other forms of subsumption, reproductive subsumption moulds to the terrain it finds, the unique social, economic and cultural characteristics of the social formations it encounters.[44] This moulding is always a complex result of the multiple forces and dynamics playing in each concrete setting; it is not unilaterally determined by either capital or the state but always mediated by the agency, resistance and class struggle of those subsumed. The struggle between the productive and reproductive functions – the different policies and 'identities' vehiculated to facilitate those functions, and further their refusal, adaptation and reworking – results in multiversal working classes.

One of the advantages of investigating 'reproductive subsumption' is that the category keeps the analytical space free: it does not pre-define specific spaces, actors or specific activities (like households, women or domestic work exclusively), therefore allowing us to identify how capitalism reshapes and re-creates reproductive spaces in different times and places by subsuming different peoples and activities differently. Labour is reproduced and replaced in manifold ways beyond households, through labour camps, dormitories, forced/migration, etc. In a nutshell, while the subordination of reproductive to productive activities remains a constant, the concrete forms and variants of these activities and who carries them out vary in time and space, at least to an extent. As it will be shown, in the *history* of capitalism reproductive subsumption has been a central driver of gender-making as gender has represented a formidable 'raw material' for the construction of reproductive labour. And because capital's mobilisation of gender cannot be easily untangled from the creation of other axes of differences – principally race – tracing the manifold histories of reproductive subsumption in different places means always digging up the *specific* articulations and intersections of class, gender, race and other axes of difference at any given time.[45]

Setting an agenda for the historical reconstruction of the subsumption of reproductive labour starts from a crucial *change* that the labour process undergoes when subsumed ('formally' or 'really') by capital: the 'revolution' between productive and reproductive activities. This revolution is twofold: it refers to the *separation* and the *reversal* of the relationship and hierarchy between production and reproduction. Fortunati elucidates this reversal through Marx: whereas in pre-capitalist communities, 'the economic purpose is "the production of use-values, i.e the *reproduction of the individual* within the specific relation to the community in which he is its basis", in capitalism it becomes the production of exchange value, *the creation of value*'.[46] Thus, while the relationship between production and reproduction characterises different epochs, capitalism creates a new hierarchy between them as the reproduction of labour and life becomes an *instrument* for the self-expansion of value. Elson's value theory of labour is the key to explaining this change, to which I turn below.

The logic of reproductive subsumption

Reproductive subsumption refers to the *separation* and *subordination* of the reproduction of life to the production of value (as surplus value) under capitalism. The reproduction of life includes different living forms, from labour to plants and animals. At the abstract level, reproductive subsumption is the *artificial* separation of two distinct *labour processes* and *forms of labour* – productive and reproductive labour – and their *hierarchical relation* vis-à-vis one another. At this level of abstraction, the lens is on labour as *work* rather than *workers*, and the separation manifests as a conflict of work, specifically work-time and energy: the day is divided between the work done within the labour process and the work/time to recover and 'live' beyond capital. As Massimiliano Tomba puts, 'The relation between the working class and capital is a struggle over time, for time. Every instant that the worker takes from capital is energy subtracted from valorisation'.[47] At the very same time, every 'instant' and 'energy' stolen from capital opens another realm, the time of social reproduction, and its own temporalities, contradictions and struggles.

How does this separation and subordination occur in the abstract? While productive and reproductive labours characterise historically all societies,[48] it is the *specific relation* they acquire in capitalism that becomes a cornerstone of the capitalist system itself. In seeking to understand how labour changes in capitalism, Elson starts by remarking that 'labour is a fluidity, a potential'.[49] To grasp this further, she follows Marx, who discerns four different aspects of labour working as 'opposing pairs', abstract/concrete and social/private. These different 'aspects' of labour are never independent of one another, they are aspects of a whole, 'one-sided abstractions'.[50] As she elaborates, to understand any social form in history, one cannot look for external causes (outside history) but must delve inside that social formation: 'going inside the form is achieved by treating it as the temporary precipitate of opposed potentia',[51] i.e. the form of labour in any society is the specific, 'crystallised' relation between different aspects of labour, yet never settled, always transient and becoming. In sum, 'Labour always has its abstract and concrete, its social and private aspects. Marx poses any particular determinate form of labour as a precipitate of these four aspects of labour. What is specific to a particular kind of society is the relation of these aspects to one another and the way in which they are represented in precipitated forms'.[52] What distinguishes capitalist societies from previous ones is that in capitalism, abstract labour dominates all other aspects of labour.

Building on this insight, I extend this analysis to two further *aspects* of labour, productive and reproductive, to make a central suggestion: in capitalism, the relation between productive and reproductive labour changes because the value relation involves the domination of abstract/social labour over concrete labour in production *and* simultaneously the domination of concrete/private labour over the abstract/social aspects of reproduction. Domination means the supremacy of a different aspect, or side, of labour towards the other, not a different type of labour, nor the obliteration of the aspect of labour that is dominated. As a result, the social and abstract aspects of reproductive labour are obscured and *seemingly* disappear. Thus, the value relation does not merely envelop and regulate productive labour, disregarding and letting loose reproductive labour in a residual form. Instead, it is a relation that reworks and transforms the relationship between production and reproduction, polarising them in opposite directions. Crucially, the dominance of the concrete aspect of labour in reproduction is functional to the dominance of abstract labour in production: reproductive work presupposes productive work.[53]

So rather than approaching productive and reproductive labour through the polarity between exchange and use value, by building on Elson's analysis, I explore their relation as established by the difference/identity of abstract and concrete labour. Emphasising how the relationship between productive and reproductive labour develops as an interplay between abstract and concrete labour, recasts reproductive labour as a direct product of the value relation. As such, the dominance of concrete labour in this realm means that labour is less subject to the direct disciplining of abstract labour (than in production) *but neither free nor independent from it*. This exposes the social character of reproductive labour behind its private appearance. Additionally, focusing on labour rather than its objectification into a product (whether a use or exchange value) allows for staying with labour's fluidity, indeterminateness and open-endedness, thus with resistance as an ever-present *potentia*. Following labour rather than its objectivisation opens a greater lens into class struggle and the imperative to overcome the capitalist relation between production and reproduction. To further understand this, I delve next into abstract and concrete labour and their relation in capitalism.

According to Elson, abstract labour becomes an 'abstract truth' only in capitalism as a disciplining compulsion ruling production and life.[54] Assuming all the logical steps through which abstract labour emerges at the outset of Marx's *Capital*, it is worth delving briefly into its nature: relational, material/temporal and intrinsically antagonistic. Abstract labour is arrived at by deducing what all commodities have in common, i.e. they are products of labour. It is 'what remains there' when comparing all different kinds of work and gradually subtracting all differences: 'undistinguishable labour', 'homogeneous labour', 'labour pure and simple' transferred and deposited in commodities allowing their commensurability and exchangeability.[55] Thus, it is an abstraction spinning out of comparison, arising from relating all labourers and *detracting* from their heterogeneity to breach their homogeneity. This homogeneity is material:[56] the physiological expenditure of brains and muscles, an *expenditure* of matter and energy, a metabolism, a bodily performance, and as such also and inevitably a temporal phenomenon.[57] As a temporality, abstract labour is inherently dynamic, variable and unstable: in Marx's own words, it is 'A way of seeing labour from the perspective of the "how much", of the *temporal* duration of labour', a form of 'simple, average labour' which 'varies in character in different countries and at different cultural epochs, but in a particular society it is given'.[58] Thus, abstract labour is always already performative, always spatially 'synchronising' the labour of different workers.[59] A crucial point is that because of all these characteristics, abstract labour is in permanent tension with concrete labour. Its detractive, relational nature works like a conforming pressure when all the heterogeneity of concrete labour is resumed. Concrete labour therefore reconciles – mediates – this homogeneity and performativity to the world of difference, both the difference of utility and wants, as well as the difference and heterogeneity of nature, labouring bodies and life.

For Marx, concrete labour is 'A way of seeing labour from the perspective of the "how" and "what" of labour'.[60] It is the qualitative, not the quantitative, side of labour; labour seen from the perspective of its infinite variability: 'Productive activity of a definite kind, carried on with a definite aim', 'Heterogenous forms of useful labour, which differ in order, genus, species and variety'.[61] It is the distinct work of the baker, the farmer and the driver. It is the seamstress seamlessly threading, piercing, holding, stitching, peddling, sliding, counting, measuring, calculating, cutting, stretching, shaping, sweating and mastering dexterity under the manager's eyes. In the labour process, hers and every other worker's concrete labour channels abstract labour's gravitational pull, a compulsion to work faster, longer and in a standardised fashion. Outside the factory, concrete labour – labour as quality, heterogeneity, utility, subjectivity and creativity – meets depleted bodies and minds, hence the work of reconciliation between capitalist production and life *magnifies*. Here, concrete labour synchronises instead with the inherent heterogeneity of nature, including its assorted temporalities and metabolisms, the time to rest, socialise, and grow plants, animals and of course humans. In sum, the dominance of concrete labour in reproduction opposes/mediates the dominance of abstract labour in production. As suggested below, the tyranny of abstract labour in production – itself emerging out of the violent separation of workers from their means and conditions of re/production, the generalised development of production for the market, and the establishment of property relations – gives this realm its *façade* of economic compulsion. At the same time, the dominance of concrete labour in reproduction – with its *façade* of natural, private work – springs from the same history of primitive accumulation, although coloured with all the extra-economic compulsions and violence deployed to subsume workers in this realm. The individualisation and privatisation of concrete reproductive work belong to this violent repertoire.[62]

How does this translate at a more concrete level? In capitalism, the day of the working-class labourer comprises a portion of work done for capital and a portion dedicated to resting, eating, sleeping and regenerating labour power. A conflict of time becomes immediately inscribed in the worker's body as an 'embodied contradiction'[63] as capital only valorises labour power, not the labour that comes attached to it. Because work, including intellectual work, is inevitably a material process involving an expenditure of energy through a body, bodies (and minds) need time and energy to restore. This portion of time is however work too, 'a cart full of "means of subsistence" does not produce labour-power as a ready-made commodity'.[64] Food does not cook itself; clothes need to be washed, houses need to be cleaned, fields need to be tended to, children need constant care. Therefore, the labourers' working day is much longer than that beginning and ending at the factory gates. Reproductive labour is necessary to counter the complete physical and mental exhaustion of workers' bodies; it is a material requirement of capitalist production, emerging from the material limits of exploitation. Yet, 'the wage (including the lack of it), has allowed capital to obscure the real length of the workday. Work appears as one compartment of life that takes place only in certain areas. The time we consume in the "social factory", preparing ourselves for work or going to work, restoring our "muscles, nerves, bones and brains" with quick snacks, quick sex, movies, all this appears as leisure, free time, individual choice'.[65]

Or to put it otherwise, 'The hidden time of the commodity is nothing other than the difference between the necessary labour time for its production and the necessary time for the reproduction of the labour-power that produced this commodity".[66] That is, *separated* from the work done for capital, reproductive work appears as the natural, private sphere of the worker. This separation holds whether visible or not concretely. It is most evident when the workplace and the home are spatially separated and much of the reproductive work is privatised in households. It is less evident, but still operating, when production and reproduction are more difficult to discern as is often the case in petty commodity production or when the home is the workplace, and 'working from home, homing from work' intertwine to ever greater degrees.[67]

What counts as reproductive work? As noted, reproductive labour involves all the work required to allow workers to go to work, the *reproduction of labour power*, and the reproduction of life more generally, daily, generationally and ecologically, so to speak. Reproductive work is quintessentially porous and potentially endless. The list of what it takes to reproduce workers both daily and generationally is long and constantly evolves in time and space. Crucially, this work includes healthcare and education systems, community work, leisure and religious centres and many other spaces.[68] Although separated from production, this sphere constantly crisscrosses and feeds the circuit of capital and that of the commodity. Much of this work is marketised, whether through the hiring of a cleaner, dining out, popping to the laundry, or going to the cinema, the list is long. Crucially, the sphere of reproduction also occurs through active, endless capitalist consumption – whether a Netflix subscription, a sachet of *Omo*, a *Maggi* cube, or the electricity bill. The wage goes back to capital via all sorts of commodities; it transits to workers' hands fleetingly and, for many, so intermittently and fortuitously. Yet even for this 'marginal mass', reproductive work hardly shies away from capitalist consumption.[69] For a huge amount of people, and reproductive workers in particular, when the wage is nowhere to be found, debt steps in. In these landscapes, debt supports or substitutes for wages and further disciplines indebted workers to the harshest and most exploitative forms of work and violence.[70] Overall, production and reproduction constantly intermingle, many reproductive moments and functions are captured on and off by capital and thus subjected more directly to the compulsions of abstract labour.

However carried out – bought, outsourced, indebted – reproductive labour is never entirely absorbed by the market. Even if the complete commodification of social reproduction can be logically imagined, 'historically we are still very far from that'.[71] There are some bare minimum functions, material and affective, that remain irreducible and cannot be absorbed entirely by the state, the market or by cheap immigrant labour. Life-making, as the realm of difference and incommensurability – an anti-abstraction – inherently resists the *full* disciplining of abstract labour. Thus, there is, and perhaps there will always be, 'this remainder that has to remain outside of market relations, and the question of who has to perform it in the family will always be, to say the least, a conflictual matter'.[72] This matter is conflictual because this work is *necessarily* unwaged, i.e. for the working classes, it is not entirely covered by the wage. This is intuitive at the most abstract level: in capitalism, it is labour that reproduces capital fully, not vice versa. A portion of labour always works for free in production (yielding surplus value) and reproduction (reproducing labour). Again, the wage, especially the family wage, masks this wage-less work.

Some key contradictions of reproductive subsumption

As a process of fictitious separation and subordination between productive and reproductive work, reproductive subsumption is inherently a contradictory process. That is, reproductive work is fraught with contradictions manifesting at different levels. As pointed out by Lise Vogel, 'from the point of view of capital, domestic labour is simultaneously indispensable and an obstacle to accumulation'.[73] Likewise, from the point of view of labour, reproductive time detracts from productive time and the wage. Thus, by its mediating role, reproductive labour exists in structural tension with capitalism, i.e. productive and reproductive times live in a contradictory relation with capital: the labour time of reproduction is necessary to, but simultaneously detracts from the labour of production and therefore direct surplus value extraction. Essentially, by ejecting reproductive labour from the capitalist labour process capital pushes this contradiction to the worker and the working class. In this way, a contradiction of capital appears as an inner contradiction of the worker and in this journey becomes a chief driver of difference and fragmentation, effectively a propellor of *horizontal antagonistic relations* within the working class. Atomised by its internal competition for wage work, the working class is also fragmented by the fundamental *rift* between production and reproduction and the attendant antagonism this generates. As such, a contradiction between capital and labour becomes an embodied contradiction between labour power and labour, which in turn becomes a contradiction between bodies: the uneven division of labour experienced in the worker's body metamorphoses into an uneven division of labour within the working class. Reproductive subsumption becomes therefore the charting of this process, the historical resolution of these contradictions in concrete settings, i.e. how this vertical antagonism between capital and labour is displaced onto the working class.

Separating reproductive from productive time and attributing a wage only to the latter holds potentially a further contradiction. It is not just structurally fundamental to securing labour's life and capacity to work, it may contribute to relative surplus value extraction by lowering the cost of living and alleviating the wage from the high costs of reproduction. The more work is done by reproductive workers for free, the greater relief for the wage, the lighter the bill for capital.[74] As Federici argues about Europe's industrialisation, 'the devaluation and feminization of reproductive labor was a disaster also for male workers, for the devaluation of reproductive labor inevitably devalued its product: labor-power'.[75] In this long and tumultuous process of housewifisation of work,[76] the monumental expenditure of hard-working dexterous bodies, nimble fingers and docile temperaments was pivotal in reducing socially necessary labour time.

The contradictory nature of reproductive subsumption – the contradictory relation between productive and reproductive work/time – deepens when reproductive subsumption is historically solved by assigning reproductive work to women and therefore the *matching* of production and reproduction through a gendered division of labour. In this case, the contradiction tilts disproportionately to women, women's bodies and capital requirements to have women working for wages as well as doing reproductive labour. In such landscapes, 'Since well-situated women are able to afford the services of underpaid female immigrant labourers, we are witnessing a redistribution of, for example, personal care and nursing within the female plane of existence'.[77] This redistribution, however, is differentiated across racial lines: the contradiction within reproductive workers is 'resolved' historically by pushing differentiation among women.[78]

Perhaps the most crucial contradiction, illustrating vividly the open-ended nature of subsumption as a process, is within the nature of reproductive labour/time as simultaneously a condition of, and a potential threat to, capitalism. Labour reproduction is a cardinal moment of capitalism through which labour power is restored and produced. Thus, reproductive labour/time is essential to production because it continually mitigates the inherently destructive forces of capitalism. So, if capitalism depletes and kills bodies and environments, reproductive labour counters that, i.e. it produces use value and metabolic value.[79] By constantly undoing what capital does, reproductive labour keeps the system running, preventing its accelerated destruction. Yet, from the point of view of labour, this space is potentially revolutionary. As Susan Ferguson recalls, 'concrete labour can never be fully identical with its abstract form, and the discrepancy between the two will generally be greater where the direct imposition of value imperatives is not available'.[80] Here, 'the production of life regularly requires resisting the subsumption of life to capital'.[81] In the momentaneous dwindling of abstract labour's gravitational pull, reproductive labour holds the potential to activate a world against capital. As Elson recalls, the seeds of anticapitalism do not fall from the sky and are always internal to the system. So, from this angle, social reproduction appears as the 'temporary precipitate of opposed *potentia*', it is always 'a moment of co-existent opposed possibilities'.[82] Bluntly, since reproductive labour oils the system, it can also set the fire to burn it down.

Overall, these contradictions highlight some important points. First, they flag how capital drastically changes the terms and conditions of human life. Holding to the category and analytical instruments of 'subsumption' is fundamental to highlight that the work of reproduction is re-created by capital under new and evolving terms and conditions. Second, these contradictions highlight the extraordinary instability of this system, and the tendency to solve these at the expense of both labour and nature. Third, the separation between productive and reproductive is a permanent act of violence. It creates wedges among labour on multiple fronts. It separates labour power – as an instance and moment of capital – from its bearer, labour as such, as the antithesis of capital. It materially dispossesses the working class from its means and realms of reproduction.[83] It thereby entails a fundamental fracture between workers and nature and among the working classes. As reproductive labour is expelled from the wage relation, it follows that the 'dull compulsion of economic forces' is insufficient to keep reproduction in a subordinate position, and while this is true for all workers, processes of naturalisation, institutionalised and non-institutionalised violence and disciplining are paramount in reproductive subsumption. Below, I turn to gender and race as some key 'raw materials' for the historical making of reproductive labour. I do that by drawing some rough historical sketches. Although partial and simplified, they help illustrate more concretely how gender and race were crucial ingredients in the subsumption of reproductive workers on two sides of the Atlantic.[84]

The violence of reproductive subsumption

As explained by Saenz de Sicilia, in Marx, 'the motif of overcoming the imposition of alien and dominating forms indifferent to the qualitative singularity of the living content they shape figures as a powerful influence on his critique of capitalist societies. The logical and abstract character of subsumption, as highlighted by Hegel, is a perfectly apt figure for the oppressive character of capital, as an alienating and one-sided form of social relatedness'.[85] The subsumption of labour under capital is thus a story of compulsion to adhere to capital's social form. As a subsumptive relation, reproductive subsumption is no different, hence central to the long history of primitive accumulation *and* beyond. Therefore, the violence necessary to separate, subordinate and devalue reproductive work needs to be historically investigated, and the dominance of concrete labour in reproduction needs to be interpreted as an artefact of capitalism as a mode of production rather than a transhistorical feature of reproductive work.[86] The vignettes below hint at these processes in the intertwined transitions in Europe and the Atlantic.

In *Caliban and the Witch*, Federici traces an overarching history of reproductive subsumption in Western Europe's transition to capitalism. The lynchpin of this four-century story is capital and states' violent struggles to divide the emerging working class and craft women as reproductive workers. It is well known that forcefully separated from 'the farm, the fen, and forest ecosystems'[87] and amidst the crumbling of the subsistence economy, peasants found themselves bonded to the market. Less acknowledged, is that the separation from the 'land' was magnified by an unparalleled process of 'social enclosure, the reproduction of workers shifting from the open field to the home, from the community to the family, from the public space (the common, the church) to the private'.[88] The overall privatisation of reproductive work hinged on the parallel expulsion of women from the wage and the general devaluation of their work: 'if a woman sewed some clothes it was "domestic work" or "housekeeping", even if the clothes were not for the family, whereas when a man did the same task it was considered "productive".'[89] Divorced from the land and married to a wage, male workers found in women's devalued/unpaid labour the lost common: 'in the new organisation of work *every woman (other than those privatised by bourgeois men) became a communal good*, for once women's activities were defined as non-work, women's labour began to appear as a natural resource, available to all, no less than the air we breathe and the water we drink'.[90] This continental gendering, naturalising, privatising and downgrading of reproductive work required the sustained disciplining of women on all fronts. Women became 'scolds', 'spinsters', 'witches', 'whores', 'shrews'; their bodies served to restock the working class, pacify its riotous spurs, or ultimately burned at the stake to eradicate magic, traditional knowledge and working-class power. Ultimately, their onslaught was key to reversing the relation between production and reproduction.

The Atlantic side of this primitive accumulation took violence to ever greater heights. The formation of workers took a different trajectory here than in Europe.[91] A key to understanding this difference resides in Jairus Banaji's distinction between 'modes of production' and 'forms of exploitation'. For him, '*historically*, capital-accumulation has been characterised by considerable flexibility in the structuring of production and in forms of labour and organisation of labour used in producing surplus value'.[92] By highlighting that in capitalism, wage labour takes multiple forms as 'capital-positing labour', i.e. 'abstract, value-producing labour',[93] this perspective allows recasting the making of a working class beyond so-called 'free wage-labour' and spreading from African coasts through the Atlantic and its plantations.

For Stephanie Smallwood, along African coastal forts and in slave ships 'traders reduced people to the sum of their biological parts, thereby scaling life down to an arithmetical equation and finding the lowest common denominator'.[94] To realise this transformation into commodities – functional to slavery as a form of exploitation – millions of 'Venuses' were dispossessed of land, kinship, culture, memory and ultimately any epistemic possibility.[95] Their formation as 'capital-positing labour' required the most violent expansion of labour power at the expense of labour, whose 'reproductive need' was denied together with all subjectivity. Constantly 'probing the limits up to which it is possible to discipline the body without extinguishing the life within',[96] this specific subsumption implied a form of racialisation aimed at turning humans into labouring machines, specifically a *class* of workers with liminal reproduction, one flattened to an intermittent caloric intake. Here, the separation between production and reproduction entailed an unprecedented squeeze, an attempted erasure of the latter by the former: for captives, any meaningful notion of reproductive labour remained in the concessions, villages and cities from which they had been uprooted. In this landscape, class-making implied an entire rewriting of the enslaved, their cultural unmaking, de-humanising and un-gendering: 'we might say that the slave ship, its crew, and its human-as-cargo stand for a wild and unclaimed richness of *possibility* that is not interrupted, nor "counted'/"accounted", or differentiated, until its movement gains the land thousands of miles away from the point of departure'.[97]

On American and Caribbean shores, this human cargo powered the plantation economy. The plantation epitomised the crudest reversal between production and reproduction. Here, women did not find themselves tending to planters' domestic needs but instead crowded tobacco, sugar and cotton fields, undertaking endless, shattering physical work.[98] Their subsumption as quintessential productive workers, however, never erased their reproductive *potential*. Women were also the potential *increasers* and pacifiers of the slave population, at once 'productive and reproductive commodities',[99] their belly 'a factory of production incommensurate with notions of the maternal, the conjugal or the domestic'.[100] Thus, if women in Europe were formally distanced from the market, the enslaved woman's 'reproductive potential ensured that her capacity to gestate a child meant that she carried the market inside her body'.[101] Subjugated by the market at the most intimate level, any protection of enslaved private lives, their corporal and cultural integrity, was a permanent site of class struggle. In the latter, the nature of reproductive labour as a 'temporary precipitate of opposed *potentia*' comes again to the fore.[102]

For Sylvia Wynter, as the plantation marked 'the reduction of Man to Labour and of Nature to Land', the fracture between production and reproduction followed the boundary between the plantation and the plot,[103] where an uneven and volatile 'shadow world of cultivation' had developed since the first generations of enslaved Africans.[104] Thus, if plots represented crevices to plant yams, 'folk culture' and 'recreated traditional values – use values',[105] living quarters permitted 'a retrieval of the man and the women in their fundamental humanity'.[106] In these precarious interstices of reproduction, women's labour was key: by performing the only labour unclaimed by the planter, and alongside continuous and open acts of counterinsurgency, 'her survival-oriented activities were themselves a form of resistance'.[107] Thus, in the most brutal landscape of capitalist subsumption marked by the *attempted* obliteration of social reproduction, incipient reproductive work – as simultaneously the condition for, and a threat to, the plantation economy – still interspersed the plantation, literally and figuratively cultivating the seeds of resistance at its margins.

Overall, these historical sketches provide some concrete examples of the emergence of a global working class that is differentiated and fragmented from the outset: they illustrate how the construction of reproductive work and workers follows different, interlinked trajectories East and West of the Atlantic. As sketches, they remain necessarily general, simplified and unfinished. They overlook detailed regional and local histories highlighting different tendencies and countertendencies operating in capitalism. Crucially, they omit the multiple colonial trails stretching through Africa and beyond, through the Pacific,[108] for which more research is needed.

Cannibal gaze

This article has sought to explain and historically trace key internal fractures within the working class – chiefly the one between productive and reproductive labour – by drawing on Elson's analysis of the specific *form* labour assumes in capitalism. As argued, this *form* takes shape through a chasm between productive and reproductive work, i.e. the artificial separation and domination of the production of value for capital over the reproduction of the individual and life. The category of reproductive subsumption is built to explain theoretically and historically this essential separation as a subsumptive process, a violent relation between capital and labour that is co-determinative, historically contingent and open-ended. At the most abstract level, this separation occurs as abstract labour dominates productive work while concrete labour dominates reproductive work. In this polarising relation, the 'dominating' form of labour always exists in *tension* and *continuity* with the dominated form. Thus, the concrete labour of social reproduction is never entirely free from the pressures and compulsion of abstract labour.

By detailing some of the specific forms of violence deployed to separate (abstract) and devalue reproductive work, histories of reproductive subsumption locate the 'production of difference' in historical processes of class formation, showing how 'the social relations of gender, race and sexuality are held as internally constitutive of class, rather than external to it'.[109] Specifically, within these diversified processes of class-making, race and gender represent violent *subsumptive forces* –'abstracting devices'[110] – *forming* reproductive workers in context-specific ways, reallocating them differently across the productive/reproductive divide and 'scaling their humanness' along the way. This illuminates again how the prism of social reproduction throws new light on different processes of racialising and gendering operating at different points and the legacies these might carry over the present.

Like other forms of labour subsumption, reproductive subsumption is never a finished project, i.e. subsumption is constantly reposited by the struggle of those subsumed and by the internal contradictions emerging from their subsumption. So, while the long period of primitive accumulation set processes of reproductive subsumption in motion, these processes remain open-ended even when capital is no longer in a state of 'becoming'. The requirement of reproductive work – whether outsourced, marketised, squeezed, or infinitely stretched to make up for erratic and thin wages – does not fade when the 'dull compulsion of economic forces' is in full swing. Albeit constantly evolving, extra-economic violence remains a pillar of reproductive subsumption, as evidenced by the recalcitrance of pervasive forms of gendered and racialised violence throughout the history of capitalism. Therefore, exposing the historical process and dynamics perpetually bundling the majority of the world's workers with 'natural work' or as 'closer to nature' remains critical. Following Suzanne Cesaire, this 'great camouflage' of capitalist social relations and hierarchies needs to be exposed and rejected. And to do that, one's historical gaze needs to be 'cannibal'.

Elena Baglioni is a Reader in Global Supply Chain Management and Sustainability at QMUL. She researches global value chains, the political economy of natural resource industries, labour regime and labour process analyses, ecology, social reproduction and transitions to capitalism. She co-edited the volume Labour Regimes and Global Production *and is an Editor of the* Global Labour Journal.

Notes

1. Diane Elson, 'The Value Theory of Labour', in *Value: The Representation of Labour in Capitalism*, ed. Diane Elson (London: Verso, 2015). I am deeply grateful to my dear friends and colleagues Liam Campling, Gerard Hanlon, Edward Legon, Matteo Mandarini, Amit Rai, Jack Sargeant and Shreya Sinha. Their insights, conversations, patience and suggestions over previous versions of this article have been invaluable. I would also like to thank the editors of *Radical Philosophy* and, not least, the ISRF, which provided much-needed time and space to undertake this project.
2. Diane Paton, 'Gender History, Global History, and Atlantic Slavery', *The American Historical Review* 127:2 (2022), 726–754.
3. Nicole Leach, 'Transitions to Capitalism: Social-Reproduction Feminism Encounters Political Marxism', *Historical Materialism* 24:2 (2016), 11–137, 114.
4. This work sides with, but differs from, the recent and important adoption of a feminist approach to subsumption by Elizabeth Portella and Larry Alan Busk, 'The Formal and Real Subsumption of Gender Relations', *Historical Materialism* (2024), 1–34.
5. Barbara Laslett and Johanna Brenner, 'Gender and Social Reproduction: Historical Perspectives', *Annual Review of Sociology* 15 (1989), 381–404, 383.
6. Mariarosa Dalla Costa and Selma James, *Women and the Subversion of the Community* (Falling World Press, 1972); Nicole Cox and Silvia Federici, *Counter-Planning from the Kitchen* (New York: Wages for Housework Committee and Falling Wall Press, 1975); Rohini Hensman, 'Wage-Labour: The Production and Sale of the Commodity Labour-Power', *Historical Materialism Blog*, originally published 1977, accessed July 16, 2025, https://www.historicalmaterialism.org/wage-labour-the-production-and-sale-of-the-commodity-labour-power-1977; Leopoldina Fortunati, *L'arcano della riproduzione: casalinghe, prostitute, operai e capitale* (Venezia: Marsilio Editori, 1981); Lise Vogel, *Marxism and the Oppression of Women* (Chicago: Haymarket Books, 2013).
7. Val Plumwood, *Feminism and the Mastery of Nature* (London: Routledge, 1993), 199; Maria Mies and Vandana Shiva, *Ecofeminism* (London: Zed Books, 1993).
8. Marcel van der Linden, *The World Wide Web of Work*

(London: UCL Press, 2023), 11.

9. Andrés Saenz de Sicilia, 'Being, Becoming, Subsumption: The Kantian Roots of a Marxist Problematic', *Radical Philosophy* 2:12 (2022), 35–47.

10. Patrick Murray, *The Mismeasure of Wealth: Essays on Marx and Social Form* (Leiden: Brill, 2016), 296.

11. Murray, *296*.

12. Jairus Banaji, *Theory as History: Essays on Modes of Production and Exploitation* (Leiden: Brill, 2010).

13. Henry Bernstein, 'Where is population in "surplus population"?', *Focaal* 97, 79–88 (2023), 83; emphasis mine.

14. Saenz de Sicilia, 'Being', 38.

15. Banaji, *Theory as History*, 3.

16. David McNally, 'The Dialectics of Unity and Difference in the Constitution of Wage Labour: On Internal Relations and Working-Class Formation', *Capital & Class* 39:1 (2015), 131–46, 142.

17. Silvia Federici, *Caliban and the Witch: Women, the Body, and Primitive Accumulation* (New York: Autonomedia, 2014), 63.

18. Gargi Bhattacharyya, *Rethinking Racial Capitalism* (London: Rowman & Littlefield International, 2018).

19. Bhattacharyya, *Rethinking Racial Capitalism*, 50.

20. Elson, 'The Value Theory of Labour', 143

21. Robert Nichols, *Theft Is Property* (Durham, NC: Duke University Press, 2019).

22. On this, see the debate in *Viewpoint Magazine* (2015): 'Gender and Capitalism: Debating Cinzia Arruza's "Remarks on Gender"'; and Andreas Bieler and Adam David Morton, 'Is Capitalism Structurally Indifferent to Gender?: Routes to a Value Theory of Reproductive Labour', *Environment and Planning A: Economy and Space* 53:7 (2021), 1749–69.

23. Saenz de Sicilia, 'Being'; and Andrés Saenz de Sicilia, 'Subsumption', in *The SAGE Handbook of Marxism*, eds. Beverley Skeggs, Sara R. Farris, Alberto Toscano and Svenja Bromberg (London: Sage, 2022).

24. Saenz de Sicilia, 'Subsumption', 614.

25. Saenz de Sicilia, 'Subsumption', 612.

26. Karl Marx, 'Results of the Immediate Process of Production', Appendix to *Capital: A Critique of Political Economy, Volume 1* (London: Penguin Books, 1990).

27. For space reasons, I omit the less-known categories of hybrid and ideal subsumption, see Murray, *The Mismeasure of Wealth*, and Massimiliano Tomba, *Marx's Temporalities* (Chicago: Haymarket Books, 2013). While Marx somehow conveys a linear development from formal to real subsumption, he also recognises the possibility of forms of formal subsumption emerging side-by-side with forms of real subsumption (Marx, *Capital*). Formal/real subsumption and relative/absolute surplus value can be co-dependent and co-determinative and non-linear. See also Raju J. Das, 'Reconceptualizing Capitalism: Forms of Labour, Class Struggle, and Uneven Development', *Review of Radical Political Economics* 44:2 (2012), 178–200.

28. Karl Marx, *Capital*, 1021; emphasis in original.

29. Banaji, *Theory as History*, 280.

30. Marx, *Capital*, 1025, 1020.

31. Marx, *Capital*, 1035.

32. See Saenz de Sicilia, *Subsumption*, for an excursion over some of the key evolutions of this category, including Negri's. On total subsumption, see also Endnotes, 'The History of Subsumption', *Endnotes* 2 (2010), accessed July 16, 2025, https://endnotes.org.uk/articles/the-history-of-subsumption. In a recent book, Saenz de Sicilia discerns three forms of subsumption: 1) via commodification, 2) via production and 3) via social reproduction. Andrés Saenz de Sicilia, *Subsumption in Kant, Hegel and Marx: From the Critique of Reason to the Critique of Society* (Leiden: Brill, 2024). The latter refers to the social reproduction of the capitalist system and thus differs from the concept of reproductive subsumption developed here. Although Saenz de Sicilia situates subsumption 'both within and beyond the bourgeois economic totality' (iv, 214), he does not systematically extend his analysis beyond production. Instead, through the concept of 'reproductive subsumption', I seek to venture into this terrain by investigating the contradictions set in motion by capitalism not at the total societal level, but between production and labour reproduction.

33. Antonio Negri, *Marx Beyond Marx* (South Hadley, MA: Bergin & Garvey, 1984), 114.

34. Real subsumption is also the most unstable, hence fragile phase of capital, characterised by the peaking antagonism between 'social capital' and 'social labour'. See *Marx Beyond Marx*; Michael Hardt and Antonio Negri, *Empire* (Cambridge, MA: Harvard University Press, 2000).

35. Samir Amin, 'Contra Hardt and Negri: Multitude or Generalized Proletarianization?', *Monthly Review* 66:6 (2014).

36. George Caffentzis, 'The End of Work or the Renaissance of Slavery?' (1998), accessed July 16, 2025, https://fadingtheaesthetic.wordpress.com/wp-content/uploads/2013/05/george-caffentzis-the-end-of-work-or-the-rennaissance-of-slavery-common-sense-24.pdf.

37. Veronica Bennholdt-Thomsen, 'Subsistence Production and Extended Reproduction', in *Of Marriage and the Market*, eds. K. Young et al (London: CSE Books, 1981).

38. Bennholdt-Thomsen, 'Subsistence Production and Extended Reproduction', 26.

39. Bennholdt-Thomsen, 'Subsistence Production and Extended Reproduction', 27.

40. Bennholdt-Thomsen, 'Subsistence Production and Extended Reproduction', 27.
41. For Banaji, capitalism works 'through a multiplicity of forms of exploitation based on wage-labour', 'these "forms" may reflect the subsumption of labour into capital in ways where the "sale" of labour-power for wages is mediated and possibly disguised in more complex arrangements' (Banaji, *Theory as History*, 145).
42. Leopoldina Fortunati, *The Arcana of Reproduction, Housewives, Prostitutes, Workers and Capital*, (London: Verso, 2025), 220.
43. Sébastien Rioux, 'Embodied Contradictions: Capitalism, Social Reproduction and Body Formation', *Women's Studies International Forum* 48 (2015), 194–202, 195.
44. Stuart Hall, 'Race, Articulation, and Societies Structured in Dominance', in *Essential Essays*, vol. 1, ed. David Morley (Durham, NC: Duke University Press, 1980).
45. Hall, 'Race, Articulation'.
46. Fortunati, *The Arcana*, 13, quoting Marx's *Grundrisse*.
47. Tomba, *Marx's Temporalities*, 135.
48. All labour is always inherently productive, in the sense that it is always an expenditure of energy, muscles and brain that change form, a metabolism of matter and energy, a material process. By the same token, because all labour is an expenditure of something, to secure its existence it must also be to some extent reproductive. It is difficult to draw a precise line between what work is and is not reproductive, given that reproduction includes satisfying one's needs beyond immediate, bare physical survival. In sum, productive and reproductive labour 'share a continuity as well as difference' (Elson 2015), 142.
49. Elson, 'The Value Theory of Labour', 128.
50. Elson, 'The Value Theory of Labour', 144. Also building from Elson's value theory, Mezzadri describes abstract, concrete, private and social labour as 'varied sides of the same multidimensional coin'. Her analysis extends the inseparability of these forms to the inseparability of the use/exchange-value of labour as labour/labour-power. See Alessandra Mezzadri, 'Value Theories in Motion: Circular Labour Migration, Unfinished Land Dispossession and Reproductive Struggles across the Urban-Rural Divide', *Environment and Planning F* (2024).
51. Elson, 'The Value Theory of Labour', 142.
52. Elson, 'The Value Theory of Labour', 149.
53. The dominance of private, concrete labour over reproductive work as a value relation has received different interpretations. Key representatives of the Wages for Housework movement (Maria Rosa Dalla Costa, Selma James, Silvia Federici and Leopoldina Fortunati, among others) have interpreted reproductive work as surplus value producing. In *The Arcana*, Fortunati argued that in capitalism, the disguising of domestic work as unproductive work is precisely what allows capital to extract surplus value from it. Slightly earlier, Rohini Hensman flagged the inconsistencies in Marx's analysis around the reproduction of labour power as a process of individual or productive consumption (Hensman, 'Wage-Labour'). Alessandra Mezzadri has developed and extended this view more recently. See Alessandra Mezzadri, 'A Value Theory of Inclusion: Informal Labour, the Homeworker, and the Social Reproduction of Value', *Antipode* 53:4 (2021), 1186–1205; and Mezzadri, 'Value Theories in Motion'. Countering this interpretation is the work of Lise Vogel, taken up by many contributors to Tithi Bhattacharya, ed., *Social Reproduction Theory* (London: Pluto Press, 2017). Both interpretations agree that reproductive labour is never entirely waged, it is precisely its naturalisation as reproductive work that is a necessary condition for capital. Reproductive subsumption traces this process of worker formation and reproductive naturalisation in historical perspective.
54. Following Marx, Elson argues that in capitalism 'abstract labour comes to have a "practical truth" because the unity of human labour, its differentiation simply in terms of quantity of labour, is not simply recognised as a mental process but has a correlate in a real social process, that goes on quite independently of how we reason about it'. Elson, 'The Value Theory of Labour', 150.
55. Marx, *Capital*, 128, 134.
56. Kohei Saito, *Capital, Nature, and the Unfinished Critique of Political Economy* (New York: Monthly Review Press, 2017).
57. It is temporal in several senses. A material process is inherently a temporal one, an unfolding of matter and energy, a metabolism occurring in time. Abstract labour is also labour seen not from a qualitative but from a purely quantitatively perspective, and the unit of quantification is time, the substance of socially necessary labour time.
58. Marx, *Capital*, 136.
59. Tomba, *Marx's Temporalities*.
60. Marx, *Capital*, 136.
61. Marx, *Capital*, 132.
62. Marnie Holborow, *Homes in Crisis Capitalism* (London: Bloomsbury Academic, 2024).
63. Rioux, 'Embodied Contradictions'.
64. Endnotes, 'The Logic of Gender: On the Separation of Spheres and the Process of Abjection', *Endnotes* 3 (2013), 4, accessed July 16, 2025, https://endnotes.org.uk/articles/the-logic-of-gender.
65. Silvia Federici, *Revolutions at Point Zero: Housework, Reproduction, and Feminist Struggle* (Oakland: PM Press, 2012), 35–36.
66. Stavros Tombazos, *Time in Marx* (Leiden: Brill, 2014), 85. Tombazos further specifies that 'The latter is, as a matter of course, "necessary" in the historical sense of

the word, and not in its physiological sense. Social needs evolve'.

67. Mark Fisher, *Capitalist Realism: Is There No Alternative?* (Winchester: Zero Books, 2009), 22.
68. Bhattacharya, *Social Reproduction Theory*.
69. Bhattacharyya, *Rethinking Racial Capitalism*.
70. Luci Cavallero and Verónica Gago, *A Feminist Reading of Debt* (London: Pluto Press, 2021).
71. Oksala, 'Capitalism and Gender Oppression', 6.
72. Endnotes, 'The Logic of Gender'.
73. Vogel, *Marxism and the Oppression of Women*, 163.
74. Wilma A. Dunaway, 'Through the Portal of the Household: Conceptualizing Women's Subsidies to Commodity Chains', in *Gendered Commodity Chains*, ed. Winifred A. Dunaway (Stanford, CA: Stanford University Press, 2014), 55–71.
75. Federici, *Caliban and the Witch*, 75.
76. Maria Mies, *Patriarchy and Accumulation on a World Scale* (London: Zed Books, 1986).
77. Roswitha Scholz, 'Patriarchy and Commodity Society: Gender without the Body', in *Marxism and the Critique of Value*, ed. Neil Larsen et al (Chicago: M-C-M, 2009), 137.
78. Angela Davis, *Women, Race and Class* (New York: Vintage Books, 1983).
79. Ariel Salleh, *Ecofeminism as Politics: Nature, Marx and the Post-Modern* (London: Zed Books, 2017).
80. Susan Ferguson, *Women and Work: Feminism, Labour and Social Reproduction* (London: Pluto Press, 2020), 139.
81. Ferguson, *Women and Work*, 138.
82. Elson, 'The Value Theory of Labour', 142.
83. Separation refers here to 'market mediation': production for the market becomes the chief vehicle to reproduce oneself. According to Mau, market 'mediation' always already implies domination and compulsion: 'what is actually transmitted through the market is not *information* but *compulsory commands* communicated through the movements of things'. Søren Mau, *Mute Compulsion* (London: Verso, 2023), 186. See Nichols, *Theft is Property*, for a sophisticated reading of 'dispossession'.
84. My current work, not included here, investigates in detail processes of reproductive subsumption in Western Africa.
85. Saenz de Sicilia, *Subsumption*, 614.
86. Hall, 'Race, Articulation, and Societies Structured in Dominance'.
87. Carolyn Merchant, *The Death of Nature: Women, Ecology, and the Scientific Revolution* (London: Wildwood House, 1980).
88. Federici, *Caliban and the Witch*, 84.
89. Federici, *Caliban and the Witch*, 92.
90. Federici, *Caliban and the Witch*, 97.
91. Eric Williams, *Capitalism and Slavery* (London: Penguin Books, 2022).
92. Banaji, *Theory as History*, 145.
93. Banaji, *Theory as History*, 54–55.
94. Stephanie E. Smallwood, *Saltwater Slavery* (Cambridge, MA: Harvard University Press, 2007), 43.
95. Saidiya Hartman, 'Venus in Two Acts', *Small Axe* 12:2 (2008), 1–14.
96. Smallwood, *Saltwater Slavery*, 36.
97. Hortense J. Spillers, 'Mama's Baby, Papa's Maybe: An American Grammar Book', *Diacritics* 17:2 (1987), 64–81, 72.
98. Barbara Bush, *Slave Women in Caribbean Society, 1650-1838* (London: James Currey, 1990); Stella Dadzie, *A Kick in the Belly* (London: Verso, 2020).
99. Jennifer L. Morgan, *Laboring Women* (Philadelphia: University of Pennsylvania Press, 2004); and Jennifer L. Morgan, 'Partus Sequitur Ventrem: Law, Race, and Reproduction in Colonial Slavery', *Small Axe* 22:1 (2018), 1–17, 18.
100. Saidiya Hartman, 'The Belly of the World: A Note on Black Women's Labors', *Souls* 18:1 (2016, 166–73, 169.
101. Jennifer Morgan, *Reckoning with Slavery* (Dale: Dale University Press, 2021), 222.
102. Elson, 'The Value Theory of Labour'.
103. Sylvia Wynter, 'Novel and History, Plot and the Plantation', *Savacou* 5:1 (1971), 95-102.
104. Judith A. Carney and Richard Nicholas Rosomoff, *In the Shadow of Slavery* (Berkeley: University of California Press, 2009).
105. Wynter, 'Novel and History, Plot and the Plantation', 99-100.
106. Angela Davis, 'Reflections on the Black Woman's Role in the Community of Slaves', *The Massachusetts Review* 13:1/2 (1972), 81–100, 86.
107. Davis, 'Reflections', 86.
108. Onur Ulas Ince, *Before the Global Color Line: Empire, Capitalism, and Race in Asia, 1800–1850* (forthcoming, Oxford University Press).
109. Bieler and Morton, 'Is Capitalism Structurally Indifferent to Gender?', 1760.
110. Brenna Bhandar and Alberto Toscano, 'Race, real estate and real abstraction', *Radical Philosophy* 194, 8–17 (2015).

Phenomenology of necessary illusion
Gillian Rose on personification and the failure to think the absolute

Robert Lucas Scott

> I shall read the writing and the meaning I shall make known to the king.
>
> Daniel 5: 17[1]

The critical task of modern philosophy, for Gillian Rose, is to provide an account of the historical barriers that prevent us from thinking philosophically and, relatedly, from achieving a collective existence free from domination – the historical barriers that prevent us, in Hegelian terms, from 'thinking the absolute'. These historical barriers, insofar as they refer to consciousness, are what Rose calls 'necessary illusions' – not 'necessary' in the Kantian sense of fundamental features of the human mind, but 'necessary' in the Hegelian-Marxist sense that they are historically produced by the society of which they are a part. As she puts it in a lecture, 'you can't just stop the mistake by knowing about it, you've got to alter the conditions that give rise to it.' The illusions are necessary not in a metaphysical sense, but in the sense that they are 'unavoidable even after we've found out about them' – for as long as that which determined them still persists.[2] Otherwise, they are in fact contingent; they could be otherwise.

Four times in *Hegel Contra Sociology*, Gillian Rose writes a version of the claim that 'Hegel's philosophy has *no* social import if the absolute cannot be thought.'[3] A twist of the argument, however, is the discovery that we cannot think the absolute – or at least not in the way we might have expected. All thought is prone to abstraction; all recognition is prone to misrecognise. A second corresponding twist, though, is that in spite of our failure to think the absolute, Hegel's philosophy still has a social import for it provides the means for comprehending this failure as a failure, necessary illusions as necessary illusions, while comprehending why and how these failures have come about. For Rose, such a comprehension 'is to think the absolute and fail to think it quite differently' from those who would simply claim to think or realise the absolute when they are failing to (Fichte) or concede the failure without understanding why (Kant).[4]

As this essay will demonstrate, Rose argues that under capitalism – or, more specifically, under bourgeois property law – necessary illusion has two halves. The first half is well known: *reification* – the misrecognition of relations between people as relations between *things*, theorised most famously by Lukács with his influential generalisation of Marx's theory of commodity fetishism. The second, frequently overlooked, half is *personification* – the misrecognition of people as *persons*, abstract and individuated legal subjects who, as bearers of rights, embody formal and abstract freedom and equality. J. M. Bernstein claims that, after her early work on Adorno and the Frankfurt School, Rose abandoned 'reification theory as the mechanism for a critically expanded Marxist social theory, opting for a (Marxian inflected) Hegelian speculation in its place'[5]. In contrast, this essay will demonstrate that Rose not only retained a theory of reification but supplemented it with a theory of personification. This is a theory she takes to be already nascent in Marx's *Grundrisse* and his subsequent development of the theory of the commodity fetish, but finds its first full articulation in Hegel's critiques of Kant and Fichte. As Rose elaborates throughout *Hegel Contra Sociology*, Hegel's critique reveals that Kant and Fichte fail to recognise the social determination of their philosophies.

In doing so, they unthinkingly recapitulate necessary illusion rather than comprehend it. Their apparently ahistorical metaphysics in fact 'smuggle' in the historical legal fictions of 'thing' and 'person'.[6]

The necessary illusion of personification has been neglected, both in the reception of Rose and in critical theory more broadly. As a result, critical theory has often unwittingly reproduced these illusions – particularly notable in a tendency towards a negative construal of freedom as freedom from historical necessity, and towards the development of abstract 'theories' to be imposed upon their objects. Recovering the concept of personification, however, opens new paths for more adequately grasping the distinctly modern illusion of the sovereign freedom of the subject which persists despite the undeniable realities of unfreedom. This illusion is perhaps more pervasive today than ever, detectable in everything from the ideological allure of individual freedom, to the rise of left- and right-wing identity politics, the hypertrophy of inner life, and voluntaristic appeals to abstract forms of freedom and the will, all in spite of endemic individual depoliticisation. At the root of this contradiction – between individual 'freedom' and 'empowerment' and individual depoliticisation – lies the juridical form of personhood that mediates modern subjectivity. For it is through the (mis)recognition of oneself as a *person* (a bearer of property rights) that one comes to (mis)recognise oneself as free, even when one does not actually own property, possesses no means of production, and has to sell one's labour-power on the market as a *thing*. To reformulate a phrase from Hegel: everything turns on grasping and expressing necessary illusion, not only as reification, but equally as personification.[7]

While contesting the idea that Rose abandoned Marxism (a view put forward not only by Bernstein but also by Tony Gorman, Peter Osborne and Martin Jay),[8] it must nonetheless be acknowledged that, in *Hegel Contra Sociology* at least (the very work where she announces her project of critical Marxism), Rose argues that Hegel has a significant advantage over Marx for his phenomenological mode of presentation, for which the 'exposition of abstract thinking and the derivation of the social institutions which determine it are completely integrated in the tracing of the education of self-consciousness at specific historical moments.'[9] She claims that Marx, by contrast, neglects this phenomenological innovation and lapses instead into a one-sided materialism which prioritises practice over theory and therefore upholds abstract dichotomies between being and consciousness, between objective determinations and necessary subjective illusions – dichotomies which Hegel shows to be socially determined. Indeed, *Hegel Contra Sociology* concludes by arguing that it is only by following Hegel and immanently presenting the contradictions between substance and subject (capital and subjectivity) that the Marxist analysis of the economy may be meaningfully linked to a comprehension of the conditions of revolutionary practice. Without this link, practice becomes a question of appealing to an abstract imperative, will, act or 'class consciousness', and to the 'pre-judged, imposed "realization"' of Marx's analysis '*as a theory, as Marxism*' – an appeal and imposition which disavows and therefore obscures the ways in which these forms have been determined. In Rose's words: 'an instrumental use of a "materialist" theory rests in fact on the idealist assumption that social reality is an object and that its definition depends on revolutionary consciousness'; this risks 'recreating a terror, or reinforcing lawlessness, or strengthening bourgeois law in its universality and arbitrariness.'[10]

This argument, framing Marx as a kind of neo-Fichtean, has been a source of controversy since the earliest reception of *Hegel Contra Sociology* – particularly in Peter Osborne's review in a 1982 issue of *Radical Philosophy* (which I will go on to address in more detail). What has been ignored, however, even in Osborne's retrospective reflections on Rose's relation to Marxism, published 33 years after his initial review, is that Rose totally abandons this criticism of Marx in all her work following *Hegel Contra Sociology*, precisely once she comes to recognise the specificity and importance of the category of the 'person' in Marx's writings. From *Dialectic of Nihilism* onwards, it is not just Hegel but also Marx, for Rose, who expounds what she calls the 'antinomy of law' – the modern separation of the realm of economic exchange from that of politics and citizenship, arising 'from specifically modern forms of private property and formal equality'. Crucially, it is this separation which, for Hegel *and* Marx, 'gives rise to the illusion of sovereign individuality', of *personhood*.[11]

It will take another essay to detail what I take to be Rose's move *towards* rather than away from Marx after *Hegel Contra Sociology*, which would counter Osborne's claim that her project of a critical Marxism turned out to be 'something of a passing placeholder or a mask within her thought.'[12] Suffice it to say for the moment, though, that where Rose complains in 1981's *Hegel Contra Sociology* that Marx's first thesis on Feuerbach 'reinforces the abstract oppositions between idealism and materialism, theory and praxis',[13] by the time of her 1986 lecture 'Does Marx Have a Method?', she says the exact opposite of the very same passage: 'it cannot be said that Marx is here or anywhere else defending materialism in opposition to idealism, for he is indicting the very opposition between objects, senses and passivity in materialism; and the will, subjectivity and activity in idealism.'[14] Likewise, in 1992's *The Broken Middle*, Rose reads Marx's *On The Jewish Question* as a sustained account of how the antinomy of law 'makes political man into an abstract, artificial man, "an *allegorical, moral* person"', which reduces 'political life and institutions to the interests of egoistic man, the member of civil society.'[15] And in the posthumously published *Mourning Becomes the Law* (1996), Rose commends an 'aporetic' reading of Marx, 'as insisting on the uncertain course of class struggle, which depends on the unpredictable configurations of objective conditions and the formation of class consciousness.'[16] In short, while in *Hegel Contra Sociology*, Rose reads Marx deterministically as another Kantian or Fichtean, as *assuming* abstract dichotomies, in all of her later work, wherever Marx is mentioned, she reads him as she reads Hegel: as *comprehending* these dichotomies and their social determination. When Rose writes in the Introduction to 1984's *Dialectic of Nihilism*, then, that '[e]mphasis on the differences between Marx's and Hegel's thinking has obscured the continuity of their preoccupation with the antinomy of law', she should be read as referring, at least in part, to her own earlier work in *Hegel Contra Sociology*.[17]

The present essay traces the early development of Rose's thought on necessary social illusion. It begins with her work on Adorno and the Frankfurt School, and her critique of a one-sided theory of necessary illusion as reification. From there, it follows her retrieval of Hegel's and Marx's focus on the juridical opposition of free subjects (or *persons*) and subjected *things* as the 'speculative core' of their work. The essay then gives a more detailed account of her recovery of Hegel's phenomenological critiques of Kant and Fichte, which discover the presupposed concepts and institutions of modern property law – principally 'persons' and 'things' – at every level of their philosophies. This is followed by a rebuttal of Osborne's criticisms of Rose, both in his 1982 review and in his 2015 retrospective essay, which misinterpret her 'retrieval' of Hegelian speculative experience for social theory as a reduction of the mechanism of social transformation to a matter of merely recognising misrecognition.[18] Finally, the essay finishes with a coda comparing Rose's insistence on thinking and failing to think the absolute with Slavoj Žižek's assertion that the absolute itself is a failure.

I pursue this comparison because Žižek is arguably the most influential left-Hegelian in recent decades – maybe even since Kojève – and because his work shares significant affinities with Rose's own attempt to retrieve Hegelian speculative thinking for Marxism. I argue, however, that by returning to *Hegel Contra Sociology*, we may see how Žižek's elevation of failure to metaphysical or absolute heights obscures the determination of this failure by a specific kind of law – a law which Rose's Hegel enables us to comprehend. Critical theory after Žižek leaves us lacking, lost and alienated, without knowing why, for he conceives of such a condition as *ontologic-*

ally necessary. And while his call for a revolutionary 'abyssal act'[19] or *'pure voluntarism'* – a 'free decision to act against historical necessity'[20] – may appear to offer a path to transforming society, this essay will demonstrate how such a call ultimately risks merely reproducing the present state of things, by overlooking how the very opposition of freedom *against* necessity which he assumes is itself an illusion arising from modern property law.

How is critical theory possible? Adorno

Rose's preoccupation with necessary illusion begins with her 1976 PhD thesis on Adorno. This was developed into her first book, *The Melancholy Science* (1978), and expanded upon in her undergraduate lectures on *Marxist Modernism* (1979, published 2024; reviewed in *RP* 2.18) – works which explore how the Frankfurt School generalised Marx's theories of the value form and commodity fetishism into theories of reification.

Marx's theory of commodity fetishism was always a theory of necessary illusion, expressing that under conditions of capitalist production and exchange, 'a particular social relation among people ... assumes, for these people themselves, the phantasmagoric form of a relation among things.'[21] The phantasmagoric form in which commodities appear to us fundamentally misrecognises what they are, and misrecognises the source of their value. For Rose, this is 'the most speculative moment in Marx's exposition of capital. It comes nearest to demonstrating in the historically-specific case of commodity producing society how substance is ((mis)-represented as) subject, how necessary illusion arises out of productive activity.'[22] And yet, for Marx, this illusion is not simply 'false'. (As Rose notes, the notion of 'false consciousness' is Engels' invention.[23]) It is instead a *real* illusion insofar as it is systematic and unavoidable given present conditions. To repeat: 'You can't just stop the mistake by knowing about it, you've got to alter the conditions that give rise to it.' Marx was primarily interested in how this real illusion functioned in the realm of commodity production and exchange. Lukács and the Frankfurt School, meanwhile, aimed to expand the scope of his analysis to other capitalist institutions (such as religion and law) and to capitalist culture (both popular and avant-garde).

According to Rose, this generalisation was both for better and for worse: 'for better' because it provides a fuller account of the intransigence of capitalist domination than Marx himself was able to derive; 'for worse' because this generalisation was taken as 'an invitation to hermeneutic anarchy'[24] – as an invitation to take liberties with the specificities, complexities and many of the crucial elements of Marx's theory. As Rose complains, the term 'reification' is 'used to evoke, often by mere suggestion or allusion, a very peculiar and complex epistemological setting which is rarely examined further or justified', thus sacrificing its critical or explanatory force.[25] She is particularly critical of those who use 'reification' to be simply 'synonymous with objectification' – that is, of those who would use it to describe any process by which something comes to be conceptualised in static terms – in a way which 'does not even pertain any longer to a specific mode of production.' She is also critical, though, of those who, following Lukács, have generalised Marx's theory of commodity fetishism 'without making it their task to rehearse Marx's theory of value' more broadly and therefore without assessing 'the various different ways in which the theory might be generalised.'[26]

For Rose, these insufficiently thoroughgoing theories of reification have arisen in part because of 'the various emphases that Marx himself put on [his theory of value].'[27] In the *Grundrisse*, Marx writes:

> Labour capacity has appropriated for itself only the subjective conditions of necessary labour ... separated from the conditions of its realization [the objective conditions] – and it has posited these conditions themselves as *things*, *values*, which confront it in an alien, commanding personification.[28]

This short description of the illusions inherent to capitalist production and exchange encompasses three subtly distinct points, each of which Marx would later emphasise as paramount at different times: 'Sometimes he stresses that a relation between men appears as a relation between things, sometimes that "value" appears to be a property of the commodity and thus a thing, sometimes that the commodity takes on a life of its own and becomes personified.'[29] As a result, theories of reification were developed that prioritised one of these aspects as the most significant. For instance, Lukács was interested in 'the way man's productive activity becomes alien and objective to them under capitalism', and Benjamin was interested in 'the phantasmagoric and personified form of commodities and the life they lead as such.' Adorno, meanwhile, was interested in 'the way a relation between men appears in the form of a natural *property* of a thing'[30] – the sociological basis of his critique of identity thinking which, like commodity exchange, asserts an abstract equivalence between concretely different things.

Rose argues that these more one-sided theories have also arisen, however, not only due to a selective reading of Marx (or else due to Marx's inconsistent emphases), but due to reification itself – that is, they can be understood as casualties of what they would otherwise seek to describe. In this sense, Rose's criticisms should be understood less as injunctions to be 'less reified' – which would commit the cardinal sin (from a Hegelian perspective) of issuing an abstract prescription not grounded in existing social relations – but instead as immanent critiques that understand reification to be a tendency of all critical thinking produced under capital, including her own. While Rose is critical of Adorno in *The Melancholy Science*, she nonetheless aligns with him over all other western Marxist thinkers for being more thoroughgoing in his acknowledgement of this unavoidable tendency.

This unavoidable tendency raises the question of the extent to which critical theory is even possible. Indeed, the subtitle of Rose's PhD thesis refers to 'Adorno's Concept of Reification and the *Possibility* of a Critical Theory of Society' (my emphasis). Rose notes that Adorno sometimes claims that society and the consciousness of society have become 'completely reified' – which seems like a claim that no critical consciousness is possible: 'It is to say that the underlying processes of society are completely hidden and that the utopian possibilities within it are inconceivable. The mind (*Geist*) is impotent; the object is inaccessible.' But even to state this thesis is to prove its empirical falsity. As Rose puts it: 'if it were true it could not be known.' Therefore, Rose argues that Adorno uses such exaggerations 'in order to induce in his reader the development of the latent capacity for non-identity thought'[31] – the thought that the concept, given the present state of society, is *not* identical with its object. In Bernstein's words: 'Critical theory posits itself as the moment just prior to complete closure.'[32]

Crucially, to think non-identically, is not to 'see through' the falsity of appearances to the 'true' reality. Non-identity thinking is instead a kind of negative capability which acknowledges that there is something more in the concept (of society, for example) than can be fully identified – and that this necessary failure of identification and its corresponding necessary illusion is socially produced. Non-identity thinking or negative dialectics identifies the non-identity or negative in what claims to be positively identifying.

This type of critical theory of society, which says that society cannot be positively identified, is in many ways different to Marx's, even though its 'negativity' is derived from Marx's theory that the commodity resists being comprehensively grasped. As Rose explains: 'For Marx, to know "theoretically" meant to know how social relations in capitalist society are determined by the production of commodities, and to endorse this analysis as the potential perspective of a universal class – the proletariat.' While Marx did of course critique the theories of classical political economy as well, a process which 'involved deriving the state of society from its appearance in those theories and concepts', this was, according to Rose, 'indirect by comparison.' For Adorno, meanwhile, 'theoretical knowledge in the former sense, to know how social relations are determined by the exchange mechanism, is now almost impossible.'[33] This can account for why the majority of Adorno's critical theory is directed not towards analysing, for example, how value is created and extracted through the exploitation of labour, or the role of money, or the circulation of capital, but instead through the analysis of how the present state of society appears in reified theories and concepts. As Rose puts it: 'Adorno does not accept Marx's ideas as an *a priori* theory of society, but *presents a dialectic*: he shows how various modes of cognition, Marxist and non-Marxist are inadequate and distorting when taken in isolation; and how by confronting them with each other precisely on the basis of an awareness of their individual limitations, they may nevertheless yield insight into social processes.'[34] I should stress that by referring to 'the analysis of how the state of society *appears*', I mean exactly that. Again, it is not that Adorno thinks that the analysis of reified theories and concepts reveals or 'identifies' the true state of society, but instead that it can reveal its ideological self-presentation, which can in turn yield some insight into the determination of this self-presentation: it can present the illusion inherent in the concept or theory *as* an illusion, and the means of its historical-social production.

The illusion of persons: Marx and Justinian

Rose's project remains an Adornian one in so far as it aims to comprehensively draw out the contradictions within culture and thought which are necessarily produced by the contradictions in society; and insofar as it resists through an unwavering focus on the diremptions of thought and society all spurious totalisations or positive abstract identifications (a focus analogous to Adorno's non-identity thinking). Nonetheless, Rose is also highly critical of Adorno. In fact, all of her sustained engagements with his work after *The Melancholy Science* (in *Hegel Contra Sociology*, *The Broken Middle*, and the essay 'From Speculative to Dialectical Thinking' in *Judaism and Modernity*) mount criticisms[35] – and even *The Melancholy Science* is less an introduction (as its subtitle claims) but an immanent critique of his thought. This is not the place to develop all of these criticisms, but here I shall mention two in particular in order to begin to account for why Rose ultimately turned from Adorno to Hegel.[36]

Firstly, Rose expresses a worry that it is 'difficult … to judge the move from revealing irreconcilable antinomies in central concepts to establishing the social origins of those antinomies.' This move always involves a leap in Adorno's work – a leap which is simultaneously achieved and obscured 'by means of chiasmus and analogy.' While these rhetorical devices may be assessed by their 'internal cogency' – that is, by the neatness of the similarities (or, ironically, the identities) being drawn – they are ultimately impossible to bear out in a more systematic way.[37] This 'move' between text and social context was later self-deprecatingly described by Fredric Jameson as both 'the crucial moment of transition' and 'the embarrassing weak link' in all Marxist criticism. 'Even so brilliant a dialectician as T. W. Adorno is capable of completing a subtle analysis of the contradictions of a given text with the vaguest of gestures toward "late capitalism" or "verwaltete Gesellschaft".'[38] In Rose's words, Adorno's work 'makes for better criticism of philosophy but for less convincing elucidation of the relationship between philosophy and society.'[39] Given the apparent aim of Adorno's project, it should not be underestimated how damning this is.

Secondly, Rose is not only critical of how reification has been insufficiently and inconsistently articulated in Marxist thought, she also argues that reification constitutes only one half of the dialectic – only one half of capital's necessary illusion. She argues that Marxist accounts of necessary illusion in the wake of Lukács miss that, for Marx, capital not only represents people as things (and things as people), but also represents people as the juridical fiction of 'persons': abstracted individuals who, as bearers of 'rights' (principally property rights), are formally but not substantially or actually free and equal. This criticism extends to Adorno. As she writes in a crucial footnote to her essay 'From Speculative to Dialectical Thinking': 'In the section of *Negative Dialectics* entitled "Against Personalism" the concept of self-alienation – and by implication "the ideological inessentiality [*Unsesen*] of the person" – is said to play no part in Marx's *Capital* …. Adorno thus overlooks the importance of "personification" as the legal correlation of the commodity form throughout *Capital* …. This may be why Adorno treats reification as the correlate of immediacy.'[40]

Rose's complaint against Adorno here is that by dismissing the concept of 'self-alienation' (in *Capital* and more broadly), he also overlooks the juridico-economic structure of personhood, and thereby misses the specificity of how capitalist social forms produce subjectivity through legal form. Adorno rejects the concept of self-alienation on the grounds that it implies an essentialist and metaphysical doctrine of the self – a pre-given or authentic being from which the subject has fallen. But in doing so, he fails to consider the possibility of a more dialectical, historically grounded, and juridically mediated concept of self-alienation whereby the subject is alienated from its capacity to be self-determining and socially realised through its legal and economic personification in the commodity form. What is missed, for Rose, is that

> capital posits people as 'persons' and as 'things': it reifies *and* it 'personifies' them. Every individual is a bearer of legal rights and obligations, and hence of commodities and money – a 'person'; but those who do not own the means of production are also 'things' – they have to treat their own labour-power as a commodity, as a thing. Things, in their turn, also become personified – the phantasmagoria of the market-place. 'Reification' and 'personification' imply each other – they are legal categories and social correlatives.[41]

One of her most direct articulations of this thesis

is in the introduction to *Dialectic of Nihilism*: 'In the *Grundrisse* Marx examines how Capital posits individuals as "persons", the bearers of rights, and as "things", the commodity "labour-power". The theory of commodity fetishism subsequently developed in the first volume of *Capital* is not simply an account of how material relations between "persons" are transformed into social relations between "things". It is an account of the "personification" *and* "reification" intrinsic to the juridical categories of "commodity", "capital", and "money".'[42] Elsewhere, in a contribution she made to a conference at the University of Lund, she says that in her work she 'revised an earlier reading of Marx drawn from Lukács and based on reification: the transformation of social relations between people into relations between things, to a reading which stresses equally reification and personification posited by Capital.'[43]

As early as *The Melancholy Science* Rose insists that the standard English definition of the commodity fetish – as a social relation between men which assumes 'the *fantastic* form' of a relation between things – misses the mark.[44] She contends that '*die phantasmagorische form*' in Marx's German 'should be translated as "the phantasmagoric form" in English. The epithet "phantasmagoric" stresses the *personifications* as well as the strangeness of the form in which the relations between men appear. "Phantasmagoria" means a crowd or succession of dim or doubtfully real persons' – an etymology that already signals the abstraction of human subjects into juridical 'persons'.[45] While Rose would go on to develop this insight (moving beyond her reading of Marx as a neo-Fichtean in *Hegel Contra Sociology*), her early work already gestures toward this dual structure of necessary illusion implied by the commodity form: not only the reification of people and the personification of things (whereby commodities 'seem to be autonomous figures interacting with one another and human beings'[46]), but also the personification of people themselves, as abstract, formally free subjects under the law: the legal fiction which grounds the illusions of freedom and equality in capitalist society.

A theory of personification is therefore crucial for a critical theory of capitalist society in order to account for the necessary illusions of freedom and equality in spite of manifest unfreedom and inequality. Adorno's thesis of 'total reification' for example, or his conception of late capitalism as an increasingly authoritarian form of state capitalism, failing to anticipate liberal and neoliberal capitalism and the ideological significance of 'freedom', neglect that the institution of property *does* establish a kind of freedom – albeit a formal and abstract freedom. This, of course, is not to defend the institution of property, but to account for its intransigence, and for how it systematically obscures unfree social relations. Again, it bears emphasising that to say that freedom and equality are illusions is not to say that they are simply false or untrue. Freedom and equality under bourgeois property law are (more or less) real – for example, persons bear more or less equal legal rights, enjoy freedom to own and transfer property, and are governed by uniform laws within a standardised framework – but these realisations of freedom and equality are abstract and relative, not concrete or absolute. Even a world in which bourgeois property rights were fully realised and extended to *everyone* regardless of gender, class, nationality, etc., would not entail substantial freedom. As we shall see, this is because the existence of people with property (persons) *necessarily* implies the existence of people without property who must sell their labour-power (people as things) – even though, with bourgeois property law, these people as things technically bear the *right* to property and are therefore technically persons too.

This insistence on personification as well as reification also has the advantage of establishing the connection between bourgeois law and Roman law, where the legal concepts of 'person' and 'thing' first found expression. This in part explains the subtitle of *The Broken Middle: Out of our Ancient Society*. While 'the broken middle' names the irreducible antinomy of capitalist modernity, the origins of this antinomy can be traced to antiquity. For example, in the preliminary remarks in the first book of *The Institutes* of Justinian, quoted in *Dialectic of Nihilism*, we find: '*Omne autum ius, quo utimur, vel ad personas pertinent vel ad res vel ad actiones* – all our law relates either to persons or to things, or actions.'[47] For Rose, tracing this connection of persons and things from antiquity to modernity provides the opportunity to 're-open the critique of religion' – or the critique of ideology or representation – 'without depending on the dogmatic opposition between base and superstructure, ideology and science, synchrony and diachrony.'[48] By returning to this antinomy of reification *and* personification, which characterises the abstractions of both Roman and bourgeois property, one grasps the antinomical character of our ancient-modern society without privileging either side. The crucial difference between Roman property law and bourgeois property law is that, in the former, only some are persons (bearers of property rights) while others are things (slaves, *res mancipium*). In the latter, by contrast, everyone is a person insofar as they are formally granted the right to property, the catch being that this recognition of universal personhood is purely formal and abstract, and masks the reality of material inequality where the actual ability to own property is unevenly distributed – where most people are things, commodified by the mute compulsion to sell their labour-power, in spite of their formal personhood. Under Roman law, society is abstract but transparent: individuals are either persons or things. Under bourgeois property law, meanwhile, the diremption of personification and reification is internalised into each individual and therefore society is ambiguous and opaque. The illusion of freedom is more intransigent precisely because it is universalised.

Phenomenology and the critique of persons and things: Hegel

For Rose, both of these problems with Adorno – the difficult move from text to context (or from subjectivity to its determination), and the neglect of personification – can be addressed with reference to Hegelian phenomenology, understood as the study of the formation of knowledge and its illusions from an immanent standpoint which follows the process of this formation. For Hegel, a 'phenomenology' which adopts an external or transcendental standpoint can never be strictly phenomenological. Instead, his philosophy traces the abstractions and presuppositions of thought and subjectivity *as they appear*, whether explicitly stated or merely implied, and reveals that in spite of their apparent naturalness or immutability, they are in fact *unnatural*, presupposed, contingent.

To give a more precise example, Hegel's phenomenology identifies how the philosophers of his day unwittingly assumed and were shaped by the legal categories of person and thing. In the words of Andrew Brower Latz, it traces how 'Fichte's concept of the self, the [Kantian] subject of *Moralität* and *Moralität* as a form of ethical life, all repeat and reinforce the structure of the property holder, which itself reflects the Roman legal person's absolute dominion over his property (*res*).'[49] For Rose, this is one of the most crucial and overlooked contributions of Hegel's philosophy to critical theory: 'Opening up an historical perspective on the development of the idea of "persons" as the bearers of equal rights and hypertrophy of inner life, Hegel expounds the antinomy of law as the characteristic compound in modern states of individual freedom and individual depoliticization.'[50] By viewing abstract notions of freedom and equality as they appear as a part of their historical-legal contexts, Hegel accounts for the paradox of modern society, characterised by formal freedom and equality within unfreedom and inequality. Although Rose argues that Marx uses the legal categories of things and persons in his account of the fetish character of commodities, she also argues (in *Hegel Contra Sociology* at least) that only Hegel and his phenomenology successfully traces them in the process of their formation: to relate actuality to its representation and to subjectivity.[51]

In Hegel's early Jena writings, principally the essay on natural law, he develops a critique of Kant's and Fichte's 'subjective idealism' – though here, he undertakes this critique not in a phenomenological style but in a style of critical detachment. In this essay, Hegel criticises Kant and Fichte for conceiving of morality as a form of subjective freedom that stands apart from or in opposition to legality, as this abstracts morality and freedom from the more difficult question of the concrete institutions and practices of ethical life or *Sittlichkeit*. 'Freedom can therefore only be conceived [by Kant and Fichte] in a negative sense, as freedom from necessity.'[52] Crucially, in the second half of the essay, Hegel argues that this negative conception of freedom is not just an arbitrary error of unthinking abstraction but 'must be understood as re-presenting a real social relation, which he calls "relative ethical life" or "the system of reality". The system of reality is the system of the political economy of bourgeois property relations in which law is separated from the rest of social life.'[53] In short, he argues that the transformation of the individual into an abstract free subject or 'person' by the dynamics of bourgeois property law is responsible for the necessary illusion of free subjectivity apart from legality found in Kant and Fichte. In their presupposition of the 'person', they have 'smuggled in' [*untergeschoben*] and affirmed a contingent social institution. In fact, Hegel argues, this notion of 'universal' personhood – assumed by Kant's notion of the universal subjective maxims of the will, and dependent upon the reality of 'universal' property rights – is a contradiction terms: 'For private property', as Rose puts it, 'is not universal: if it were universal, it would, *ipso facto*, be abolished as private property.'⁵⁴ While personhood and its implied rights may be formally universal, they can never be actually so. This argument already makes Hegel an enemy of liberalism, for which the problem with property rights is always only the inconsistency of their application.

The advantage of the essay on natural law, for Rose, is that 'the connection between Hegel's critique of Kant and Fichte's epistemology and the analysis of property relations is particularly clear.' The disadvantage is that 'the text is not a phenomenology.'⁵⁵ This means that, as we saw with Adorno's attempts to link the antinomies of concepts and theories to the antinomies of society, these connections are only made analogically and externally which makes judging their validity impossible.

Rose argues that Hegel's *System of Ethical Life*, however, written around the same time as his essay on natural law, does not have this particular weakness. Like the essay on natural law, the work attempts to demonstrate that i) there are dichotomies present in the philosophies of Kant and Fichte (and Schelling is implicitly criticised here too), and ii) that they correspond to the dichotomies of specific social relations. In this case, Hegel focuses particularly on the separation between concept and intuition. However, while in the essay on natural law 'the first part of this proposition [i] is discussed in the second section, while the second part of the proposition [ii] is addressed in the third section', in the *System of Ethical Life* 'the discussion of the two parts of the proposition is integrated. It is thus the first "phenomenology".'⁵⁶ As Rose puts it, the *System of Ethical Life* 'is set out in a way designed to derive one by one the social institutions re-presented by the philosophical dichotomies between concept and intuition'⁵⁷ – either those which correspond to the domination of intuition over concept (for example, the interest of particular individuals, the division of labour and the institution of private property), or those which correspond to the domination of concept over intuition (for example, the institutions of exchange and contract).⁵⁸ 'These derivations continue up to the point where it becomes possible to leave the sphere of individualistic misunderstanding, of relations (*Verhältnisse*), and to reconsider them as relative ethical life.'⁵⁹ As with the later *Phenomenology of Spirit*, knowledge is presented on and in its own terms, not in order to justify the *status quo*, but precisely in order to draw out what this naturalised stasis obscures: its incompleteness, contingency and conditionality. Therefore, when Rose writes that 'it becomes possible to leave the sphere of individualistic misunderstanding', this does not mean that one is elevated to a God-like standpoint apart from relative ethical life, but that one is able to simply reconsider this 'ethical life' *as* relative.

It is in this complex work that Hegel most substantially develops the bourgeois juridical fictions of property and personhood – fictions which guarantee rights but abstract from all particular content, and which produce the apparently but not actually ahistorical dichotomy of concept and intuition. In the part entitled 'Infinity, Ideality in its Form or in its Relation', Hegel first shows how the dominance of intuition over the concept manifests in the interest of particular individuals and the division of labour. In Rose's summary, we begin with a situation in which 'each individual produces according to his particular interests with the result that the labour and the products become increasingly diverse and fragmented. This division of labour gives rise to surpluses which cannot be used by the individual who produced them, but can be used to satisfy the needs of others.'[60] Therefore, although the particular individual is presented here as primary, it nonetheless, through the production of a surplus, feeds into a universal interest. This essentially reproduces Adam Smith's myth of the 'invisible hand' whereby self-interested people inadvertently end up contributing to a public good.

Someone must possess these surpluses, however, in a stable and guaranteed way. The ownership of these surplus goods is therefore recognised by law. This is the category of 'property', and the owner of this property is recognised by law as a 'person'.[61] In these categories, the particular properties of goods and their owners are abstracted into formal categories. The inverse dominance of concept over intuition is therefore derived and manifested in the corresponding institutions of exchange and contract, the institutions which maintain and guarantee these fictions of property and personhood. Unlike, for example, the division of labour, which refers to particular and different people making particular and different things, and which only inadvertently contributes to a universal interest, '[e]xchange and contract depend on making things which are particular and different formally comparable or abstract, turning them into value or price'; they depend on 'the recognition of formal equalities.'[62]

In the third part of this phenomenological movement, these notions of property and person, on the one hand, and exchange and contract, on the other, are 're-cognised' (Rose's hyphenated formulation emphasising acknowledgement, cognition and repetition) to draw out their antinomies – that is, Hegel reveals how the recognition of formal equalities by the institutions of property and personhood presuppose but obscure material inequality:

> The concept of equal persons, meaning equal right to own property, presupposes people without property. It presupposes people in all those relations which have not been taken up into the legal concept of 'person'. People who are not persons, who do not have even the right to property, are, in Roman property law, thing, 'res'. The formal recognition of private property right presupposes this relation or subordination of others.[63]

What does this have to do with Kant, Fichte and Schelling? Again, Hegel's essay on natural law which I discussed earlier has the advantage of being especially clear in setting out the case that the antinomies of society are reproduced in the antinomies of Kant and Fichte's thought, but the disadvantage of developing this schematically and externally. The advantages and disadvantages of the *System of Ethical Life* are exactly the inverse, meaning that the critique of Kant, Fichte and Schelling is totally integrated into the critique of society and only implicit. Their thought is not mentioned by name, but instead suggested by Hegel's use of their philosophical manoeuvres and concepts to describe social institutions, to show how they have purchase, or else run into contradictions, not only on the lofty planes of the intellect but in reality.

The punchline of the work comes with Hegel's revelation that 'intellectual intuition is real intuition.' For Rose, this is the 'great achievement' of the *System of Ethical Life*.[64] 'Intellectual intuition' (etymologically 'intellectual *seeing-into*', '*An-schauen*') is Kant's name for a kind of non-sensory intuition which provides immediate and direct knowledge of an object. For Kant, it is a purely hypothetical kind of intuition given the gap between knowledge and the thing in-itself: there is no direct access to the object. Fichte and Schelling, meanwhile, assert that the idea of intellectual intuition can be used to resolve the aporias of Kant's philosophy by re-cognising it as the original free act (the self-positing of the *I* in Fichte's terminology) which precedes all empirical consciousness: the foundational move or decision upon which all knowledge and reality can be constructed. It entails an abstract freedom from necessity and reality: a pure act to get things going. Hegel's 'great achievement', according to Rose, is that, through an analysis of social antinomies (such as the example I gave above), he reveals that the kind of abstract and formal freedom entailed by intellectual intuition to be fundamentally contradictory. For Hegel, such implied notions of abstract freedom are systematic illusions.

What, then, must intellectual intuition be – understood as that which allows us to 'see into' things – if it is not to be merely hypothetical (Kant) or else unthinkingly abstract (Fichte and Schelling)? It must, for Hegel, be an intuition which entails a real freedom, not as a negative ideal, but as realised in society itself. This is the origin of Hegel's concept of *recognition*. In Rose's words, it would be 'a seeing into (*An-schauen*) which does not dominate or suppress but recognizes the difference and sameness of the other.'[65] Or in Hegel's words: 'Through ethical life and in it alone, intellectual intuition is real intuition, the eye of spirit and the loving eye coincide: according to nature man sees the flesh of his flesh in woman, according to ethical life he sees the spirit of his spirit in the ethical being and through the same.'[66] While Fichte and Schelling's notion of intellectual intuition stands opposed to and above its other, as the free act of a *person*, Hegel's notion of real intuition sees the other as 'different and as the same as oneself, as spirit not as a person, as a living totality not as a formal unity.'[67]

The problem, for Hegel, is that this kind of intuition or recognition 'can only be achieved in a just society'[68] – that is, real intuition is incompatible with and impossible under bourgeois law which, through its necessary illusions of persons and property, ensures systematic misrecognition. And yet, the difference with Fichtean or Schellingian intellectual intuition is that Hegelian real intuition or recognition, when not elevated again to the level of an abstract ideal (as found in the work of Rita Felski or Axel Honneth, for example), is a kind of knowledge which can account for its own present impossibility.[69] Real intuition is thought of as the kind of intuition which would transcend the dichotomies of concept and intuition, but as it is not realised – that is, as these dichotomies and their determination are not transcended in capitalist reality – it can only be thought of for now as an ought or *Sollen*.

This appeal to an ought, for Hegel, is a failure to think. True philosophy should never propose what ought to be. But, as Hegel comes to realise the present impossibility of true philosophy itself due to the dominance of abstraction, 'true philosophy' is itself an ought. As he puts it in the *Differenzschrift*: the day is yet to come 'when from beginning to end it is philosophy itself whose voice will be heard.'[70] Hegel's phenomenological realisation of these necessary failures is itself a necessary failure to think, but it is a failure to think *better* than Kant, Fichte and Schelling, because it acknowledges the historical determination of this failure. The ought is not imposed from without, but arrived at through a confrontation of the limits of what is. This epitomises Hegel's 'thinking and failing to think the absolute' and it is the key to 'the social import' of his philosophy.[71]

Pyrrhic victory? Osborne

For Osborne, in his early review, this is 'something of a Pyrrhic victory, both sociologically and practically. For while the acknowledgement and explanation of an unjustifiable element of *Sollen* in speculative experience reasserts its theoretical consistency, it also serves to emphasise both its theoretical and practical impotence.'[72] In part, Osborne is right – certainly, it is a problem for us who wish to transform the existing state of things to confront the difficulty of revolutionary change. But is it a problem with the argument itself? Osborne criticises Rose for failing to 'specify *concretely* what this new mode of transformation is.'[73] Yet this misses Rose's central criticism of Marxism *qua* theory: that the very demand for a concrete theory of transformation, one that can be simply implemented or imposed in practice, risks reproducing social illusion – and, in doing so, risks 'recreating a terror, or reinforcing lawlessness, or strengthening bourgeois law'.[74] Critique does not provide a concrete specification for transformation. What it can offer, however, is a concrete specification of the historical barriers to transformation. Critique is the logical explication of reality not changing.

On the other hand, Osborne's review overstates the impotence of Hegelian phenomenology and misses what is at stake in Rose's 'retrieval' of it. First, he claims that speculative experience does not really involve the comprehension of the determination of relative ethical life, only 'the fact that ethical life is determined.'[75] I hope that the present essay has sufficiently dispelled this idea. Speculative experience involves the comprehension of the determination of ethical life by *the antinomy of law*: the separation of economic life (in which a social relation between people appears in the form of a relation between *things*) from the realm of what now passes for politics (in which people appear in the form of juridical, abstract *persons*) – a separation which arises from specifically modern forms of private property. This is the speculative core of Hegel *and* Marx's work, as well as *Hegel Contra Sociology* and all of Rose's subsequent major works.

Second, Osborne claims that there is a fundamental

incompatibility between phenomenology and any social theory, including Marxism, due to the former's restriction to the standpoint of consciousness. 'Phenomenology', he writes, 'does not involve a social theory. "Theory" is precisely what it rejects.'[76] His suggestion is that, by remaining within the subject-object problematic of modern epistemology, Rose is *only* interested in the recognition of the formation and deformation of phenomenal knowledge, at the expense of understanding the concrete dynamics of the capitalist mode of production and exchange. But Rose's point is precisely to 'retrieve Hegelian speculative experience *for* social theory' – not to replace social theory with speculative experience.[77] What social theory lacks, according to Rose, is an adequate theory of the relation of actuality to representation and subjectivity – but she is not saying that this is all that social theory should be. Osborne concedes that '[s]he does not object to the analysis in *Capital*',[78] but nonetheless he seems to not want to let her have it.

By the time of his retrospective essay on Rose, Osborne also seems to have changed his mind on the fundamental incompatibility between phenomenology and social theory – as demonstrated when he calls for a kind of social critique 'which includes but is not reducible to its phenomenological dimension. Just as Marx's *Capital* ... includes but is not reducible to a phenomenological dimension.'[79] As I have argued, this was Rose's argument too, both regarding social critique and later (after reassessing her accusations of his neo-Fichteanism) Marx's *Capital*. But still Osborne insists that Rose reduces social reality to 'relations of (mis)recognition' and that she thereby misses those 'forms of social being that cannot be "transformed" (or "negotiated") on the basis of the recognition of misrecognition alone.'[80] As this essay has sought to demonstrate, Rose's entire point is that a social theory *combined* with the insights produced by Hegelian speculative experience is the means by which the impossibility of this 'transformation' or 'negotiation' via recognition of misrecognition is made most explicit. Misrecognition, for Rose, is a *necessary* illusion – and recognition of misrecognition, while a necessary condition of radical social transformation, does not in itself substantially transform anything. To repeat Rose's words from the first paragraph of this essay: 'you can't just stop the mistake by knowing about it, you've got to alter the conditions that give rise to it.'

Coda: Žižek

Let me finish with Slavoj Žižek, whose work represents the most influential attempt in recent decades, arguably more so than Rose's, to recover Hegel's thought for the left – and who, like Rose, insists against more 'deflationary' accounts of Hegel that 'the absolute is not an optional extra.' While he has not substantially engaged with Rose's work in his writing, he does cite her across a couple of pages of his 1991 *For They Know Not What They Do: Enjoyment as a Political Factor* for the stress she places on the importance of grasping 'the fundamental paradox of *the speculative identity*.'[81] He has also praised *Hegel Contra Sociology* as one of the best books on Hegel.[82]

There are some significant overlaps which set Rose and Žižek apart from the majority of academic Hegelianism. Like Rose, for whom the dialectic 'is multiple and complex, not as its critics would have it, unitary and simply progressive',[83] Žižek also stresses the openness, contingency and antagonism of Hegel's thought, against the cliché that everything in Hegel tends towards closure, necessity and reconciliation or harmony. The thesis of

Žižek's early and arguably greatest work, *The Sublime Object of Ideology* (1989), is that 'far from being a story of its [antagonism's] progressive overcoming, dialectics is for Hegel a systematic notation of the failure of all such attempts.'[84] Similarly, for both Rose and Žižek, this notion of constitutive antagonism (or 'diremption', in Rose's later vocabulary) does not imply a preexisting or future unity, nor a wholeness from which logic fell or towards which it is destined. Instead, as Žižek puts it, 'there is no unity prior to sundering (not only empirically, but also in logical temporality): the unity lost through sundering retroactively emerged through sundering itself';[85] or, in Rose's words (quoting from Adorno), '"diremption" [...] implies "torn halves of an integral freedom to which, however, they do not add up" – it formally implies the third, *qua* sundered unity, without positing any substantial pre-existent "unity", original or final, neither finitely past or future, not absolutely, as transcendent.'[86]

The defining difference between Rose and Žižek is that, for Rose, as I have sought to show, this diremption is and must always be historicised, while for Žižek, diremption must be transposed into a fundamental feature – *the* fundamental feature – of reality itself. For Žižek's Hegel, the notion of an epistemological obstacle to thinking the absolute, for which the failure is necessarily ours (Kant) or contingently ours (scientific naturalism), must be viewed instead as an ontological obstacle, for which the failure is inherent to the absolute itself. For Žižek, the absolute is absolutely inconsistent and so simply cannot be thought consistently. 'There is no new positive content brought out here', he writes, 'just a purely topological transposition of the gap that separates me from the Thing into the Thing itself.'[87] Hegel accepts the Parmenidean idea that thinking and being are the same, with the twist that, in Žižek's words, 'the limitations (antinomies, failures) of thought are also simultaneously the limitations of being itself.'[88] For Žižek, therefore, it makes no sense to speak of a consistent reality prior to its signification, or even of a separation between reality 'out there' and the way in which it appears to us within its transcendental horizon. Instead, 'at its most basic, reality is not what is but what fails to be what is',[89] and the transcendental horizon is not merely a frame through which we view reality but what Lacan would call its 'quilting point': it is a fundamental part of reality through which that reality becomes determinate.[90]

Since his 1996 work on Schelling, *The Indivisible Remainder*, Žižek has not only ontologised but even naturalised this obstacle with reference to quantum physics. He argues that Heisenberg's 'uncertainty principle', for instance, which states that one cannot simultaneously know both the exact position and momentum of a particle (and therefore affirms the inherent unpredictability of quantum systems), not only illustrates but demonstrates his thesis of the failed absolute.

> The [uncertainty] principle is thus profoundly 'Hegelian': what first appeared to be an epistemological obstacle turns out to be a property of the thing itself; that is to say, the choice between mass and momentum defines the very 'ontological' status of the particle. The inversion of an epistemological obstacle into an ontological 'impediment' which prevents the object from actualizing the totality of its potential qualities (mass and momentum) is 'Hegelian'.[91]

Or, as he puts it in his more recent *Sex and the Failed Absolute*, the systematic uncertainty of quantum mechanics shows that 'ignorance is not just the limitation of the observer who cannot ever acquire a full knowledge of reality, ignorance is inscribed in the structure of reality itself.'[92] It is not simply that we do not know whether Schrödinger's cat is dead or alive (to use the famous thought experiment), reality does not 'know' either. In various talks, Žižek likens this revelation to catching God with his pants down: God (the absolute) *is* ignorant. In a rare moment of explicit disagreement with the master (not God, but Hegel), this means for Žižek that a 'pure pre-ontological real (and not logic, as Hegel thought) is the "shadowy world" that precedes reality.'[93] Underlying reality is an indeterminate proto-reality of quantum oscillations, a fundamental failure of being or 'primordial gap' that only stabilises into an ordinary reality of objects and temporal processes, determinate being, with what quantum physicists call 'the collapse of the wave function' – that is, when it is registered by an observer. He draws parallels here with Lacanian theory, for which symbolic reality at its most basic 'is a multiplicity of "floating signifiers" which can be stabilized only through the intervention of a Master-Signifier'[94] – suggesting that the primordial indeterminacy described by quantum theory 'somehow reemerged' in human subjectivity.[95]

This linking of the 'gap' at the core of subjectivity (as described by Lacan) or spirit (as described by Hegel) to a pre-ontological gap or indeterminacy (as described by quantum physics) is anathema to Rose's conception of modern philosophy and its critical task. This is not necessarily because of any scientific implausibility. That is for others to judge. It is rather because it obscures the possibility that the 'failures' and 'ignorances' of subjectivity or spirit (its illusions, inconsistencies, alienation, and so on) might instead or at least also be mediated by historically determinate structures and social forms – and not, as Žižek would have it, that they are to be simply transposed into features of all reality, from the level of the subject to the level of the quantum. In other words, the worry is that by elevating this failure to metaphysical heights, it overlooks how these failures might be better attributed and more clearly grasped by being understood as a necessary illusion of an otherwise historically contingent reality: a specific mode of production or property law. As Osborne writes in his review of Žižek's *Less Than Nothing*, despite his criticisms of Rose, what Rose understands (but what goes unacknowledged by Žižek) is that 'Hegel's philosophy is grounded on a distinctive conception of, and relation to, historically determinate social forms; and our relation to it must negotiate the historical ontology of such forms, *from which the structure of dialectical logic itself derives*.'[96]

This is not say that we should just dismiss Žižek's dialectic of the failed absolute, but instead that we should return to the social contexts from which it is derived, instead of reifying it into a metaphysics. There may well be trans-historical universalities, as Žižek claims in his rebuttal to Osborne's criticism, albeit universals that only become 'formally valid' or available at a specific historical juncture.[97] (Hegel's logic, for example, might be one of them.) But such universals are not so easily won, and we should always be wary of instrumentalising them as methodological principles or formula. By generalising failure to absolute levels, Žižek risks leaving us only with the facticity that, in the words of the Lacanian slogan, the lack of the subject is the lack in the Other, which not only, as Osborne observes, reduces all specific historical social forms to a single structure,[98] but turns 'lack' (or else 'failure' or 'ignorance') into the unaddressable and unknowable source of history.

In *Dialectic of Nihilism*, in passing, Rose alludes to a story from the book of Daniel. At a feast hosted by the neo-Babylonian king Belshazzar, a disembodied hand suddenly appears and writes a mysterious phrase on the wall. The prophet Daniel is summoned to interpret the writing, which predicts the king's demise. That night, Belshazzar is killed, and his kingdom falls. Rose observes that 'Daniel's interpretation did not alter the course of events – Belshazzar would have perished anyway. But in the Biblical story he perished knowing the judgement.'[99] Žižek would have us perish and fail, but without knowing why. Rose, meanwhile, is like Daniel. Her interpretation may not alter the course of events. It does not prescribe or proscribe any course of action or specific mode of transformation. But her exposition of necessary illusion provides an essential account of why we do not yet know ourselves as the subject of absolute knowing. This is the crucial difference between Rose's thoroughgoing failure to think the absolute and Žižek's premature 'success' of thinking the absolute as a failure.

Robert Lucas Scott is an Arts Research Fellow at Jesus College, University of Cambridge. He is the author of Reading Hegel: Irony, Recollection, Critique *(University of Chicago Press, 2025) and an editor of Gillian Rose's* Marxist Modernism: Introductory Lectures on Frankfurt School Critical Theory *(Verso, 2024).*

Notes

1. *The Hebrew Bible: A Translation with Commentary*, trans. Robert Alter (New York: W. W. Norton, 2018). I am grateful to Rosie Woodhouse and Michael Rizq for their comments on an earlier draft of this essay. A substantially abridged version was presented to the special session 'Broken Middles' (on the work of Gillian Rose) at the virtual Annual Meeting of the ACLA 2025.
2. Gillian Rose, 'Does Marx have a method?', *Thesis Eleven* 186:1 (2025), 4.
3. Gillian Rose, *Hegel Contra Sociology* (London: Verso, 2009). 'As we shall see, Hegel's philosophy has *no* social import if the absolute is banished or suppressed, if the absolute cannot be thought' (45). 'Hegel's philosophy has no social import if the absolute cannot be thought' (98). 'Hegel's philosophy has no social import if the absolute cannot be thought' (218). 'This is why Hegel's thought has no social import if the absolute cannot be thought' (223).
4. Rose, *Hegel Contra Sociology*, 218.
5. J. M. Bernstein, 'Reification in the age of climate catastrophe: After Gillian Rose's critique of Marxism', *Thesis Eleven* 186:1 (2025), 2.
6. Rose, *Hegel Contra Sociology*, 61.

7. Cf. 'everything turns on grasping and expressing the True, not only as *Substance*, but equally as *Subject*.' G. W. F. Hegel, *Phenomenology of Spirit*, trans. A. V. Miller (Oxford: Oxford University Press, 1977), §17.

8. As Adrian Wilding summarises it: 'For Gorman, Rose's early work is a "phenomenological account of the relation between substance (objective ethical life) and subjectivity" which aims at overcoming "the continued domination of bourgeois law and private property". In the late works, this "objective" treatment of subjectivity "is displaced by a contrary emphasis on faith, inwardness and an ethic of singularity". Even if this ethic "continues to demand an engagement with the political, the terms of this engagement are no longer predicated upon a politics of revolutionary transformation." For Jay, "the young Rose favoured critical over speculative reason, outrage at social injustice over affirming the unending dialectic of law and violence, the promise of a different future contained in aesthetic form over believing that eternity exists in the here and now for those with faith". For Osborne, Rose "came progressively to distance the general project, decisively, from its initial 'critical Marxist' formulation, to the point of incompatibility". In effect, each of these three critics suggests the same thing: the mature Rose renounced critical theory for *philosophia perennis*.' Adrian Wilding, review of *Marxist Modernism* by Gillian Rose, *Historical Materialism*, accessed 4 June 2025, https://www.historicalmaterialism.org/gillian-rose-marxist-modernism-introductory-lectures-on-frankfurt-school-critical-theory/; with reference to Tony Gorman, 'Gillian Rose and the Project of a Critical Marxism', *Radical Philosophy* 105 (2001), 25–36; Peter Osborne, 'Gillian Rose and Marxism', *Telos* 173 (2015), 55–67; and Martin Jay, 'Afterword', in Gillian Rose, *Marxist Modernism: Introductory Lectures on Frankfurt School Critical Theory*, eds. Robert Lucas Scott & James Gordon Finlayson (London: Verso, 2024), 129–43.

9. Rose, *Hegel Contra Sociology*, 197–98.

10. Rose, *Hegel Contra Sociology*, 235.

11. Gillian Rose, *Dialectic of Nihilism: Post-Structuralism and Law* (Oxford: Basil Blackwell, 1984), 2.

12. Osborne, 'Gillian Rose and Marxism', 55.

13. Rose, *Hegel Contra Sociology*, 230.

14. Rose, 'Does Marx Have a Method?', 7.

15. Despite being Rose's most sustained reading of Marx in all of her work, the passage goes conspicuously unmentioned in Osborne's article on Rose and Marxism. Gillian Rose, *The Broken Middle: Out of Our Ancient Society* (Oxford: Blackwell, 1992), with reference to Karl Marx, 'On the Jewish Question', in *Early Writings*, trans. Rodney Livingstone & Gregor Benton (London: Penguin, 1977), 234; italics in original.

16. Gillian Rose, *Mourning Becomes the Law: Philosophy and Representation* (Cambridge: Cambridge University Press, 1996), 8.

17. Rose, *Dialectic of Nihilism*, 3.

18. 'The essay is an attempt to retrieve Hegelian speculative experience for social theory ...'. Rose, *Hegel Contra Sociology*, 1.

19. Slavoj Žižek, *Less Than Nothing: Hegel and the Shadow of Dialectical Materialism* (London: Verso, 2012), 963.

20. Slavoj Žižek, *First as Tragedy, Then as Farce* (London: Verso, 2009), 154.

21. Karl Marx, *Capital: Critique of Political Economy*, trans. Paul Reitter (Princeton: Princeton University Press, 2024), 49.

22. Rose, *Hegel Contra Sociology*, 232.

23. Rose, 'Does Marx have a method?', 4.

24. Rose, *Hegel Contra Sociology*, 31.

25. Gillian Rose, *The Melancholy Science: An Introduction to the Thought of Theodor W. Adorno* (London: Verso, 2014), ix.

26. Rose, *Melancholy Science*, 39.

27. Rose, *Melancholy Science*, 39.

28. Karl Marx, *Grundrisse*, trans. Martin Nicolaus (London: Penguin, 1993), 452–3. The interjection in squared brackets is Rose's own; *Melancholy Science*, 39.

29. Rose, *Melancholy Science*, 39.

30. Rose, *Melancholy Science*, 40–1.

31. Rose, *Melancholy Science*, 62.

32. Bernstein, 'Reification in the age of climate catastrophe', 8.

33. Rose, *Melancholy Science*, 65.

34. Rose, *Melancholy Science*, 66.

35. See Rose, *Hegel Contra Sociology*, 29–39; Rose, *The Broken Middle*, 8–16; Gillian Rose, *Judaism and Modernity* (London: Verso, 2017), 53–63.

36. Bernstein provides an excellent summary of eight criticisms that Rose makes of Adorno across *The Melancholy Science* and *Hegel Contra Sociology*, some which he finds just, some not. The two criticisms most central to my argument – that Adorno does not proceed phenomenologically and does not have a theory of personification – are not included. The criticisms Bernstein identifies are as follows: i) Adorno's inheritance of Friedrich Pollock's theory of late capitalism as state capitalism fails to provide both a theory of the historical development of capitalism and a theory of the state; ii) Adorno neglects Marx's distinction between abstract and concrete labour, and fails to incorporate an analysis of surplus value extraction; iii) contra Adorno, reification does not apply to all concepts, as some concepts (such as value and money) have no non-reified application; iv) Adorno lacks an Hegelian account of self-reference, unable to account for his own practice beyond his modernist style; v) Adorno fails to specify the conditions for a non-reified society; vi) Adorno has no theory of state power except as a mechanism for sustaining capitalism, ignoring political reason and democratic self-determination; vii) Adorno does not discuss the technological domination of nature; and viii) Adorno's approach ultimately remains within a neo-Kantian framework. Bernstein, 'Reification in the age of climate catastrophe', 9–10.

37. Rose, *Melancholy Science*, 98.
38. Fredric Jameson, 'Marxist Criticism and Hegel', *PMLA* 131:2 (March 2016), 432.
39. Rose, *Melancholy Science*, 72.
40. Rose, *Judaism and Modernity*, 63n29. Cf. Theodor W. Adorno, *Negative Dialectics*, trans. E. B. Ashton (London: Routledge, 1990), 278: 'he [man] never was that being-in-itself, and what he can expect from recourses to his ἀρχαί is therefore nothing but submission to authority, the very thing that is alien to him. It is not only due to the economic themes of *Das Kapital* that the concept of self-alienation plays no part in it any more; it makes philosophical sense.'
41. Rose, *Judaism and Modernity*, 58.
42. Rose, *Dialectic of Nihilism*, 3.
43. Gillian Rose, 'Seven Notes for a Letter to the Workshop', *Proceedings of the International Conference on Parts and Wholes* (June 1983), 99. I am grateful to Rosie Woodhouse for drawing my attention to this article, and for her contribution to the panel on Gillian Rose's *Marxist Modernism* at the Historical Materialism Twenty-First Annual Conference (2024) which addressed as part of its argument the neglected importance of personification as well as reification for Rose's reading of Marx. See also Woodhouse's essay on Evgeny Pashukanis which, while only mentioning Rose in passing, demonstrates some close parallels through a reading of Pashukanis, Marx and the abstractions of legal form and capitalist exchange. Rosie Woodhouse, 'The politics of abstraction: property, subjectivity, legal form', in Cosmin Cercel, Gian-Giacomo Fusco and Przemysłaz Tacik, eds, *Legal Form and the End of Law: Pashukanis's Legacy* (New York: Routledge, 2025), 47–69. Another essay in that collection draws more specific parallels between Pashukanis and Rose: Hugo Lundberg, 'From critique of abstraction to speculative legal form', in *Legal Form and the End of Law*, 179–202.
44. Karl Marx, *Capital: A Critique of Political Economy*, trans. Ben Fowkes (London: Penguin, 1990), 165. Paul Reitter's new translation does not make this error. See Marx, *Capital* (Reitter), 49.
45. Rose, *Melancholy Science*, 40.
46. Marx, *Capital* (Reitter), 49. Cf. Marx, *Capital* (Fowkes), 165.
47. Rose, *Dialectic of Nihilism*, 20; with quotation from *The Institutes of Justinian*, trans. Thomas Collet Sanders (London: Longmans, Green and Co., 1917), Lib. I Tit. II 12.
48. Rose, 'Seven Notes', 99.
49. Andrew Brower Latz, *The Social Philosophy of Gillian Rose* (Eugene, Oregon: Cascade Books, 2018), 75.
50. Rose, *Dialectic of Nihilism*, 3.
51. Hegel also traces the emergence of the category of the person – and by extension the emergence of formally free individuality – to Roman property law. 'Here, in Rome ... we find that free universality, that abstract Freedom, which on the one hand sets an abstract state, a political constitution and power, over *concrete* individuality; on the other side creates a *personality* [my emphasis] in opposition to that universality – the inherent freedom of the *abstract* Ego, which must be distinguished from individual idiosyncrasy. For Personality constitutes the fundamental condition of legal Right: it appears chiefly in the category of Property, but it is indifferent to the concrete characteristics of the living Spirit with which individuality is concerned.' G. W. F. Hegel, *Lectures on the Philosophy of History*, trans. J. Sibree (London: George Bell & Sons, 1894), 290.
52. Rose, *Hegel Contra Sociology*, 58.
53. Rose, *Hegel Contra Sociology*, 59.
54. Rose, *Hegel Contra Sociology*, 61.
55. Rose, *Hegel Contra Sociology*, 63.
56. Rose, *Hegel Contra Sociology*, 64.
57. Rose, *Hegel Contra Sociology*, 68.
58. See the table outlining the structure of the *System of Ethical Life* in Rose, *Hegel Contra Sociology*, 65–6.
59. Rose, *Hegel Contra Sociology*, 68.
60. Rose, *Hegel Contra Sociology*, 71. The following account is chronological but according to logical rather than historical order. As with Marx's *Capital*, which follows the same procedure, this does not make it ahistorical. In Rose's words: 'It is irrelevant to describe this procedure as non-historical, for even in Hegel's "historical" works the logical order is prior to the historical material. All Hegel's works roam backwards and forwards over history to establish the connections between property forms and property relations.' Rose, *Hegel Contra Sociology*, 69.
61. Rose, *Hegel Contra Sociology*, 71–2.
62. Rose, *Hegel Contra Sociology*, 72.
63. Rose, *Hegel Contra Sociology*, 73.
64. Rose, *Hegel Contra Sociology*, 75.
65. Rose, *Hegel Contra Sociology*, 74.
66. G. W. F. Hegel, quoted in Rose, *Hegel Contra Sociology*, 74; Rose's own translation. Cf. 'Intellectual intuition is alone realized by and in ethical life; the eyes of the spirit and the eyes of the body completely coincide. In the course of nature the husband sees flesh of his flesh in the wife, but in ethical life alone does he see the spirit of

his spirit in and through the ethical order.' G. W. F. Hegel, 'System of Ethical Life' and 'First Philosophy of Spirit', trans. H. S. Harris & T. M. Know (Albany: State University Press, 1979), 143.

67. Rose, *Hegel Contra Sociology*, 74.

68. Rose, *Hegel Contra Sociology*, 74.

69. For my critique of the assumption of 'recognition' as a methodological principle in the work of Axel Honneth and Rita Felski, see Robert Lucas Scott, *Reading Hegel: Irony, Recollection, Critique* (Chicago: The University of Chicago Press, 2025), 135–45.

70. G. W. F. Hegel, quoted in Rose, *Hegel Contra Sociology*, 216.

71. Rose, *Hegel Contra Sociology*, 218.

72. Peter Osborne, 'Hegelian Phenomenology and the Critique of Reason and Society', *Radical Philosophy* 32 (Autumn 1982), 14.

73. Osborne, 'Hegelian Phenomenology', 14.

74. Rose, *Hegel Contra Sociology*, 235.

75. Osborne, 'Hegelian Phenomenology', 13.

76. Osborne, 'Hegelian Phenomenology', 14.

77. Rose, *Hegel Contra Sociology*, 1.

78. Osborne, 'Hegelian Phenomenology', 14.

79. Osborne, 'Gillian Rose and Marxism', 63.

80. Osborne, 'Gillian Rose and Marxism', 62.

81. 'Let us recall the case evoked by Rose herself: that of the ultimate identity of religion and State, the Hegelian proposition that "In general religion and the foundation of the State is one and the same thing; they are identical in and for themselves." ... in the overlap of the two lacks, in the co-dependence between the deficiency of the State (its lack of identity with religion) and the inherent deficiency of the determinate form of religion to which this State refers as its foundation – State and religion are thus identical *per negationem*; their identity consists in the correlation of their lack of identity with the inherent lack (deficiency) of the central term that grounds their relationship (religion).' Slavoj Žižek, *For They Know Not What They Do: Enjoyment as a Political Factor* (London: Verso, 2008), 103–4; with quotation from Rose, *Hegel Contra Sociology*, 51.

82. *Hegel Contra Sociology* is mentioned alongside Béatrice Longuenesse, *Hegel's Critique of Metaphysics*, trans. Nicole J. Simek (Cambridge: Cambridge University Press, 2007); Catherine Malabou, *The Future of Hegel: Plasticity, Temporality and Dialectic*, trans. Lisabeth During (London: Routledge, 2004); and Rebecca Comay, *Mourning Sickness: Hegel and the French Revolution* (Stanford: Stanford University Press, 2010). See 'The Dash: A discussion with Slavoj Žižek, Rebecca Comay, and Frank Ruda', from 3:18, accessed 7 February 2025, https://www.youtube.com/watch?v=SoRlMXFy5Mw&t=3632s.

83. Rose, *Dialectic of Nihilism*, 3.

84. Slavoj Žižek, *The Sublime Object of Ideology* (London: Verso, 2008), xxix.

85. Slavoj Žižek, *Sex and the Failed Absolute* (London: Bloomsbury, 2020), 23.

86. Rose, *The Broken Middle*, 236. In *Sex and the Failed Absolute*, Žižek illustrates this point that there is no prior unity only the appearance of unity that appears retroactively by paraphrasing Samuel Beckett's Malone: one does not divide into two (as the famous Maoist slogan has it), but 'a thing divides itself into one' (23). 'There it is then divided into five, the time that remains. Into five what? I don't know. Everything divides into itself, I suppose.' Samuel Beckett, *Three Novels: Molloy, Malone Dies, The Unnameable* (New York: Grove Press, 2009), 176.

87. Žižek, *Sex and the Failed Absolute*, 22.

88. Žižek, *Sex and the Failed Absolute*, 21.

89. Žižek, *Sex and the Failed Absolute*, 32.

90. See, for example, Žižek, *Sex and the Failed Absolute*, 283.

91. Slavoj Žižek, *The Indivisible Remainder: On Schelling and Related Matters* (London: Verso, 2007), 211.

92. Žižek, *Sex and the Failed Absolute*, 287.

93. Žižek, *Sex and the Failed Absolute*, 283. A few pages later, however, Žižek tries to reconcile this 'pure pre-ontological real' with the first words of Hegel's *Logic*: 'Being, pure being – without any further determination.' For Žižek, '[t]he first being is not yet pure being which coincides with its opposite, but a pre-ontological "less-than-nothing"' (285).

94. Žižek, *Sex and the Failed Absolute*, 283.

95. See 'How philosophy got lost: Slavoj Žižek interview', from 28:09, accessed 8 February 2025, https://youtu.be/06KiOj6gjbs?si=OWIIR7h9cnF_u3yc&t=1689

96. Peter Osborne, 'More than everything: Žižek's Badiouian Hegel', *Radical Philosophy* 177 (January/February 2013), 25.

97. Slavoj Žižek, *Absolute Recoil: Towards a New Foundation of Dialectical Materialism* (London: Verso, 2015), 34–5.

98. Osborne, 'More than everything', 24.

99. Rose, *Dialectic of Nihilism*, 168.

On the bourgeois concept of real abstraction

For a non-dualistic ontology of capital

F.T.C. Manning

While some theorists take up the term 'real abstraction' as shorthand for 'what Marx said about abstraction',[1] most of the work on 'real abstraction' over the last few decades uses the term to say something *more*. Contemporary Marxian theorists use 'real abstraction' to theorise gender,[2] Nature and Society,[3] property and race,[4] the bourgeois concept of social equality,[5] State, money, and capital,[6] the general intellect,[7] natural slavery,[8] the 'time of value',[9] religion,[10] and abstract labour,[11] to name a few examples. In each case, the term 'real abstraction' is invoked to elucidate the thing it describes. But what does it mean for something to be a 'real abstraction'? To what in these concepts does the term refer? What question does 'real abstraction' answer for us, what occluded process does it reveal?

As I will suggest below, these theorists use the term 'real abstraction' to elevate something beyond 'mere' material relations, enshrining it in an immaterial realm that structures and dominates our lives. As such, contemporary scholarship reifies the term 'real abstraction' in a way that brings in, through the back door, an ontological split between ideal and material. This dualism is ultimately Kantian – based on the ontological dualism between a 'here' (where we live) and 'there' (where the abstractions are). In fact, Alfred Sohn-Rethel (broadly agreed upon as the originator of the term 'real abstraction') explicitly seeded the concept of real abstraction with a Kantian ontological dualism – albeit a historicised, rather than transhistorical, one.

Furthermore, 'Real abstraction' as a concept obfuscates the relations it purports to describe. It inhibits the posing of deeper questions; instead of asking 'how exactly is x phenomenon created and reproduced in or as capitalism, and how does it fit into the bigger system of the reproduction of capitalism' we are emboldened to say 'x is very powerful, because it is a real abstraction.'

Much extant criticism of the theory aims to correct Sohn-Rethel's origin story for real abstraction. Most famously, scholars such as Moishe Postone, Roberto Finelli and John Milios argue that Sohn-Rethel fallaciously locates the origin of real abstraction in exchange, when actually (they suggest) it originates in the capitalist production process and/or the abstraction of labour.[12] In a similar vein, Elena Louisa Lange points out that the 'praxis of exploitation' and the 'social nexus of production' drop swiftly out of Sohn-Rethel's analysis.[13] From a different perspective, McLaughlin and Schlaudt postulate that real abstraction could have its origin in technology.[14]

Others criticise specific applications or emphases of real abstraction. For example, Kurz and Jappe argue that real abstraction refers specifically to abstract labour and money, respectively, rather than the panoply of social relations brought under the umbrella of real abstraction by other theorists. Jappe suggests that Sohn-Rethel rejects Marx's concept of abstract labour in favor of his own concept of real abstraction.[15] O'Kane criticises many theorists of real abstraction on the basis that they eschew its 'subjective components' which occludes 'the experience of domination' and its 'shaping of subjectivity' – dynamics to which a new 'critical reading of real abstraction' should, on his account, be directed.[16]

Rather than questioning its misapplication or incorrect origin, in this essay I challenge the concept of real abstraction itself. First I discuss contemporary uses of real abstraction, then I show through an exegetical reading of Sohn-Rethel, how the concept is built upon a Kantian ontology. I then suggest a way of reading abstraction without dualism. Many theorists using real abstraction do so in order to either (1) theorise oppressive social dynamics in capitalism, or (2) extend and enrich a value-form or *wertkritik* approach to understanding capital. Like some theorists of real abstraction, I share the ambition to understand categories such as gender, race, nature and the state via (in part) Marx's thought, and I am likewise committed to an analysis of capitalism that engages the contributions of value-form theory and *wertkritik*. My contention here is that using the term 'real abstraction' functions as a distraction or impediment to both of these avenues of inquiry.

On contemporary uses of 'real abstraction'

Abstraction qua abstraction is not bad. Insofar as abstraction is considered in terms of its etymological roots 'to draw away' or, according to Bhandar and Toscano, 'pulling out, extracting', abstraction is the mundane separation of an egg from the uterine lining, or the pull away from darkness of heliotropes. More often, we use abstraction to mean something akin to linguistic abstraction: words like 'tree', 'running', 'anxiety', 'pottery', are abstractions because they refer to something shared in common amidst multitudinous differences. These are ultimately 'mental abstractions', or in Kurz's words, 'CONCEPTUAL abstractions, i.e. mental achievements of the human mind that reflect something real in the mind.' As concepts, these abstractions can be judged as more or less 'right' or 'wrong' insofar as they correspond accurately or not to something in the world.[17]

Real abstraction, on the other hand, is meant to say something more than this. To say that a social relation 'morphs into a real abstraction' is to endow it with some further meaning beyond naming a common, consistent dynamic across variegated space and time.[18] Value, supposedly, sits at a different level of abstraction than gravity.

Heinrich attempts to show that 'real abstractions' are distinct from 'mere abstractions' by highlighting the non-homology between 'abstract labour' and 'tree':

Abstract labor is not visible, only a particular concrete labor is visible, just as the concept of 'tree' isn't visible: I'm only capable of perceiving a concrete botanical plant. As with the term 'tree', abstract labor is an abstraction, but a completely different kind of abstraction. Normally, abstractions are constituted in human thought. We refer to the commonalities among individual examples and then establish an abstract category, such as 'tree.' But in the case of abstract labor, we are not dealing with such a 'mental abstraction' but with a 'real abstraction', by which we mean an abstraction that is carried out in the actual behavior of humans, regardless of whether they are aware of it'.[19]

First, a good deal of human behaviour can be considered to induce abstractions, more or less consciously. Think: sex, sadism, generosity or friendship. We could argue that these are all abstractions that emerge from human praxis, and are to varying degrees obscured from conscious and intentional activity (one can be sadistic whether or not one is aware of the concept of 'sadism'). Especially any 'social form' can be considered as an abstraction carried out in 'the actual behavior of humans' – Freud's incest taboo, totalitarianism and marriage can all easily be described as such.

Second, properly speaking, 'real abstraction' *is* a 'mental abstraction' in exactly the same way that 'tree' is a mental abstraction. After all, the abstraction 'tree' – insofar as it refers to some qualities such as requiring sunlight, nutrients and water, or having a main thick stem often called a trunk – is carried out in the actual existence and reproduction of those individual living things-we-call-trees. Tree is the mental abstraction based on these processes, patterns, relationships. 'Value', 'abstract labour' and 'real abstraction' are mental abstractions in the same sense: they allow us to name certain consistent processes, patterns, relationships. The question is, does 'real abstraction' refer to something qualitatively different than 'tree'?

Kurz argues that it does. He writes that real abstraction refers to something which is itself abstract, and thus represents a 'doubling of abstraction'. In this, his is one of the most explicit and coherent attempts to define 'real abstraction'. Kurz argues that abstraction of value is fundamentally different to that of 'tree' or 'animal' because a general 'tree' or general 'animal' does not 'actually' 'exist', whereas 'value' *does*.[20]

Or does it? Here, I want to suggest that the only sense in which 'value' could be an abstraction of a different, 'doubled' sort than 'tree', is if there is a different ontological realm in which abstract labour and value operate – an 'immaterial realm', 'noumenal plane', 'socialus spatium', 'realm of consciousness'. (Otherwise, value is merely the actual material/concrete processes of value reproduction and realisation, and there is no 'doubling' of abstraction.) And lo, it is upon this very basis that Sohn-Rethel forged the concept of real abstraction – on a historicised, but nonetheless transcendental ontological dualism (I will address this in Part 3, below).

The most common features of the contemporary definitions of real abstraction are as follows:

> *(a) real abstractions arise from actual concrete human activity rather than anyone's mental faculties; hence the existence of real abstractions does not depend on whether or not humans are aware of them.*

As we have seen, Heinrich describes real abstraction as 'an abstraction that is carried out in the actual behavior of humans, regardless of whether they are aware of it'.[21] In Fineschi's words, this conceptualisation of real abstraction is likewise 'an abstraction that is not posited by thought, but the result of a practical process.'[22] Lange suggests that real abstraction does not originate in thought, 'but in human activity itself', and is 'obscured from the conscious and intentional activity of the participants of the exchange process.'[23] While Elbe suggests that 'Real abstraction means that the general attribute of acts of labor of being human labor as such, in and through exchange, obtains – without the conscious intervention of those engaging in exchange – the specific significance of being the social form of private acts of labor.'[24]

> *(b) real abstractions, while abstract, act upon the world, and have great power to do so. They are also particularly difficult to affect/destroy/dismember through human activity.*

Real abstractions wield uncanny power over humans in much contemporary literature – Soren Mau writes, 'capitalist society is ruled by social relations morphed into real abstractions', which involves the transformation of certain relations into a 'quasi-autonomous system' which imposes itself through 'an impersonal and abstract form of domination.'[25] Here, real abstractions are strong enough to maintain a level of autonomy (from our actions upon them, we presume) and dominate us with an inhuman power. Toscano similarly writes that real abstraction dominates society 'by an empty reality principle',[26] while Jason Moore describes real abstractions as having 'operative force in the material world.'[27] Elbe notes that real abstraction's validity as a concept is proven by the 'increasing uncontrollable capitalist mode of production that almost completely takes hold of individuals.'[28]

For Bonefeld, 'In capitalism, Man is ruled by economic abstractions over which he has no control ... The term real abstraction articulates the vanishing appearance of Man as an embodiment of the ghost-walking economic categories'.[29] Bonefeld's words epitomise the affect that dominates writings on real abstraction. Without doubt, many parts of capitalism can appear as cold, impersonal, empty and overwhelming. Some of us need to be shaken into awareness of this complex and powerful system, and sometimes it is through these vivid descriptors that we can get there. At the same time, we must remain wary of the way such mystical and beguiling categories might come to occlude an accurate understanding of the world.

There is a problem, for example, if we come to consider real abstractions to be acting subjects in their own right – Fineschi writes of theories of real abstraction: 'In general terms, one of the most important focuses is that, in capitalism, abstractions become real and work in the system as acting subjects.'[30] Toscano goes so far as to suggest that this type of real abstraction is the *differentia specifica* of capitalism (although Fineschi argues the contrary).[31]

Three central problems arise from these features. First, in insisting that real abstractions are neither an action of the mind, nor are they material, these theorists (wittingly or no) invoke an ontological dualism between matter and 'the abstract' that approximates a Kantian divide between phenomena and noumena. As in most ontological divides, one side of the dualism – here, the realm of 'the abstract' – wields extraordinary, even quasi-supernatural powers. Consequently, the abstract both dictates the structure of our lives, and is particularly unyielding to the influence of intentional material/concrete human activity. This shows that the first premise (a) tends to yield to the second; (b) ontological dualism tends to imply the existence of supernatural power. Marx and Engels famously invoke the supernatural in the *Communist Manifesto*, analogising bourgeois society to a 'sorcerer' and capitalist production to the 'powers of the netherworld' in a clear attempt to impress upon the reader the sheer strength and vast powers of capitalism.[32] While metaphor and poetry are essential to the project of apprehending the totality of what we must destroy, we cannot forget that Marx's critique of the *fetish* is also a critique of worshipping processes that have been reified into conceptual objects which possess magical powers.

Reification and fetishisation of the concept of 'real abstraction' is the second major problem arising from the contemporary use of the term. When we say that certain phenomena become 'real abstractions', this quickly comes to mean that they turn into a specific sort of thing which acts in a specific way. This formulation can mislead and/or cut short inquiry into the topics it is meant to elucidate. For example, if we find the capitalist state form to be deleterious, hooked into capitalist production at every juncture, and almost unimaginable to dislodge, and we decide to label it a 'real abstraction', we can attribute its durability, strength and seductive force to its nature as a 'real abstraction' rather than inquiring into the actual material processes which consistently render it strong, dynamic and self-justifying.

Third, once real abstraction has been reified as a concept, insisting on the 'impersonality' and 'emptiness' of real abstractions becomes axiomatic, apparently needing little explanation or justification – it is *in the nature* of the realm of abstraction. Mau's now infamous concept of 'mute compulsion' is a theory of capitalism as the domination of real abstractions, and emphasises its 'mute'-ness, its impersonality, emptiness, etc. For Mau, impersonal power is distinguished from 'personal relations of dependence' because people are bound 'to capital as such, not to a particular capitalist.'[33] This is drawn from Marx's statement that

> The worker leaves the capitalist to whom he hires himself whenever he likes, and the capitalist discharges him whenever he thinks fit, as soon as he no longer gets any profit out of him, or not the anticipated profit. But the worker, whose sole source of livelihood is the sale of his labour, cannot leave the whole class of purchasers, that is, the capitalist class, without renouncing his existence. He belongs not to this or that bourgeois, but to the bourgeoisie, the bourgeois class, and it is his business to dispose of himself, that is to find a purchaser within this bourgeois class.[34]

Similarly, Postone names the categories of 'the commodity' and 'value' as expressing 'impersonal social forms'. He writes: 'Capitalism is a system of abstract, impersonal domination. Relative to earlier social forms, people appear to be independent; but they actually are subject to a system of social domination that seems not social but "objective".'[35]

Concepts of emptiness and impersonality evoke some important realities of capitalism. However, insofar as *impersonal* domination refers to people being exploited and dominated by an abstract capitalist class instead of particular individuals or cohorts, this is only the general condition of the most affluent echelons of the global proletariat. To the majority of the people of the world under its control, capital's domination is vicious and acute, attending to particularities of people who are being exploited. If capitalism demanded and produced modern chattel slavery and the Atlantic slave trade,[36] if precarious immigrant labour forces are strategically produced to fill labour needs where working conditions are vile, life-shortening, and shielded from labour laws,[37] these all require an actual personalisation within the 'emptiness' of value, a relentless discrimination and reproduction of heirarchised difference within the often-forced process of abstract labour – an immanent, unstoppable force of racialisation. Furthermore, the systematic oppression, repression, sexual abuse and conscription into relations of psychic, physical and emotional subordination of feminised people, grounded as it is between the capitalist separation of the spheres of 'work' and 'non-work', is a guarantee that the majority of feminised individuals will be subjected to extremely personal violences throughout the duration of their lives.

Capital forces a hierarchy between the people who live in luxury, who live on the edge of luxury, who live in unyielding stress and destitution, who live in ethnic cleansing and constant war. Between people who can expect social recognition, respect, bodily autonomy and care, and those who can expect social diminution, exclusion, death, rape and negligence. Capital and capitalists 'care' about creating these different groups, insofar as they *need to and do so*. Capital would not 'be happy' for everyone to be equal, unracialised, ungendered, content automatons. This would disable superprofits, the acceleration of value extraction, increases in ground rent extraction, and any number of other holy grails that guide the activities of the capitalist and landowning classes.

In Bhandar and Toscano's 'Race, real estate, and real abstraction', they outline capitalist property relations and race as two of many possible 'real abstractions'. Their goal is to use the framework of Althusser's and Hall's 'articulation' to show that capitalist property and race are deeply entangled ('articulated'), even though, on their reading, capitalist property is inherent to capitalist social relations, and race is not.[38] This enables them to think through the deep connections between race and property – noting for example, that the 'racial anthropology of the human is smuggled into the ontological grounding of the possessive individual.'

Bhandar and Toscano aim to address the question of 'how capitalist property relations preserve and rely upon'[39], in Stuart Hall's words,'other relations that are not ascribable within the "social relations of production"'[40] (meaning: how capitalist property relations preserve and rely upon race even when race it is not inherent to the capitalist mode of production). To do so, they take these 'other relations' (here, race) and elevate them to 'real abstractions' alongside the real abstraction of property. Once this is achieved, a process of 'articulation' can be posited as uniting them in mutual reproduction.

What do we gain in our analysis of race and property by saying that they are real abstractions? Setting aside the possibility that race is in fact inherent to capitalist social relations (an avenue of inquiry that I find much more fruitful), surely we can approach the question of how race and capitalist property are related to one another without having to impose the concept of 'real abstraction' upon them. All of the creative theoretical work Bhandar and Toscano do in the paper does not properly *require* this use of real abstraction. However, this method of dubbing certain social relations 'real abstractions' has the unintended effect of reifying them – truly thing-ifying them. Hence, in their conclusion, Bhandar and Toscano state that 'it seems that justice might require a disarticulation of the fetishes produced by racial and propertied abstractions.'[41]

But racial and propertied abstractions do not 'produce fetishes'; they *are* fetishes. Insofar as 'racial and propertied abstractions' are considered as 'real abstractions' which act upon us, they are themselves fetishes thrown up by larger processes. To say that 'racial abstraction' causes racial violence, for example, is to mystify the fact that complex material processes of racialisation – enacted by individuals, groups, institutions, to name but a few scales of analysis – cause and enact racist violence.

Similarly, to say that the value form does this or that mystifies, to a certain degree, the fact that the consequences of the value form are consequences not of a mystical immaterial force, but of real material structures and processes that we comprehend through a study of the abstract concept of the value form as a social relation.

Let us consider Bhandar and Toscano's quotation of Gilmore:

> 'Racism', writes Ruth Wilson Gilmore, 'is a practice of abstraction, a death-dealing displacement of difference into hierarchies that organise relations within and between the planet's sovereign political territories'. Processes of abstraction, Gilmore notes, figure humans in relation to inhuman persons in a hierarchy that produces the totalising category of the 'human being'.[42]

Of course racialisation is a process which 'abstracts' certain physical or cultural qualities from people and elevates them to levels of importance in categorising different groups. Specific abstracted traits become central to how people understand hierarchical racial categories. But the violence of this is not in the process of abstraction itself. As mentioned above, any 'process' which has consistent effects across space and time will be unthinkable without mobilising our faculty of 'abstraction', and of considering that process 'abstracted' from any one specific context. As such, race is not more abstract than respiration, music or weaving. The problem of racism is not that it abstracts, but rather, the 'death-dealing displacement of difference into hierarchies that organise relations within and between the planet's sovereign political territories.'

In sum, the contemporary use of 'real abstraction' invokes an ontological dualism that impedes critical inquiry into the capitalist mode of production. In the following section, I will excavate the development of this dualism in Sohn-Rethel's development of the concept of real abstraction. As we go, I also want to keep in mind that when we are swayed by the mysticism embodied by the term 'real abstraction' we stop asking *what are the processes which the mental abstraction 'value' names?* What are the processes which the mental abstraction 'gender' names? What are the processes which the mental abstraction 'race' names?

Sohn Rethel: Anti-Kantian Kantianism

As many have noted, Alfred Sohn-Rethel, rather than Marx, originated and developed the concept of 'real abstraction', which pushes into an increasingly wide field of Marxian subdisciplines today.[43] Though most writers agree that Marx never used the term 'real abstraction', many argue that a concept *akin* to that of real abstraction was *at work* in Marx's theories. Mau, for example, states that real abstraction is 'clearly visible' in Marx's writing even though he doesn't use the term.[44] Jappe insists that 'the concept – if not the word – is present, and is absolutely crucial in [Marx's] writings'.[45]

I turn to Sohn-Rethel to explore real abstraction's early development in the marxian lexicon. But rather than give a holistic assessment of Sohn-Rethel's theory, I want to highlight the fact that his concept of real abstraction is defined by a Kantian ontological dualism between thought and matter (the abstract and the concrete).[46] (Some argue that Marx himself imposes such a dualism in his theory of value, but I will argue in section 4 that this need not be our interpretation.)

To name something a 'real abstraction' is, too often, to consider it sorcery. 'Real abstraction' answers our confusion with recourse to a mystical 'other' place where abstractions live. As such, real abstraction is the distilled example of a practice that goes far beyond the use of that specific term; many theorists effect the same manoeuvre – offshoring the explanation of something vast and complex to an 'immaterial' realm – with other conceptual tools.[47]

Ironically, Sohn-Rethel orients his book on real abstraction around a critique of Kant. Kant functions as Sohn-Rethel's conceptual foil, representing the *pure bourgeois perspective* in the field of epistemology. This enables Sohn-Rethel, in his own terms, to treat Kant's work in a similar way to how Marx treats Adam Smith's interventions into the field of political economy. Sohn-Rethel convincingly shows that Smith and Kant both elaborate 'a coherent, all-embracing ideology to suit the production relations of bourgeois society',[48] marking them both as high philosophical defenders of capitalism. Sohn-Rethel considers Smith's 1776 *Wealth of Nations* and Kant's 1781 *Critique of Pure Reason* to be 'above all others, the two works which, in completely unconnected fields and in total systematic independence from each other, strive towards the same goal: to prove the perfect normalcy of bourgeois society.'[49] Kant's theory of science is

> the classical manifestation of the bourgeois fetishism of intellectual labour ... Kant might at his time have been introduced to an English public as the Adam Smith of epistemology, and at the same period Smith could have been recommended to a German audience as the Immanuel Kant of political economy.[50]

Thus, Sohn-Rethel considers his critique of Kant's epistemology as analogous to Marx's critique of Adam Smith's political economy. As Marx showed of Adam Smith's work, Sohn-Rethel hopes to reveal, through this project of uncovering the assumptions and fetishes of bourgeois philosophical epistemology, essential truths about Capital.

Sohn-Rethel considers Kant's fundamental fallacy to be his transhistorical account of the division between the material and ideal. Comparable to Adam Smith's treatment of the categories of a capitalist economy as transhistorical, Kant elevates this division of ideal and empirical realms to transhistorical truth – there is no beginning to the division, and so, conveniently, there is no end. This division between realms is fundamental, ontological, eternal. Sohn-Rethel argues that 'Kant was driven to this conclusion because he could not imagine that non-empirical concepts could possibly have natural or historical, or in any case spatio-temporal, roots.'[51] The fact that Kant could *not imagine* the material production of non-empirical concepts is, according to Sohn-Rethel, the result of the same material processes which give rise to the division in the first place. This resembles Adam Smith's treatment of homo economicus as transhistorical.

Sohn-Rethel argues, contra Kant, that the division between the conceptual and the empirical is generated by the social act of exchange. Exchange, here, is a historical rather than a permanent feature of human social life, emerging at specific moments in time and growing to dominance. Specifically, argues Sohn-Rethel, when exchange moves beyond an act occurring between societies or groups, and becomes an intra-societal activity performed by individuals with other individuals, it instigates a particular cognitive process amongst these exchanging individuals which is qualitatively dissimilar to all others, which becomes the faculty of *cognitive abstraction*.

Sohn-Rethel's notion of *cognitive abstraction* is important – it is not the mere use of abstract terms or concepts (for all language functions on a level of abstraction, where for instance the term 'bird' comes to refer to a complex multitude of beings). In fact, Sohn-Rethel suggests that there are '*levels* of abstraction' (a common form of expression in marxian thought today), and as these levels ascend, at some point mental labour attains 'intellectual independence which severs it inherently from manual labour without the need of caste divisions or mystifications.'[52]

Thus, for example, while some mathematics are possible before the development of this intellectual independence, a *theorem* 'lies on a level of abstraction too high for [some] kind of "mathematics".' For example, the practice of rope-stretching in Ancient Egypt does not ascend to the level of theorems, even though it certainly 'gets the job done', according to Sohn-Rethel. The proto-abstract forms of mathematics such as those of Ancient Egypt are characterised by 'the lack of the logical foundation and systematic coherence by which it later assumes its intrinsic division from manual labour.'[53] These forms cannot reach higher levels of abstraction because generalised exchange – the origin of intellectually independent abstractions – remains absent in this historical period.

Sohn-Rethel's eurocentrism here becomes even more obvious when he names the work of Bronze-age Egypt and Syria 'proto-intellectual' while the activity of the Greeks (claimed by the West as its progenitor) establishes 'real intellect'.[54] Sohn-Rethel gives additional depth to the white supremacist map of human progress forged in colonialism and solidified in the history of Western Philosophy through Kant and Hegel (among others). This white supremacist geography grounds the concept of real abstraction – something which cannot be considered irrelevant to its contemporary use.

Only the onset of capitalist social relations can instigate the formal rift between mental and manual labour, according to Sohn-Rethel. So long as the economic context could 'be likened to that of a huge state household',[55] the act of exchange had not yet taken a central enough place in society to begin to develop a purer expression of cognitive abstraction.[56]

With this historical narrative (that takes cues, consciously or not, from Hegel's racist and paternalistic Lectures on the Philosophy of History), Sohn-Rethel replaces Kant's transhistorical account of the metaphysical realm of pure ideas with his own historical-material genesis story of that metaphysical realm. Sohn-Rethel considers this move to be a 'liquidation' of Kant's 'critical dualism' between thought and matter. Sohn-Rethel considers his approach superior to Hegel's resolution of the dualism, in which thought and matter 'perform a process' together.[57] But here we must note that Sohn-Rethel's approach does not liquidate the dualism between thought and matter, it *historicises it*; the *reality* of that dualism, in Sohn-Rethel's account, is shored up. Here, Sohn-Rethel betrays his own goal of treating Kant as Marx treated Adam Smith, for while Marx aptly shows that *homo economicus* does not exist, and is merely an appearance, Sohn-Rethel alleges that a mind-body dualism does in fact exist as a result of generalised commodity exchange. And it is here in this dualism that real abstraction emerges, historically.

And so, real abstraction as a concept ensures the continued reification of distinct ideal and material realms. What's more, 'real abstraction' gives those realms a means of communication. Kant's system invoked the human faculty of thought as a potential connection between the noumenal and phenomenal realms, and here real abstraction similarly offers a means by which the two realms are connected; real abstraction is immaterial but borne from material-concrete human activity, and has the power to then act upon the material-concrete world, dominating and controlling people. Furthermore, real abstraction is the ground for the pure human intellect, which conceivably functions for Sohn-Rethel in some similar ways as it does for Kant.

Thus, despite articulating a set of convincing arguments that dethrone the Kantian dualism, Sohn-Rethel retains a *real*, if historically emergent and materially produced, division between thought and matter. Sohn-Rethel denotes this dualism in the old German style – as First Nature and Second Nature. Sohn-Rethel tells us that while certain concepts and notions – for instance, the individual private intellect – are fetish-concepts produced by the exchange abstraction, the existence of a second nature, separate from the first, is *real*.

But are not first and second nature also 'fetishes'? They do not describe something real so much as affirm an appearance, an 'illusion in human consciousness' to use Isaak Rubin's words, thrown up by material processes. Sohn-Rethel does not appear to consider the actual non-distinction between the empirical world and abstract cognition. Thus, he appears to fall into the same trap to which he confines Hegel, who

> could not himself step out of the bourgeois world of his epoch, and so he attained the unity outreaching Kant only by dispensing with the epistemological critique, and hence by way of hypostasis. He did not *make* 'thinking' and 'being' one, and did not enquire how they would be one. He simply argued that the idea of truth *demands* them to be one, and if logic is to be the logic of the truth it has to start with that unity, as its presupposition.[58]

This passage, early on in the book, seems to indicate Sohn-Rethel's commitment to making 'thinking' and 'being' one, but in fact he affirms them as *two*, albeit one originating in the other; and albeit temporarily two, rather than transhistorically two.

In order to *make* thinking and being one, instead of letting them play out as one process, Sohn-Rethel finds a story, a history, of their coming-into-being-as-two. Ultimately their coming into being is resolved in their eventual collapse (ostensibly concomitant to a communist revolution), and the temporary nature of their bifurcation is what proves their unity.

But why this historicisation rather than a straightforward claim of the transhistorical nondistinction between abstract thought and matter? More Kantian than he could admit, and caught in the same trap as Kant who could not conceive of abstraction arising empirically, Sohn-Rethel could not conceive there to be *no real ontological dualism whatsoever* in the world he knew.[59] Thus he argues that a material social process has the capacity to, in itself, give rise to a separate ontological plane, but offers no ontological ground on which such a thing could make sense. The ontological dualism is a given:

> The duality of sources of knowledge we accept as an incontrovertible fact. The question we ask is, what is the historical origin of our logical ability to construct mathematical hypotheses and the elements contributing to them?[60]

But: the two spheres do not actually exist in reality as separate, just as commodities do not really emerge smoothly and cleanly of their own volition onto the Walmart shelves. The oddity is that the two spheres appear to 'really' exist – not, as Sohn-Rethel argues, that the two spheres are historically determined. Their *fetish* is historically determined.

Rubin writes that eventually, 'Illusion and error in men's minds transform reified economic categories into "objective forms" (of thought) of production relations of a given, historically determined mode of production – commodity production'.[61] Thus, with Kant, we observe the fabulous examples of the increasingly reified categories of thought and matter incarnating into pure and purely separated realms. The problem is not, as Sohn-Rethel argues, that Kant neglects to account for the emergence of this division, but that Kant takes the division, which is an illusion, as real. Sohn-Rethel proceeds to accept and reify these illusions in a different way, preserving them from true liquidation as 'real abstractions'.

Abstraction without dualism

While many interpret Marx's words on abstraction, abstract labour and value, as supporting this Sohn-Rethelian concept of real abstraction, I believe real abstraction reintroduces an idealism that Marx was trying to demystify, a dualism he abandoned early on in life. I share V. A. Martin's assessment of Marx, that 'in his own field of research during his maturity – political economy – Marx managed to overcome the dichotomy that opposed real to metaphysical objects, a dichotomy that goes back to Plato.'[62] And Marx did not overcome this by the Hegelian trick of, pace Sohn-Rethel, making the two 'perform a process'. Rather, he denied a separate, operative realm where ideal objects ('real abstractions') acted as subjects. Here, I'd like to consider how to read abstraction and abstract processes in a non-dualistic way. What is 'abstract' about our abstractions is the fact that they refer to complex patterns of repeating processes amidst widely different geographies, peoples and times. In other words, 'social relation', like 'process' and 'motion', are patterns immanent to matter, not immaterial forms which exist apart from matter.

Birds in a flock of millions move and dart together in complex patterns. Abstract labour differs from the flight patterns of birds not because the former is abstract while the latter is not. 'Abstract labour' refers to a pattern of human behaviour that pulls in, impacts and transforms an astonishing breadth of living and non-living beings and relations the world over – moreover, it does so to the devastation of the vast majority and the enrichment of a few. As such, 'abstract labour' is quantitatively distinct from 'flight patterns',[63] and it is more germane to any movement towards liberation, peace and collective well-being. However, we cannot say one is a real abstraction and the other is not.

The backdrop to a non-dualistic, non-idealistic understanding of the capitalist mode of production would be a Spinozist monism – or an Einsteinian physics, which is the same. Sohn-Rethel was unable, or unwilling, to consider such a challenge to Kant's dualism. An elaboration of such a system and how it may ground Marx's critique of capitalism is beyond the scope of this paper. Instead, I will discuss several points in the critique of capitalism that are often interpreted through Kantian (or Hegelian) dualism, and how we can offer an alternative, monist reading.

In his introduction to Galileo's 'Dialogue Concerning the Two World Systems', Einstein notes that he and Galileo both worked to reject hypotheses that introduced a conceptual object that transcended the material but acted upon it.[64] He noted that transcendence is 'not exactly inadmissible from a purely logical point of view', but, we can add, its logical coherence depends on ontological dualism.

But then, what is abstract labour, or value, if not something supersensible, immaterial? Marx writes:

> To measure the exchange-value of commodities by the labor-time they contain, the different kinds of labor have to be reduced to uniform, homogeneous, simple labor, in short to labor of uniform quality, whose only difference, therefore, is quantity. This reduction appears to be abstraction, but it is an abstraction which is made every day in the social process of production... This abstraction, human labor in general, exists in the form of average labor which, in a given society, the average person can perform ...[65]

Familiar as we are with Marx's assertion that labour has *two* aspects, concrete and abstract, Marx offers little to elucidate the meaning of this split-into-two. Marx also is not particularly concerned to conceptualise in detail the ontology implied in the process of labour splitting into its abstract and concrete qualities – he does not give us, you might say, a clear ontological understanding of what this means. However we can learn something from his description of the abstract. And here we find that 'abstract' need not mean 'immaterial' in Marx.

Marx describes the emergence of an object as a commodity as a moment in which 'it changes into a thing which transcends sensuousness.'[66] Rather than interpreting this as the emergence of an abstract supra-sensible realm, consider that this could mean merely that the commodity-form of an object *bears no relation* to the material particularities of that object.

The commodity character of a thing – say, a wooden chair – is not based on an atom of its own matter. It is not found in the wood or the nails, nor in their particular arrangement as wrought by their maker(s). The sensuousness of the specific chair is, in a sense, 'transcended', but only by larger material processes, NOT by something immaterial. The chair's commodity character is not immaterial – it is based on the real, material relationships of the production and circulation and exchange of that chair (which involve necessarily the totality of social relations that compose capitalism, as its nature is to irrevocably imbricate every thing and person in that totality), all of which operate in and as ponderable matter (and perhaps, as Einstein would have added, fields).

These material relationships become *more important* to its social character than the wood and nails comprising the thing's 'own body', because these larger processes are what determines which chair will get created – and where, and how – more than any maker, any wood or any nail.

Abstract labour, for its part, is abstract insofar as it produces value. What does this mean? This is *shorthand for a whole system*. To say abstract labour produces value is to say that it is happening in capitalism, that it is waged work, and that its products will be commodities that enter the sphere of circulation. To say labour is abstract is to refer to its embeddedness in (inextricability from) a larger process which exceeds the given labour in space and in time.

To say labour is abstract is to note that it produces commodities for the market and it is organised within a larger system of wage labour. Its abstractness refers to the qualities pertaining to any specific instance of labouring which connect it to the whole of the capitalist mode of production. But does the abstractness of abstract labour mean it transcends this material, phenomenal realm? No. This additional ontological level is unnecessary for the concepts to function in a rich and provocative description of the system – and, in fact, to impose ontological dualism weakens the analysis, for it offloads an important dynamic of our world onto another, literally untouchable realm of being.

What of value? What is it to say that value is abstract? Value is the quality of commodity production which brings together its disparate parts – to say it is 'congealed labour time' doesn't clarify much here. Value is not a material substance like ice, snow, blood or beans, but the name of one aspect of a process. Value represents the fact that a person has worked for some amount of time in this death-dealing global system. It is the name for the product of (abstract) labour. It is a measurement we can take of capitalist exploitation. It is not an immaterial substance, any more than centimetres are immaterial substances.

Abstraction can also describe some of the consequences of the existence of abstract labour's production of commodities as a system – for example, to the 'abstract' social life of commodities which only occurs because of the value that they hold – in common.[67]

The objectivity of commodities as values differs from Dame Quickly in the sense that 'a man knows not where to have it'. Not an atom of matter enters into the objectivity of commodities as values; in this it is the direct opposite of the coarsely sensuous objectivity of commodities as physical objects. We may twist and turn a single commodity as we wish; it remains impossible to grasp it as a thing possessing value. However, let us remember that commodities possess an objective character as values only in so far as they are all expressions of an identical social substance, human labour, that their objective character as values is therefore purely social. From this it follows self-evidently that it can only appear in the social relation between commodity and commodity.[68]

Atoms of matter *of the commodity* do not enter into value composition – but this does not mean value is immaterial or ontologically separate from matter any more than gravity exists in a separate sphere of existence from falling rain. Gravity is a force which is *in and of matter*, and value is no less so. Here, value manifests in the social relations of commodities – social relations which themselves do not transcend matter but occur in matter. To say that value exists and that it is abstract, then, is to use shorthand to refer to the complex totality of capitalist social relations.

To be sure, value is so strange and complex a system that we have yet to fully comprehend it (and likely won't until long after we destroy it), which can tempt us to ascribe to it a spectral or mystical substance. Such metaphors and allusions can drive home the real vastness and permeation of value into all human life (such that 'human life' itself is a concept inextricable from value). If you had to describe the Grand Canyon to someone who had never seen it, you may say something more than its metric measurements. So, we may both forgive and appreciate those authors whose poetic nuancing of the concept of value has assisted us in grasping it more fully.

However, poetry notwithstanding, value is the product of wage labour in a capitalist system, and all the things that this entails. Value is *not* an ontologically distinct, 'abstract' substance, existing in some other plane of reality, birthed into that plane by the demonic machinations of capital. Value – like gravity – is a conceptual representation of a complex process that is difficult for all of us to comprehend.

To repeat: value is not an object, but a process. Many have said this, but the implication I emphasise here is this: if value is not an object, but a process (or set of processes) it cannot be a 'real abstraction', insofar as this term is commonly understood to refer to something immaterial.[69] Everything that creates value happens here, in this world, and is explainable within it, without need for reference to a wicked Narnia where a white queen of value coordinates our realm through her interdimensional spyglass.

F.T.C. Manning is a writer, researcher and educator based in San Francisco, California.

Notes

1. Gianluca Pozzoni, 'Chapter 11: Real Abstraction', in *Marx: Key Concepts* (Cheltenham: Edward Elgar, 2024). Thanks to O. L. Silverman, Caitlin Manning, and Nader Hasan for their excellent critiques and suggestions on the following essay.
2. Maya Gonzalez and Jeanne Neton, 'The Logic of Gender', *Endnotes* 3 (2013).
3. Jason W. Moore, 'Nature/Society & The Violence of Real Abstraction', (2016), accessed 14 July 2025, https://jasonwmoore.wordpress.com/2016/10/04/naturesociety-the-violence-of-real-abstraction/.
4. Brenna Bhandar and Alberto Toscano, 'Race, Real Estate and Real Abstraction', *Radical Philosophy* 194 (Nov-Dec, 2015), 8–17.
5. Werner Bonefeld, 'On Capital as Real Abstraction' in *Marx and Contemporary Critical Theory: The Philosophy of Real Abstraction*, eds. Antonio Oliva, Ángel Oliva and Iván Novara (Cham: Springer, 2020), 159.
6. Roberto Fineschi, 'Real Abstraction: Philological Issues', in *Marx and Contemporary Critical Theory*, 71.
7. Paolo Virno, 'General Intellect' in *Lessico postfordista Dizionario di idee della mutazione*, eds. Adelino Zanini and Ubaldo Fadini (Milano: Feltrinelli, 2002).
8. Sara-Maria Sorentino, 'Natural Slavery, Real Abstraction, and the Virtuality of Anti-Blackness', *Theory and Event* 22:3 (2019), 632.
9. Bonefeld, 'On Capital as Real Abstraction', 153–70.
10. Alberto Toscano, *Fanaticism: On the Uses of an Idea* (London: Verso, 2010).
11. Michael Heinrich, *An Introduction to the Three Volumes of Karl Marx's Capital* (New York: Monthly Review Press, 2012).
12. Moishe Postone, *Time, Labor, and Social Domination: A Reinterpretation of Marx's Critical Theory* (Cambridge: Cambridge University Press, 1996); John Milios, 'Value Form and Abstract Labor in Marx: A Critical Review of Alfred Sohn-Rethel's Notion of "Real Abstraction"', in *Marx and Contemporary Critical Theory*, 25–39.
13. Elena Louisa Lange, 'Real Abstraction', in *The Sage Handbook of Marxism*, eds. Beverley Skeggs et al. (London: Sage, 2022), 593–608.
14. Peter McLaughlin and Oliver Schlaudt, 'Real Abstraction in the History of the Natural Sciences', in *Marx and Contemporary Critical Theory*, 311.
15. Anselm Jappe, 'Sohn-Rethel and the Origin of "Real Abstraction": A Critique of Production or a Critique of Circulation?', *Historical Materialism* 21:1 (2013), 3–14.
16. Chris O'Kane, 'The Critique of Real Abstraction: From the Critical Theory of Society to the Critique of Political Economy and Back Again' in *Marx and Contemporary Critical Theory*, 281–82.
17. Robert Kurz, 'Abstrakte Arbeit und Sozialismus', *Marxistische Kritik* 4 (Dez. 1987).
18. Søren Mau, *Mute Compulsion: A Marxist Theory of the Economic Power of Capital* (London: Verso, 2023).
19. Michael Heinrich, *An Introduction to the Three Volumes of Karl Marx's Capital*, trans. Alex Locascio (New York: Monthly Review Press, 2012).
20. Kurz, 'Abstrakte Arbeit'.
21. Heinrich, *An Introduction*.
22. Roberto Fineschi, 'Real Abstraction: Philological Issues', in *Marx and Contemporary Critical Theory*, 62.
23. Lange, 'Real Abstraction'.
24. Ingo Elbe, 'Reification and Real Abstraction in Marx's Critique of Political Economy', in *Marx and Contemporary Critical Theory*, 255.
25. Mau, *Mute Compulsion*, 82.
26. Alberto Toscano, 'The Open Secret of Real Abstraction', *Rethinking Marxism* 20:2 (2008), 277.
27. Moore, 'Nature/Society'.
28. Elbe, 'Reification', 249.
29. Bonefeld, 'On Capital as Real Abstraction', 154.
30. Fineschi, 'Real Abstraction', 70.
31. Toscano, 'Open Secret', 273; Fineschi, 'Real Abstraction.'
32. Karl Marx and Friedrich Engels, *Manifesto of the Communist Party*, in *Marx and Engels Collected Works, Volume 6, 1845-1848* (London: Lawrence & Wishart, 2010), 489.
33. Mau, *Mute Compulsion*, 136.
34. Karl Marx, *Wage Labour and Capital*, in *Collected Works of Karl Marx and Friedrich Engels, 1849, Vol. 9: The Journalism and Speeches of the Revolutionary Years in Germany* (London: Lawrence & Wishart, 2010), 203.
35. Postone, *Time, Labor, and Social Domination*, 125.
36. See, for example, Eric Williams, *Capitalism and Slavery*, (Chapel Hill: University of North Carolina Press, 1994); Walter Rodney, *How Europe Underdeveloped Africa* (Brooklyn: Verso, 2018); and Karl Marx, *Poverty of Philosophy*, in *Marx/Engels Collected Works*, vol. 6 (New York: International Publishers, 1976), 167.

37. Exemplified in Mostafa Henaway, *Essential Work, Disposable Workers: Migration, Capitalism and Class* (Toronto: Fernwood Publishing, 2023).
38. Bhandar and Toscano, 'Race, Real Estate and Real Abstraction', 13.
39. Bhandar and Toscano, 'Race, Real Estate and Real Abstraction', 13.
40. Stuart Hall, 'Race, Articulation, and Societies Structured in Dominance', *Black British Cultural Studies: A Reader* (1996), 16–60.
41. Bhandar and Toscano, 'Race, Real Estate and Real Abstraction', 16.
42. Bhandar and Toscano, 'Race, Real Estate and Real Abstraction', 11.
43. 'Realabstraktion' was not used by Marx (Finelli, 61), though 'reelle Abstraktion' was in *Contributions to the Critique of Political Economy*. See, Lange 'Real Abstraction'.
44. Mau, *Mute Compulsion*, 184.
45. Jappe, 'Sohn-Rethel and the Origin of "Real Abstraction"', 6.
46. Žižek appears to be one of the only theorists who has clearly apprehended the Kantian transcendental core of the concept of real abstraction. See Slavoj Žižek, *The Sublime Object of Ideology* (Verso, 1989), 10–13.
47. See, for example, Andreas Malm on 'substance monism, property dualism' in Andreas Malm, *The Progress of This Storm: Nature and Society in a Warming World* (London: Verso, 2020); and various authors who mobilise a first nature / second nature divide, e.g. Neil Smith, *Uneven Development: Nature, Capital and the Production of Space* (Oxford: Blackwell, 1984).
48. Alfred Sohn-Rethel, *Intellectual and Manual Labour* (London: Humanities Press, 1983), 14.
49. Sohn-Rethel, *Intellectual and Manual Labour*, 35.
50. Sohn-Rethel, *Intellectual and Manual Labour*, 14.
51. Sohn-Rethel, *Intellectual and Manual Labour*, 74.
52. Sohn-Rethel, *Intellectual and Manual Labour*, 92; emphasis mine.
53. Sohn-Rethel, *Intellectual and Manual Labour*, 91.
54. Sohn-Rethel, *Intellectual and Manual Labour*, 99.
55. Sohn-Rethel, *Intellectual and Manual Labour*, 92.
56. It is relevant to mention here Moishe Postone's critique, that Sohn-Rethel fallaciously perceives the 'commodity form as being extrinsic to commodity-determined labor'. See Moishe Postone, *Time, Labor, and Social Domination*, 177–78. Indeed, Sohn-Rethel looks at commodities and commodity exchange as something which predates commodity-determined labour proper and instigates the formation of abstract cognition which enables abstract mathematics and other scientific developments. However, it might still be argued, in defense of Sohn-Rethel, that these pre-capitalist abstractions are but proto-abstractions, arising from societies *increasingly oriented around* but not *defined fundamentally by* commodity exchange proper.
57. 'The Hegelian dissolution of the Kantian antithesis is not achieved by dissolving them, but by making them perform as a process. The Hegelian dialectics has no other legitimacy than that it is a process occurring. Questioned as to its possibility it would prove impossible.' Sohn-Rethel, *Intellectual and Manual Labour*, 13.
58. Sohn-Rethel, *Intellectual and Manual Labour*, 15.
59. Slavoj Žižek pointed out a redeemable aspect of Sohn-Rethel's theory, which is that through his work on real abstraction, Sohn-Rethel 'has confronted the closed circle of philosophical reflection with an external place where its form is already "staged"'. In this sense, Žižek suggests, Sohn-Rethel brings in a theory of the unconscious. Slavoj Žižek, *The Sublime Object of Ideology* (London: Verso, 1989), 13–14
60. Sohn-Rethel, *Intellectual and Manual Labour*, 38.
61. I. I. Rubin, *Essays on Marx's Theory of Value* (Montreal: Black Rose Books, 1973), 5.
62. Maurício Vieira Martins, 'On Real Objects That Are Not Sensuous: Marx and Abstraction in Actu' in *Marx and Contemporary Critical Theory*, 191–202.
63. I disagree with Kurz here that real abstractions involve a *doubling* of abstraction, whereas other mental abstractions do not. Either they are all doubled, or none of them are.
64. Galileo Galilei, J. L. Heilbron and Albert Einstein, *Dialogue Concerning the Two Chief World Systems: Ptolemaic and Copernican*, eds. Stillman Drake and Stephen Jay Gould (New York: Modern Library, 2001).
65. Quoted in Martins, 'On Real Objects That Are Not Sensuous', 193.
66. Karl Marx, *Capital: Volume 1: A Critique of Political Economy*, trans. Ben Fowkes (Harmondsworth: Penguin, 1992),163.
67. It is nowhere clearer that contemporary theories of society and 'the social' have their basis in this society of value rather than the reverse as when we consider these passages from Marx.
68. Marx, *Capital: Volume 1*, 138–39.
69. Perhaps the concept of 'field' and the supersession of the 'law of gravity' by 'general relativity' could offer a perspective to aid us in deepening our understanding of value.

Smash the feminist family
An interview with Sophie Lewis

Sophie Lewis is an independent writer and scholar based in Philadelphia. Full Surrogacy Now: Feminism Against Family *and its follow-up* Abolish the Family: A Manifesto for Care and Liberation *were published by Verso in 2019 and 2022. In this interview with* Radical Philosophy, *Sophie is in conversation with Victoria Browne, Hannah Proctor and Rahul Rao, discussing their latest book,* Enemy Feminisms: TERFs, Policewomen, and Girlbosses Against Liberation, *published this year by Haymarket.*

Radical Philosophy Can you tell us something about the decision to construct a history of 'enemy feminisms' largely through a series of biographical portraits? What does this narrative device help you to do? Should we read these individuals as social symptoms?

Sophie Lewis At the heart of *Enemy Feminisms*, the original impetus, is a reckoning with the instinctive charity with which feminists read feminists. This charity is based on correct impulses: not to entrench the ignoring of women's intellectual and activist contributions, not to capitulate to societal seductions for women to build their careers on tearing other women down, a wariness of trashing as well as 'matricide'. But it is also a dangerous impulse that leads to too much papering over and whitewashing. My title calls out a mistake – our habit of not counting opponents as feminists – where we try to resolve the problem in such a way that we can love all feminists, simply by excluding those we cannot like.

It's a necessarily intimate project. I'm not making sweeping taxonomical gestures, but rather looking concretely at how brilliant women – legitimately and recognisably feminist in aim – make sense of their times in such a way as to produce a feminism of fools. I see this engagement as practical and urgent, not academic or purely historical, because it's about interrogating how messy and complicated our current and future battle lines are. Additionally, it was important to get biographical because such specificity is what cuts through our epistemic resistance to the idea that 'real' feminists wrought 'real' evil. I found it interesting in its own right to make my theoretical intervention via this 'storytelling' mode, precisely because it forced me to grapple with the extent to which people both are and aren't social symptoms, i.e. phenomena merely 'of their time', manifesting bigger forces and logics. People, after all – for better and worse – are constantly doing things that bring new times, worlds and horizons into being. While it is a peculiar effect of much classic feminist historiography *not* to give women from the past 'full credit', as it were, for their misdeeds, I am insisting that women (specifically feminists, in this case), while embodying the femin*isms* they created, share responsibility for the dark sides of history, not just the light.

RP How have you come to your style of writing? Your last two books could probably be understood as manifestos whereas you have described this one as a 'bestiary'. Why did that seem like the appropriate genre? And what underpins your intentionally anachronistic use of a contemporary argot to describe historical figures (Victoria as girlboss, the KKK as proto-Mumsnet and so on)?

SL Are style and genre interrelated, or are these separate questions? When it comes to the latter, I'd probably start by pointing to what certainly *appears* to be a shift towards the 'negative' in the most recent book: my prescriptions here arise from descriptions of tragedies and mistakes, whereas the earlier work was limning a 'positive' possibility by unearthing forgotten family-abolitionist and motherhood-abolitionist political lineages. *Full Surrogacy Now* and its short follow-up are part of the same proposition – a single thought, really – and their titles are both affirmative utopianist injunctions. (However, I should mention: I'm not sure they *are* true manifestos at all, despite the claim to being one in the subtitle of *Abolish the Family: A Manifesto for Care and Liberation*.) In contrast, on its face at least, *Enemy Feminisms* is totally different. Rather than boldly and optimistically turning the capitalist kinship-form inside out, here I am chewing uncomfortably on a two-hundred-year legacy of mutant, liberal and fascist, political DNA, only to insist: these enemies are our enemy *kin*. Underlyingly, though, this means that the manifesto and the bestiary are linked. The first articulates feminism qua care communisation, a.k.a. family abolition, and the second fills out the picture with this communist feminism's uncanny doppelgängers, seductive opposites and counterinsurgent antagonists (what feminism also *is*, as opposed to what it *ought* to be, and happily sometimes has been). The first gesture was 'feminism against family' (*Full Surrogacy Now*'s subtitle). Could we paraphrase the second as 'smash the feminist family too'?

Style-wise, I imagine the only really relevant fact is that I embarked in 2017 on a career as a working non-academic, or ex-academic, or para-academic writer. I'm trying to make the reader's experience flow, and I like to communicate via humour, via jokes. I attempt to attend to things like rhythm. (Again: writing is how I pay my rent, not any academic job.) As for my penchant for argotnautical anachronism: I've never thought about it, but it's part of the quest for warmth, insight and pleasure. I trust that my linking of 1920s KKK feminism and Mumsnet will not – cannot – be understood as trivial or trivialising. In fact, I am confident that analogies like that serve as illuminating defamiliarisations, jolting us into self-awareness. If they're additionally funny, then all the better. It occurs to me, on that note, that laughter and irony are explicit ingredients of the ultra-earnest message of the 'Cyborg Manifesto', a text whose style and politics both marked me profoundly at an early age. I suspect that my writing (like Donna Haraway's) will always be rooted in and in conversation with formal academic prose at the same time as, aspirationally, playing and singing. Perhaps the least I can do – or should I say the most? – is infuse a little warmth into my sentences, so as to undermine the unearned power of stuffy academic claims to seriousness even as I remain, as Haraway puts it, 'deadly serious'.

RP How have you navigated the move from academia to being a public intellectual on the left – both in terms of the shifts in style this necessitates but also in terms of audiences and public exposure? Is there a desire to speak to people who might not already share your political commitments and persuade them to shift to the left?

SL I sense that what I want is to seduce people into antiwork communism, rather than 'persuade' them; and my strategy, quite often, it seems, is to talk as though it were already so. In other words, there's a playful (or is it totalitarian?) assumption I operate on, that everyone is already on my side, so it's all just a question of clarifying that fact – or, alternatively, forcing a disavowed enmity into the open. To the extent that I've 'navigated' my passage from the ivory tower to the culture industry with any kind of purpose or clue, I've tried to reach bigger audiences – yes, of course – by gaining practice as a public speaker, learning about effective communication in that context, and writing in journalistic formats when given the opportunity. Nonetheless, I have found that these bigger audiences often come when one isn't trying at all (e.g. I notoriously gained major visibility in the winter of 2019 over some idly tweeted analysis of a Netflix octopus documentary). In other words, the routes to a wider readership are often unpredictable, fairly arbitrary and uncontrollable. Moreover, mere 'exposure' is worth very little by itself: contrary to the popular wisdom, not all publicity is good publicity. Who would want to be misread as a provocateur or 'ragebaiter'?

I invite and delight in comradely critique and disagreement, but I have no desire to accrue haters (even if it's anthropologically interesting to observe oneself becoming the repeated subject of pile-ons because of one's positions on abortion, trans liberation, children's bodily autonomy or Palestine). It's a simple fact: to write in the name of gestational and sexual freedoms, or abolition of the family, or anti-Zionism, is to suffer online abuse. I accept it. I cannot remember a time before I wanted to be a writer, and it's an unfathomable honour, a wildly strange feeling, for that dream to have 'come true', especially because it never exactly felt like I was being brave or clear-eyed enough to *decide to quit* academia. My gradual half-conscious leaning-out of institutional space – to which I am, it seems, allergic – took many years, and I have no way of knowing where I'd be today if the former Verso editor Rosie Warren hadn't invited me to write *Full Surrogacy Now* in 2016, on the strength of an essay she'd found by me, online, about the TV show *First Dates*.

That debut book is based on my PhD, which was in Geography, but, candidly, *Full Surrogacy Now* isn't neatly distinguishable, from my point of view – either in method or aim – from what I do now, or for that matter from whatever I was doing beforehand when I was in English Literature or Politics. I don't feel like I've ever been up to meaningfully different things, not least because there's only really one thing I feel I know how to do. All in all, the transition I've made has been piecemeal, circumstantial, improvised; I know firsthand what 'workaholism' is and about being broke, and/but my choices suggest I would rather remain precarious into my late thirties than be 'secure' and institutionalised. All this time, despite occasionally trying to force myself, I hardly applied for any jobs. Sure, all my degrees are in different disciplines anyway, and I moved joblessly – for love – to the US in 2017, where my C.V. is possibly even more illegible and unemployable than it would be elsewhere. But equally, it's undeniable that a stubborn streak of Bartleby-esque '*I would prefer not to*' asserted itself in me. A certain cussedness, down for the extra-mural hustle.

RP The metaphors we work with reflect and engender certain ways of thinking about and doing politics, including *broad churches*, *big tents* and *umbrellas*, as well as military metaphors like *the trenches* and *doing battle*: can you speak to your own use of metaphor?

SL It's one of my core questions: how to intervene in the conversation around 'white feminism' in such a way as to introduce alternatives to the 'tent' and 'umbrella' metaphors operative there? That particular imagery is all about inclusivity but, you know: if a tent is made of cissexist cloth, why would you want to enlarge it? Similarly, 'problematic' feminisms have typically been described in the mainstream discussions of recent years as 'leaving other women behind' – yet why would we assume that the destination is somewhere the 'other' women would want to visit in the first place? I'm constantly floating counter-metaphors in

Enemy Feminisms: I suggest we might 'break up the house of feminism', and that some of the ideologies living in our very own neighbourhoods are fascisms against which barricades must be built. In other contexts, I've invited us to think of feminism as containing, per the popular meme, 'two wolves'. The ongoing plea is that we move beyond metaphoric repertoires that purify feminism by holding it conceptually apart from 'other' potentially contaminating historical forces (e.g. 'strange bedfellows').

How else might we talk about the ugliness haunting our ancestors' records? As I've already suggested, the grammar of *linkage* (i.e. A and B get into bed together) is ultimately a sanitising, not to mention consolatory, tactic. Instead of allowing that a given feminism might be reactionary, or a form of exploitation meaningfully feminist – which would mean grappling with the discomfiting consequences of that thought – we say that feminists have become complicit in, co-opted by, opportunistically weaponised by, insincerely instrumentalised by, or tricked into something else: a completely distinct, separate evil. But what if the feminism itself has been a big enough girl, as it were, to do its own weaponising, co-opting, attracting, recruiting, and so on? The language of 'enmity' aims to equip us to think about feminism as non-synonymous with antifascism, even as feminism is necessarily central to any effective antifascist struggle.

RP Early in the book, you note a difference between 'forgiving enemies and giving up the fight against them'. Can you say a bit more about this? Why forgive at all?

SL I specifically don't say that forgiveness is imperative or even desirable (I don't think I have a view on that question). What I'm considering, in that passage, is the possibility that forgiveness of one's enemies is common and – for better or worse – *likely*, be that witting or unwitting. The point is that the human social mechanism whereby 'to understand all is to forgive all' poses a challenge for antifascism. So, the message I'm offering to feminists who are struggling to treat other feminists as fascists is this: Forgive and understand all you want! – but if a sister crosses one of the lines that your group has identified as 'red lines', make her life hell, do not hesitate. Deplatform, disempower, denounce; *force* her to stop being a fascist. That's all I'm saying. If one finds that one is feeling empathetic vis-à-vis an enemy, what does one do? Simple. One still fights them.

RP Related to the question of forgiveness, would it also be possible to talk about 'frenemy feminisms'? Your generously critical earlier articles on Donna Haraway and Shulamith Firestone suggest that they could maybe be understood as frenemy feminists and perhaps we could add Silvia Federici to the list (if the term is defined as feminists who have said deeply problematic things but whose work nonetheless remains valuable).

SL I have used the term 'frenemy' in a different context – in my essay 'Amniotechnics', which became the final chapter of *Full Surrogacy Now*, where that word describes the human relationship to water – because I think it usefully captures a contradictory state of nurture and danger. I feel far more hesitant to talk about 'frenemy feminisms', however, and I certainly wouldn't characterise my critical paeans to Haraway and Firestone in those terms. My disagreements there, for me, are comradely ones, because these bodies of work are truly vital – i.e. anything but disposable – in my eyes. Are Haraway and Firestone 'problematic'? If the word 'problematic' ever had any purchase on its objects, it feels to me as though it now has absolutely none; it amounts to a memed and ridiculed moral posture. What position could possibly be un-problematic? We must be more specific and say what we mean when we call something or someone out, as in, 'technophobic', 'racist', 'misanthrophic', 'bioconservative', 'cissexist', 'femmephobic', and so on.

As multiple reviewers noted at the time of its publication, there are absurdly sloppy elements of transphobia in Silvia's essay collection *Beyond the Periphery of the Skin*, themselves embedded in a wider argument about 're-enchantment' that represents a substantial reversal of her 1970s *Wages Against Housework*-era theorising. For me, what I know of her meagre recent contribution to anti-trans philosophy does not (yet) rise to the level of an enemy feminism, especially in light of my intuition that one could easily turn Federici against Federici, so to speak, using the denaturalising tools from her earlier body of work to combat the lazy, half-baked bits of pro-cisness in her later takes. In *Enemy Feminisms*, obviously, I am interested in how we hold on to each another, not just how we draw lines and face off. I showcase the transfeminist activist Bryn Kelly's compassionate approach to Adrienne Rich (who helped Janice Raymond write the transmisogynistic fountainhead *The Transsexual Empire*). Bryn's is the approach I would probably reach for in relation to Federici: 'Hey, did you know you hurt me? Can we talk about that?'

RP How do you negotiate the tension between identifying red lines and resisting the purgative impulse of fascistic politics? For instance, using the word 'enemy' insists on a strong sense of disidentification (us/them) but on the other hand you argue that these enemies should still be understood as part of feminism and not positioned outside of it. If we understand all of these 'enemy feminist' strands of thought – colonial, racist, transphobic, pornophobic, antiabortion, etc. – as being so firmly part of the histories and theories of feminism, then how is feminism defined, and is feminism still something worth fighting over and for? And, relatedly, how are these different feminisms related to one another? Do they have a dialectical relationship? Is there an internal dialectic to feminism?

SL It is a real tension, one that I observe in everyday life, in the sense that sometimes we have to punch fascists in the face even when we understand them to be, in a sense, our kin. Hatred (even of fascists) and enmity (even vis-à-vis fascists) are emotions that get a very bad rap; I think it's fair to say we're phobic of these types of relation and unwilling to explore how to inhabit them honourably. Negativity in general is viewed as unconstructive, and it is commonplace to demand a complement of 'good news', like a wine pairing, alongside every piece of 'bad news' about our cultural or political ancestors. Editors at larger presses tried to pressure me a little to this end, in fact, before I ultimately sold my proposal for *Enemy Feminisms* to Haymarket. Couldn't I showcase a comrade feminist side-by-side with every enemy? Couldn't I concentrate on bridge-building and reconciliation, instead of performing, if you will, conflict escalation, highlighting utterly opposed interests and agendas, making irresolvable antagonisms visible? The thing is: no, I couldn't. That would be a different book. My bottom line is that the disidentificatory space of 'us versus them' is unavoidable in politics. Solidarity boils down, so often, in practice, to *which side are you on?* – and the trick is to make sure that one's own 'side' keeps on becoming and morphing unceasingly, never calcifying into a 'nation'. Enmity *is* a dangerous intimacy; it has to be constantly prevented from crystallising into something ontological and turning into naturalised otherness. The process of line-drawing has to be repeated all the time, and comradely disagreement, 'impurity', hospitality and non-disposability among our own ranks have to be cherished values. In short, yes: if the book tried to determine exactly where red lines should be, or imagined itself as showcasing a perfect, pure, unerring, un-messy, blemish-free politics, then it would indeed be repeating the purgative logic at the core of the fascistic politics I'm attempting to crack open.

There is a dialectic internal to feminism, one I think of as generative. One expression of it is that famous phrase 'pleasure and danger'; another, the transcendence of sex, on the one hand, and the valorisation of women's autonomy, on the other. But there is also an opposition that may not be dialectical at all, and this is what I've already said I half-jokingly think of in terms of 'two wolves'. My mental shorthand for that core axis of enmity is: cisness versus abolition, or *the feminists of securitisation* versus *the feminists of care-communisation*. Put differently, what I'm proposing is that canonical Western feminism has an imperfect and messy (of course) but nonetheless anticolonial, anti-propertarian, expansively sex-radical, fugitive proletarian 'undercommons', and the latter has suffered systematic counterinsurgent repression and erasure at the hands of the former's respectability politics. It is because of that 'shadow' feminism – this utopian antifascist legacy that we must not dishonour or forget, even if we sometimes only find ghostly traces of it in the archives – that we cannot cede the name of 'feminism' to the enemy feminists. It would be a shame for this term to become the exclusive name of those forces that have staged internal bourgeois counterrevolutions against gender liberation again and again (while trying to convince us that they themselves were the only ones around).

It would also be a mistake, because 'feminism' remains one of the best names communists have for the adequately radical critique of capital that extols the priority of lifemaking over accumulation while laying bare the violence, not only of the wage, but all capitalist work. The potential collective *eros* of revolutionary feminism, or family abolition, or anti-colonial queer-utopian feminism (whatever we want to call it) is certain to continue to elude us,

I feel, if we can't move past the uneasiness and discomfort of the prevalent terms of the 'white feminism' conversation, wherein 'problematic' feminisms are imagined as undesirable variations on a single theme – rather than genuine historic antagonists of our politics. It can only do us good, ultimately, to admit it: feminism can also be a weapon of class discipline, a fully-fledged colonialism in its own right, or one of racism's forms of appearance; it can be a sex-nationalism or sex-Zionism; it can be a carceral-humanitarian weapon of the state.

After all, feminism, as I understand it, is any woman-led vindication of 'women's interests' against some kind of critical definition of patriarchy. (I think we need these three elements – [a] woman-led, [b] pro-women, and [c] against patriarchy in order to capture *pro-life feminism*, for example, in our net – because pro-life feminists view abortion as patriarchal and as anathema to female flourishing – while excluding tradwifery, which is woman-led and imagines itself to be in women's best interests, but rejects the idea that patriarchal injustice exists.) It's a definition that discards the many forms of organised womanhood that would, of course, say that they benefit women, yet are explicitly pro-patriarchal and understand themselves as antifeminist. As you know, my book is careful only to address formations that pitted themselves against a representation of male supremacy in their own self-understanding, no matter how minor (*pimps*...), racialised (*immigrant rapists*...) or fantasmatic (*the toilet interloper*...) this representation might be. A comradely feminism, by contrast, is one that understands its own constituency as porous, intimately implicated in the system it is unmaking, and non-innocent.

RP At a number of junctures in the book, you suggest that the psychic formation of white feminism is shaped by the fact that it is an 'easier' response to gender oppression ('A woman swallows her own conspiracist and pseudoscientific bullshit about Black men's savage lasciviousness ... because it's easier than indicting her own husband, uncle, priest, dad or the family form itself'; 'Divisions like "productive-reproductive" and "private-public" feel rather abstract ... it would be easier to be able to paint a picture of our tormentor! ... Easier, anyway, than figuring out what unmaking the mode of production that underlies the logic of gender would entail. Easier to visualize the problem as a glass ceiling, a wage differential, an office sex pest...'). Is there a particular theory of psychic formation at work here? Are we psychically lazy?

SL That's an interesting question. I, for one, am quite often very lazy in certain ways. But I suspect that the mechanisms that pull us into conspiracism, fascism, political 'diagonalism' and dangerously truncated anticapitalist critiques have less to do with an insufficient psychical 'work ethic' and more to do with the pleasure of refusing responsibility for the world. As such the implicit theory of psychic formation I'm working with is probably loosely borrowed (at least, this was the unconscious intention) from Paul Gilroy's essay 'Black Fascism' (2000) where he concludes that 'a susceptibility to the appeal of authoritarian irrationalism has become part of what it means to be a modern person.' Gilroy calls on 'blacks' to recognise that they 'are not, after all, a permanently innocent people' but, rather, 'modern folk who can think and act for ourselves.'[1] So – how can antifascists make the pleasures of non-innocence irresistible? This is a question less about overcoming laziness than about overcoming a fantasy of one's own innocence.

RP You talk about the improper use and appropriation of the term 'abolition' to describe some patently non-abolitionist campaigns such as those by the 'New Abolitionists' against sex work.

We see this with many terms that are in danger of becoming empty signifiers – 'decolonisation', 'intersectionality', etc. What should we do in the face of this danger? Stand our ground and fight for the most subversive interpretations possible, abandon the terms, or something else? How do we make decisions about when concepts have become so compromised that they need jettisoning or revisioning?

SL Honest answer: I don't know. I am holding a torch for the definition of 'abolition' as 'positive supersession' even as I am painfully aware that the phrase 'abolish the family' conjures, inside many of the heads it reaches, visions of a nightmarish top-down process – carceral dystopia – rather than communisation. Is that irrational of me? Possibly! However, it's hard to think of an important concept that isn't widely misunderstood or hasn't long been in danger of losing its radical significance. 'Queerness', for me, is the go-to example: what was a signifier of collective anti-proprietary insurgency becoming a widespread normative identity label. (Again, is it just stubbornness that drives my insistence on *remembering* that outmoded, anticapitalist valence of the 'queer'?) 'Intersectionality' was done dirty by legal scholars, whereas it was originally an anti-imperialist movement-rooted heuristic. 'Communism', which I take to be an antiwork and antistate project, is similarly 'compromised' by the term's association with state-capitalist historic regimes. 'Feminism' itself is a word some of us link to a struggle revolutionising every aspect of life, even as others (e.g. the historian of patriotic women, Elizabeth Cobbs) beamingly propose that nothing needs to change, in fact, nothing *ever* really needed smashing, it only needed gentle debugging – such that, job done, 'we are all feminists' now. When terms become so abused, it makes sense to consider jettisoning them. I'm just skeptical that any term is immune.

RP The chapter on feminism and fascism tells a powerful story about the genealogical connections, overlaps and resonances between the suffragist movement and British fascism. One question you ask and answer is 'what happens to a feminism ... when it relies too heavily on terrorism ... the answer is always: it lurches inexorably to the right.' Is this an argument you would extend to all political movements? Is this an argument against terrorism or political violence generally, or one about its particular incompatibilities with feminism?

SL I welcome this question, since I regret not only that I didn't expand properly on this point, but also that I apparently phrased it in such a way that I can be heard as denouncing left political violence per se. I reject the premise that one can be meaningfully 'against' political violence, since the state's political violence is already the status quo. I am not making an argument about a particular incompatibility between feminism and political violence, either. What I am gesturing towards is a dynamic where an organisation comes to rely 'too heavily', be that because it has no other choice or for some other reason, on methods of 'terror' such as bombing. My claim is that going underground paramilitaristically as a tiny vanguardist cell, to make and plant nitroglycerine-and nail-bombs (as Emmeline Pankhurst's army of suffragettes did), opens up psychic arenas of hardened self-romanticisation and adventurism, via the imperative to crush all self-doubt as one crushes one's fear. (N.B. This is not the case when a guerrilla armed struggle is grounded in mass popular support.) Of course, Mrs Pankhurst's paramilitary was already widely viewed as right-wing and totalitarian by other feminists, even before its terror campaign kicked off in 1908; but thereafter, its proto-fascistic, braggadocious internal culture, predicated on an assumption of women's innocence, worsened. So, I am pointing to an authoritarian internal modality that seems to follow when a turn is made –

albeit in 'understandable', depressing historic circumstances, and often (unlike the WSPU) in conscious desperation and despair – towards using stochastic spectacular violence via incendiary devices, in lieu of, rather than in addition to, mass organising and large-scale direct actions such as strikes and building occupations. I recognise that what constitutes 'too much' here is utterly subjective, and I also want to repeat that I think there is a role for these tactics. But it also seems clear to me – from what I know of the histories of groups one could describe as 'relying too heavily' on bombs, from the Rote Zora to the Red Brigades to the Weather Underground – that there are ideological dangers to taking that kind of path.

RP There is a biggish temporal jump in the book from the 1940s to the 1970s when you describe the advent of an anti-porn culturalist feminism (genuinely 'merely cultural') that focused on 'objectification' of women rather than defying the state or capital and that called itself 'radical feminism'. This chapter feels quite pivotal, not least because the stakes are quite literally visceral. Would you say that this is the origin story of contemporary TERFism and that we might 'still' be in this moment?

SL Exactly. I would. I imagine the book in two halves, organised on either side of that temporal gulf you mention, and the narrative of the second half (beginning with 1970s anti-prostitution and culminating in 2020s anti-abortion, anti-sex, anti-trans feminism) is designed to periodise today's 'ultimate' feminism of cisness – TERFism – within that long shadow. This is a story about the ('visceral', as you say, but specifically also sexually *nationalist* and border-securitising) casting-out of penile corporeality from the innocent circle of female flesh, such that even the practice of 'topping' and 'bottoming' within lesbian eroticism eventually gets assimilated with heteromasochism and male violence, alongside all forms of penetration, and alongside the actual human 'refugees' of gender – trans  people – whose yearning for female embodiment and active pleasure in it undermines the 'cultural feminist' definition of femaleness *qua* bodily suffering. It's a story about the defeat of the Long Sixties and specifically the tragic triumph of pornophobia – i.e. the sex-worker exclusionary repudiation of *porn*, as in, whoreness – over the radical feminism whose face and name it ate. It is an ongoing source of consternation to me that pornophobia is misnamed 'radical feminism' in so many circles today, not least amongst a new generation of self-described 'radfems' who embrace a deeply anti-utopian Dworkinism. (I describe this in a recent piece arguing against the ongoing literary revival of Andrea Dworkin,wherein I revisit Dworkin's penultimate – virulently Zionist – book *Scapegoat*, which is a plea for a kind of sex-Zionism she wants women to carry out in a manner modelled on the Israeli occupation of Palestine.[2]) From the fleeting popularity in the West of Korean '4B' female-separatist girlboss discourse, to the ongoing enthusiasm for nihilistic 'femosphere' self-help online ('Andrew

Tate for women …'), and from 'feminism's Brexiteers' (as Sarah Franklin once called TERFs) to the ambient 'heteropessimism' that Asa Seresin identified in 2019 – which conspicuously does not seek to *change* the drastic disappointingness of men – I see hauntings from the 'femopessimist' intrafeminist counterrevolution of the 70s everywhere I look.

RP The recognition that women of colour might themselves be agents of white feminism (e.g. Ayaan Hirsi Ali) is a powerful and salutary corrective to the facile tendency to assume that diversity of representation is in itself ever an advance. Yet it is an argument that feminists who happen to be white often find themselves unable to make because of positionality politics. It does not seem to be enough to say that the possible socialist and antiracist credentials of such feminists might give them the necessary legitimacy to do this work, given that some of the most troubling feminists of colour themselves emerge from such a politics (one thinks here of some WoC feminists in the UK who emerge out of a tradition of socialist antiracist feminism but have latterly taken problematic TERFy and Islamophobic positions as part of a more general state feminist turn). Who is best placed to call out this shift, or should the question of 'legitimacy to call out' trouble us less than it does?

SL I don't think, though, that today's non-white advocates of annihilationist politics – feminist or no – necessarily represent a 'shift': rightism has long had non-white exponents, architects and apologists. (I reference this in several places in the book, actually, for instance when I mention nineteenth-century black feminist eugenicism and frame it as structurally aligned with white supremacy.) Already almost a century ago, as Gilroy writes in the aforementioned essay 'Black Fascism', there were 'fascist' logics in Marcus Garvey's Universal Negro Improvement Association (UNIA) and Elijah Muhammad's Nation of Islam. Now, in the twenty-first century, as you indicate, we've seen the rise not only of far-right black female antifeminists like Kemi Badenoch and Candace Owens, alongside 'the 2022 Group' in the UK and 'Black Conservative Federation' in the US, but also of black 'enemy' feminists who sometimes have backgrounds in left movements, such as the anti-trans 'sex-based rights' activists Linda Bellos, Allison Bailey and Sonia Appleby or – elsewhere in the world – Chimamanda Ngozi Adichie and Laetitia Ky (an Ivorian artist in her twenties).

The latter crowd makes a lot of noise about the positional illegitimacy, i.e. usually whiteness or perceived maleness, of their critics. But if we are truly speaking a liberatory critique, I don't see why we should hesitate, regardless of how we are positioned. There is nothing inherently delegitimising about speaking from a relatively privileged standpoint against reactionary views that happen to be emanating from an historically marginalised person or group. Often, as you say, it is uncomfortable (and subject to mockery) to call out these political actors as racist, colonialist and white-supremacist when one happens to be white oneself. But anti-racism and anti-cisness obviously aren't the precinct of nonwhite and noncis people alone, not least became racism and cisness brutalise us all. So, we're going to have to get much more agile on this terrain fast, since the age of what we might call *fascism with an intersectional face* – from Latinx-feminist CIA adverts to Suella Braverman, from the trans YouTuber and MAGA stalwart Blaire White to the black Moms for Liberty officer Tia Bess – is long since upon us.

RP In your chapter on anti-abortion feminism, you write that 'as part of my "critical utopianism", I wonder if we could arrive, one day, at the as-yet-unthinkable place where giving fetuses ethical consideration *has* become practically possible, perhaps thanks to gestator-controlled ectogenetic technologies, advances in obstetric medicine, and a reorganization of life's work, beyond the private nuclear household.' Please could you explain that thought in more detail for us, and also comment on how it illustrates or fits into your critical utopian project more generally?

SL In this fleeting thought-experiment, or little aside, I'm essentially asking: Do we know for sure that anthrogenesis – the manufacture of human beings – will always be organised the way it is now? Pregnancy is very deadly – currently, it claims about 300,000 adult lives a year – and I simply refuse to believe that things have to be this way. Could not science research and technological development, obstetric support investment and radical pro-gestator social change somehow coalesce into a situation where fetuses are *collectively* held, rather than holding a single adult gestator hostage (communal ectogenetic tanks, as famously seen in Marge Piercy's 1976 novel *Woman on the Edge of Time*, would be one such scenario)? If so, and only if so, I think, the question then logically arises: Would there be considerations worth taking seriously *other* than – as is the case now – a gestational progenitor's prerogative to stop giving life to a specific fetus? In the first place, will it always be the case that every new human person emerges in the same violent and miraculous way they do currently, i.e. through the matrix of a labouring non-individual body ('the motherfetus', to use Chikako Takeshita's term)? And in a society in which children generally are no longer viewed as personal property or private possessions, would there be room in a politics like mine – an uncompromisingly pro-abortion, as well as aspirationally child-liberationist politics – to give weight to the idea that fetuses should be kept alive even when they're extracted from the motherfetus? It seems to me that there probably would, simply because killing is something that should always be undertaken thoughtfully and seriously.

I say that abortion is 'killing' – that's the starting point for all of the above. In my view, to pretend that nothing and no one dies when gestational labour is stopped is, actually, to denigrate gestational labour. As such, the headline that *The Nation* chose for my article in 2022 after the fall of Roe v. Wade – 'Abortion Involves Killing, and That's OK!' – rather misrepresents one of my core arguments, which is that killing is probably never or hardly ever OK (in the sense of 'ethically unremarkable'), even though it is often *good* (in the sense of 'productive of happiness'). Admittedly this difference between 'good' and 'OK' is a slippery thing, but it is real, and rests on the distinction between politics and ethics. Like most (all?) communists I'm far more interested in the political than the ethical, and that's why my long-term project has attempted to bring the whole topic of gestation out of the latter (bioethical) sphere, into the former (labour), which is where it can be animated in terms of needs, desires, violence and freedoms, as opposed to rights, principles, adjudications and categorical imperatives. I guess you could say I've been trying to think antiwork Marxism vis-à-vis this specific human labour, babymaking, for over a decade.

I've more generally been thinking with the unorthodox marxian feminist Donna Haraway's framework of interspecies 'responsibility' for almost *two* decades. Per her *When Species Meet*, it is a dangerous fantasy and straight-up empirical falsehood to imagine that people can meaningfully aspire to 'not kill' in the context of contemporary capitalist-colonial society. After all, not only do we kill all the time – participating in myriad forms of state- and market-mediated killing with every cent we put into circulation – but many instances of killing are actively beneficial: the Italian Resistance's execution of Mussolini comes to mind. 'Perhaps', suggests Haraway, 'the commandment should read, "Thou shalt not make killable." The problem is actually to understand that human beings do not get a pass on the necessity of killing significant others.' Reading these words, I recalled how, even as a teen, I felt vaguely felt dissatisfied with the 'clump of cells' line of argumentation in 'pro-choice' politics – wherein there is nothing *to kill* inside the labouring uterus. Thus, in my twenties, I started reaching for Haraway's orientation to what she calls 'the necessity and labor of killing' in order to try to think through abortion.[3]

Of course, a human fetus is not an organism of a different *species* to the gestator. Yet despite this, fetuses, as I contend in my wannabe-Harawavian intervention 'Amniotechnics', *are* fundamentally alien, underwater creatures whose relationship to the gestators they corporeally co-compose is usefully illuminated through the lens of the nonhuman other; of xenohospitality and multispecies *response-ability*. Basically, one of the things I think I've been attempting to articulate over and over in different ways ever since *Full Surrogacy Now* is that we can and must find a way of full-throatedly vindicating abortion – i.e. the gestational labourer's absolute prerogative to self-extricate from the gestational workplace that is her own placenta, which currently is the same thing as killing and maybe will always be – without however rendering the fetus 'killable' in the process. We can and ought to resist that impulse, to ethically 'tidy up' feticide, not least because seeking recourse in a notion of anything's inherent 'killability' is a fascistic manoeuvre that is liable to shape other aspects of our dealings with the rest of the living world. To say so does not take away from, but actually strengthens in the long-term, the absolute prerogative of gestational labourers to be universally supported – no questions asked – to stop being pregnant for free, on demand. To reiterate what I mean here: gestational labour literally creates people, what could possibly deserve more trust than that? How can we accomplish an adequate valorisation of gestational labour if we aren't willing to admit that gestational labour *stoppage* involves killing? Death is the flipside of life. As Emma Heaney suggests in her forthcoming book *This Watery Place* (2025), 'The miracle of life is obscured', actually, by the premature identification of the fetus with human beings' entitlement to stay alive, 'and the resulting erasure of the valour of gestation.'

Notes

1. Paul Gilroy, 'Black Fascism', *Transition* 81/82 (2000), 70–91, 91.
2. Sophie Lewis, '"Are Women Weak Jews?" On Andrea Dworkin's Zionism', *Spectre*, May 27 2025.
3. Donna Haraway, *When Species Meet* (Minneapolis: University of Minnesota Press, 2008), 80.

Breaking out of the circle
On the life and work of Ghassan Kanafani
Francesco Anselmetti

Ghassan Kanafani, *Selected Political Writings*, eds., Louis Brehony and Tahrir Hamdy (London: Pluto Press, 2024). 308pp., $29.95, 978 0 74534 937 4

Ghassan Kanafani, *The Revolution of 1936-39 in Palestine: Background, Details and Analysis*, trans. Hazem Jamjoum (New York: 1804 Books, 2023). 101pp., $20.00, 978 1 73685 004 6

No definitive account exists of Ghassan Kanafani's life, a fact quite remarkable for a writer of his stature; perhaps the finest – certainly the most versatile – Palestine produced in the 20th century. Its main contours are fairly well-known: his birth in 1936, just ten days before the announcement of the strike that triggered the Great Revolt; his expulsion from Acre during the *Nakba*; his adolescence as a young refugee in Damascus; a brief but formative stint working as a teacher in Kuwait; literary success, militancy and martyrdom in Beirut at the age of thirty six. The detail however is often fragmentary, leaving us with more questions than answers. We hear, for instance, that before his family was driven out of Palestine his father was detained for some time by the British. What exactly he was held for (political activity or otherwise) is unclear. Of his early intellectual formation we know he attended a French missionary school in Yafa as a young boy, and was later mocked as a teenager in Damascus for his poor command of Arabic, only rectified after months of concerted study, but exactly who might have guided his early writing, in either influence or teaching, remains to us unknown.[1]

When it comes to his political trajectory we stand on firmer ground. Over the course of his short but astonishingly rich career Kanafani left his mark as an editor and commentator on almost all the major newspapers and political journals of his time – leaving a paper trail which in volume far exceeds the fiction for which he is better known. Indissociable from his work as a journalist was his involvement in two related organisations at the forefront of the Arab and Palestinian liberation movement over the course of the long 1960s: the Arab Nationalist Movement (ANM) and the Popular Front for the Liberation of Palestine (PFLP). As the mode of the regional struggle against Zionism and imperialism shifted, so too did the strategic calculi of these groups. In its first decades the struggle for Palestine was wedded to a state-driven project of Arab liberation; only as a result of this project's defeat did a discrete Palestinian Revolution emerge in the form of a localised insurgency. A battlefield of narrowing scope and scale: this was the fundamental terrain of Kanafani's political thought. His extraordinary capacity to visualise and chart this topography – the battle's requirements, its traps, its opportunities – should be grasped as both the kernel of his theorising and the highest moment of its articulation.

The permanence of empire

The political leadership that had led the joint Arab forces in the 1948 war in Palestine did not survive long after its defeat. In Palestine itself, what remained of the Arab Higher Committee ultimately dissolved under Egyptian and Jordanian pressure; in Syria a wave of military coups in 1949 effectively suspended civilian rule until the mid 1950s. In July 1951, King Abdullah of Jordan, accused of bartering with the Zionist leadership to secure personal control of the West Bank, was assassinated at the entrance to the al-Aqsa Mosque in Jerusalem. The following year, a group of Egyptian officers – vanquished heroes of the war of '48 – successfully rose up against an ailing monarchy, promising wide-ranging agrarian reform and confrontation with imperialism's continued presence in the region.

It was during this period of regeneration that a group of young nationalist students first met at the American University of Beirut. Most of them had been in Palestine in some capacity during the war: George Habash and Wadie Haddad, two medical students (from Lydd and Safad respectively) had been expelled from their homes along with their families; Hani al-Hindi, from Damascus, had fought in the Galilee as part of a force of Arab volunteers known as the Arab Salvation Army headed by the noted nationalist commander Fawzi al-Qawuqji. Important early members included the Kuwaiti Ahmad al-Khatib, another medical student who was instrumental in establishing support in the Gulf for what was soon to be known as the Arab Nationalist Movement (alternatively, and more accurately, translated as the 'Movement of Arab Nationalists' (*Harakat al-Qawmiyyin al-'Arab*)). Constantine Zurayk, a Syrian historian teaching at AUB, was the first to develop a vocabulary to make sense of the unfolding present in the immediate aftermath of the war in his *Ma'na an-Nakba* (*The Meaning of the Disaster*), published in August 1948. This spirit of elaboration was a determining influence on the student group, which initially coalesced around a literary association, *al-'Urwa al-Wuthqa,* which bore the same name as an influential Egyptian anti-colonial journal of the late 19th century. For the circle, no division existed between the loss of Palestine and the continued subjugation of the Arab world. The former, in fact, was merely an expression of the latter, since the political community envisaged by Arab nationalism was one which could overcome the colonial segmentation inflicted after the end of the First World War.[2]

Right-wing visions of the Arab nation did exist, but for the most part Arab nationalism had different preoccupations from its *völkisch* European cognates. Unity had very practical, strategic connotations: 'five, or six, or seven states', Zurayk wrote, 'each completely independent of the other, each concerned with its own affairs and internal interests, each subjected to various foreign influences and to internal forces with conflicting interests – states in this condition cannot repel the harrowing blows of our time.'[3] Other aspects of the ANM's programme were still under development – the question, for instance, of the primacy of Palestine had not yet emerged. Would the achievement of unity be a prerequisite to defeat Zionism? Or, conversely, would the liberation of Palestine be a necessary step on the path to achieving unity? Well-defined answers were not strictly required in order to begin the work. By 1950, recruitment began to extend beyond the confines of the university, with members from across the Arab East, from Iraq to Yemen, Kuwait to Lebanon. As early cadres returned from Beirut, cells emerged in Damascus, Amman, Baghdad and Aden that began agitating for Arab unity and liberation.[4]

Habash and Haddad spent much of the early 1950s in Jordan, treating the sick in various refugee camps and contributing to the opposition mounting against the regime, led by Abdullah's grandson, King Hussein – a lingering satellite of British colonial rule. In a similar spirit, al-Hindi returned to Syria, where he fostered ties with figures in the military and security apparatus sympathetic to the nationalist cause (much of the ANM's later activities would be enabled by al-Hindi's connections, especially in Syria). In 1954, when the Jordanian government forced Habash to cease publishing the party's newspaper *al-Ra'i*, al-Hindi took over its editorship from Damascus. It was in the Syrian capital that Habash first met Kanafani. The latter was barely a teenager – 14 or 15 by his own recollection – and was working part-time as a proof-reader in a printing house.[5] A teaching job at an UNRWA school in Kuwait took him away from Damascus in 1955, but by then his talents had become clear to the group's leadership. His first short stories – the literary form he would privilege and excel in – date from this period. Very soon he would begin contributing to *al-Ra'i*, publishing 18 texts in 18 months between June 1957 and December 1958, the first release of an astonishing creative energy that would scarcely relent over the next decade and a half.

Politically, Kanafani and the rest of the ANM drifted steadily towards Nasserism over the course of the 1950s. The Syrian experience with military rule (from 1949-54) had proved largely inimical to the ANM's goals, so optimism around the Free Officers' coup in Egypt was, at least initially, tempered with caution. But Nasser's success in repelling the British, French and Israeli aggression over Suez in 1956 and, perhaps more importantly, his union with Syria (to form the United Arab Republic) in 1958 won him the support of the majority of the nationalist camp. The ANM, for its part, played a central role that year in the peripheral struggles ignited by the founding of the UAR: risings in Jordan (for which Haddad was imprisoned for two years) and the civil war between Lebanese and Arab nationalists that was only pacified by direct American intervention in July 1958.

Early texts associated with the ANM tended to focus on the postwar landscape of imperial power in the Middle East: studies of Israel's early development, the nature of the new Arab states' independence and the relative prospects of the nationalist cause. The relationship between Zionism and imperialism, on the one hand, and class power and exploitation, on the other, remained largely opaque, the latter usually circumscribed as a phenomenon endemic to internal social structures of individual Arab states. The majority held, as a result, that the question of class struggle would be suspended until after unification. In 1960, the movement launched a new weekly, *al-Hurriya*, headquartered in Beirut, which would serve as its official mouthpiece for the subsequent decade. At its helm was a young cadre from South Lebanon named Muhsin Ibrahim, roughly the same age as Kanafani and emerging alongside him as one of the movement's brightest lights. On Habash's recommendation, Kanafani was to leave Kuwait, join Ibrahim in Beirut, and start working for the new publication. It wasn't long after Kanafani arrived that divisions began to emerge between the movement's leadership, now centred around Damascus, and the younger generation converging on Beirut.

Soon after its launch, Ibrahim began using *al-Hurriya* to critique the movement from the left. 'There is no longer a political national question', he wrote in an article published on May Day of 1960, 'standing separately and posing against a specific social question called "the worker's question" or "the peasants question" or the "question of social progress".'[6] Ibrahim's argument elevated class struggle to a position equivalent to that occupied by national liberation; the implication was that one could think of the two as mutually dependent, and not, in the more purely nationalist vein, as separate stages of ascending importance. But the ambiguities inherent in the Nasserist project left ample room for disagreements of this kind. The ensuing factionalism within the movement had as much to do (as is often the case) with personal enmities as with substantive questions of theory and strategy. The split was precipitated by a dramatic reversal of fortune for the Arab revolution. In 1961, the UAR collapsed following a coup in Syria; two years later, the very idea was buried definitively as Ba'athists consolidated their control of Syria in a wave of fratricidal purges of their former Nasserist allies. Returning to Beirut in 1963 after a spell in jail during the turmoil in Syria, Habash found his movement in a state of disarray.

Two successive party conferences cemented the ANM's division between a 'left', led by Ibrahim and Nayef Hawatmeh, a young Jordanian who had just returned from leading the ANM in Iraq, and Habash loyalists, comprising the majority of the movement's Palestinian membership. In terms of their political line, though, there was still much in common between the two groups: Ibrahim's circle still saw Nasserism as the primary vehicle for Arab liberation, whilst to those around Habash who had initially been skeptical, class analysis presented itself as an increasingly compelling way of explaining the challenges faced by the nationalist movement, especially with regards to fraying Egyptian-Syrian relations. The limits of the ANM's drift left were well-defined, however. True to the Nasserist line both wings stood firm in their suspicion of communism (or more accurately, communist parties) not only because of Soviet ambivalence over Zionism, but more importantly on account of the potential threat Moscow represented to Cairo's regional leadership. At stake was also the rivalry between Nasser and 'Abd al-Karim Qasim, an Iraqi general who himself successfully overthrew Iraq's monarchy with the support of the Iraqi Communist Party – by far the largest and best-organised in the Arab world. The mass incarceration and torture of communists was a defining period in the history of the Egyptian left. Other groups that populated Egypt's carceral system under Nasser include the Muslim Brotherhood, viciously persecuted, and, oddly enough, Palestinians: the writers and militants Mu'in Bseiso and Sahbaa' al-Barbari would both write about their time as political prisoners in the early 1960s under Nasser's administration of their native Gaza.[7]

Ideological subtleties notwithstanding, the schism within the ANM would have profound repercussions: Kanafani, on account of his proximity to Habash, was transferred from *al-Hurriya* to an editorial position at *al-*

Muharrir, a privately-owned Nasserist daily. The move proved pivotal. The paper significantly broadened his audience, becoming under his direction the second most read in Lebanon, and cemented his reputation as one of the leading literary voices in Beirut (a city, by that point, awash with writers). More importantly, though, his new position helped him to acquire Lebanese citizenship, affording him unprecedented freedom and stability. He had spent the first few years in Beirut undocumented, and had thus tended to keep a low profile, though in his limited mobility he did however have time to work on several projects, including his first and perhaps most famous novella, *Men in the Sun*, in which three Palestinian migrant workers die attempting to cross the Iraq-Kuwait border – an extended allegory of displacement based on his own observations of the Palestinian condition in the Gulf.[8]

Arab summitry

The earliest piece included in the recently published anthology of Kanafani's translated political writings, *Ghassan Kanafani: Selected Political Writings*, dates from this period, from his first months as editor of *al-Muharrir*. 'Yemen and Iraq: One Story or Two?', published in November 1964, is a skilful report connecting the nationalist struggle underway on two seemingly distant fronts: the nationalist insurgency in North Yemen, in which Egypt had been directly involved since 1962, and renewed discussions between Egypt and Iraq on unification, antagonised at that moment by the aligned interests of Syria, Turkey, Iran and internal Kurdish opposition. The piece gives a sense of scale to the Nasserist revolution at its apex: by 1964, some 40,000 Egyptian troops had been deployed in North Yemen in what amounted to an open war with Saudi Arabia for control of the southwestern Arabian peninsula (in training and arming forces loyal to the deposed King Muhammad al-Badr the Saudis were aided by a motley crew of colonial counterinsurgents, including Belgian mercenaries drafted in from Katanga).[9]

Attempting to take stock of the revolution's gains on the occasion of a temporary ceasefire agreed by Egypt and Saudi Arabia, Kanafani notes how nationalist advances are met with counter-offensives elsewhere, as anti-Nasserist forces intensify their activities in Iraq. 'Coincidence?' Kanafani asks. 'No, it is unacceptable to attribute such things to coincidences when a coherent analytical line is at hand.'[10] Counterrevolution may have proceeded unevenly across different fronts, but these were to be grasped as instances of a single, overarching imperial strategy which produced combined effects.

In truth – and despite Kanafani's optimism around the agreement – by the time the Egyptian-Saudi truce in Yemen was signed in late 1964 the revolution had already undergone a profound transformation. Nasser, saddled with foreign debt incurred to finance the war and the coveted dam at Aswan, had at the close of 1963 already begun to publicly abjure the possibility of a military confrontation with Israel (the rhetoric would return, rather belatedly, in the immediate prelude to the Six Day War). In response to an Israeli proposal to redirect water in the upper Jordan Valley westwards towards its coastal cities, in January 1964 Nasser opted to convene the Arab League, a body which had never met before, and which included amongst its members a number of imperial client states, including Saudi Arabia – an early sign for many that the Arab revolution had all but been renounced in favour of a more feeble strategy of 'summitry'.[11]

The main result of the Arab League meeting was the establishment of the Palestinian Liberation Organisation (PLO), a body the majority of Palestinians hitherto active in the nationalist struggle viewed with profound suspicion. There may have been differences amongst the ANM's ranks on the primacy of the Palestinian question in the broader battle for Arab liberation, but even the factions most focussed on Palestine rejected the idea that the main driving force behind the struggle should be a nationalised 'entity', one which risked relieving the Arab regimes of their responsibilities in the struggle, and, in keeping with the conditions that produced it, seemed better equipped for negotiation than war.

Kanafani clearly saw the dangers of such efforts. As early as October 1963 he had written of his hope for the 'appearance of a revolutionary organization that would put an end to all schemes, plans, trusteeships, governments and projects whose objectives are the pulverization of the Palestinian people.'[12] A related problem was one of leadership: the man Nasser chose to head the PLO was Ahmad al-Shukeiri, a lawyer and former member of the Arab Higher Committee in his late fifties. Kanafani, in all likelihood, knew him well: Shukeiri's father, Sheikh Asa'ad, had been a leading notable in Acre in the first decades of the twentieth century, representing the city in the Ottoman parliament in the 1910s and heading the Supreme Muslim Council under British rule. The discredited political class of the Mandate period had resurfaced, but the generation of Palestinian militants that had come of age in the wake of their debacle had no intention of submitting to its authority.

The rejection was shared by what was, by the mid-1960s, the fastest-growing Palestinian group within the movement for national liberation. Since its inception in Kuwait in the late 1950s, Fatah had always privileged the battle for Palestine over the broader regional revolution, and as such had felt impatient toward the reigning principle that armed struggle could only be waged once favourable conditions for Nasser and allied Arab armies had matured. An armed PLO with sponsorship from the Arab League threatened Fatah, organisationally and strategically: it represented both a blow to its legitimacy and the subordination of Palestinian militancy into a tool Nasser could leverage to tilt diplomatic settlements in his favour.

Rejection, defeat, rebirth

On New Year's Day 1965, Fatah militants infiltrated the Galilee and sabotaged Israel's water carrier, not coincidentally the very object of the Arab League summit Nasser had hosted the prior year. Fatah would go on to claim over thirty operations over the course of 1965 – three hundred by the summer of 1967. The phase of armed struggle under the autonomous leadership of Palestinians had officially begun, on the date that by most accounts marks the start of the Palestinian Revolution.

Fatah's acceleration was not ignored by other factions. A number of armed groups emerged in the subsequent months, united in Fatah's opposition to the PLO but in competition with it for recruitment and following. The ANM, which had initially admonished Fateh for baiting Nasser into a premature war, calling it 'a suspect movement' acting on behalf of US imperialism, soon busied itself with rising to the challenge it had posed. Since the controversial conferences of the mid-1960s the party had increasingly fragmented along national lines; those closest to Habash ultimately founded the Organisation of Avenging Youth, a paramilitary force which began recruiting members in Lebanon, Jordan, Gaza and even amongst Palestinians in Israel. Publicly, their pronouncements had to adapt to the shifting discursive terrain of Palestinian politics, balancing growing support for direct armed confrontation with loyalty to the Nasserist doctrine of revolutionary patience: *fawq al-sifr, wa taht al-tawrit* ('above zero, but below entanglement') was the desired balance according to Kanafani, who had by now risen to the executive ranks of the ANM's Palestinian branch.[13]

The Arab armies' defeat in June 1967 thus merely intensified dynamics that had been underway for some years. Where exactly to locate the demise of the Arab revolution is a crucial question: the collapse of the UAR, for instance, or the ruinous war in Yemen in their effects certainly hold more explanatory power than the *naksa* (which should be understood less as a turning point in itself, and more as the culmination of these longer-term processes). An equally important question to ask is when, if at all, the break with Nasserism occurs amongst his disciples. Having already taken the initiative to lead the struggle against Nasser's designs, Fatah gained the most from his exit from the field of battle. By the autumn of 1967 it was clear even to his staunchest partisans that the time for stalling was over. Perhaps the greatest testament to the scope of the defeat lay in the fact that the Palestinian 'entity' that the ANM had repudiated in previous years as a dramatic narrowing of the nationalist vision no longer appeared such an intolerable compromise. A sense of critical, begrudging resignation permeates Kanafani's verdict on the war published in *al-Adab* in October of that year.

By the summer of the following year, Fatah accounted for half to two thirds of all Palestinian fighters in Jordan (around 2000, by some estimates). Arafat capitalised on the moment to seize the deliberative and executive institutions of the PLO, with a view to transforming them into the unified, internationally recognised vehicle of the revolution, now under his effective command. The Palestinian branch of the ANM had by now broken off completely from the wider organisation. Save a few early mergers and splits, the core of the resulting group formed the Popular Front for the Liberation of Palestine (PFLP), which essentially amounted to the circle that had begun coalescing around Habash as early as 1963. The PFLP's relationship to the PLO under Arafat would be one of near constant turbulence; both the principle of national unity and the PLO's international legitimacy prompted the PFLP to join its National Council, though crucially Habash would refuse to participate in its centralised military command, thus retaining for him and his group a significant degree of ideological and strategic autonomy, at least until the middle of the following decade.

At the heart of the anthology of Kanafani's political writings are a series of theoretical documents – many anonymously authored as part of a collective of writers within the PFLP – that date from this period of active struggle and coincide with the Habash circle's development of a distinctly Marxist-Leninist line. In their attempt to give theoretical sense to a seemingly endless web of practical conundrums and temporal scales that balance a coherent theory of imperialism, the political manoeuvrings of rival factions in the struggle, and the exigencies of an active front, the texts are quite extraordinary. They are, simultaneously, somewhat cryptic as documents, replete with lengthy theoretical justifications and veiled attacks on adversaries and rivals, expressing a balance of power in constant flux within and outside of the movement.

Their legibility improves a great deal when historicised, a task which the anthology falls short of performing consistently. The anthology's editors, and many of the scholars and activists convened to introduce its individual texts, give great importance to the Marxism espoused by Kanafani and the PFLP; the common thread uniting the texts that form the volume's core being the indivisibility of anti-colonial and social liberation, the fusion of nation and class as a single front of struggle. Less obvious in the majority of their remarks is the fact that these positions were the outcome of a marked transformation in the group's thinking that had been maturing over the course of the 1960s. Ramzy Baroud and Romana Rubeo offer important insights in this regard, but these arguably come too late, in the form of a short excursus at the very end of the volume (the addenda, as well as

Funeral of Ghassan Kanafani, Beirut Martyrs Cemetery, July 10, 1972. Photograph © Robert Azzi.

the bibliographic and translation notes are on the whole highly useful, and all too often missing from existing editions).[14] And though careful work is done by the volume's editors in situating Kanafani's thought within the global tradition of Tricontinental Marxism, the early Nasserism of Kanafani and his comrades deserves a lengthier and more direct treatment, especially if the aim is to introduce new readers to his political thought. Dedicating the bulk of the volume to the five last years of the author's life of course makes sense – these were, after all, the high point of his militancy, certainly his most creative years theoretically. But insofar as they were the outcome of a *turn* to Marxism, one precipitated by a specific conjuncture, the texts are not timeless – a quality often erroneously thought, at the expense of historicity, to be the measure of relevance. Alongside, or perhaps beyond any individual diagnosis of the Palestinian predicament produced by Kanafani that may still speak to the present (there are plenty), it is precisely the historical boundedness of his theorising, produced by an unerring dialectic of thought and action, that one cannot but marvel at from our contemporary standpoint.

Kanafani was neither born a Marxist, nor can his ideological turn as part of the Popular Front's emergence be adequately described as an 'adoption' of Marxism. The necessity of an idea tends to precede its arrival: if the former is adequately accounted for, the latter rarely appears a matter of pure choice. As the limits of the Nasserist project became painfully evident over the course of the late 1960s, nationalist politics required an increasingly theoretical elaboration to make sense of its retreat. Marxism provided such a theory of practice. It had come in and out of the ANM's debates over the course of the decade, but now, for Kanafani and many Palestinians around him, it answered questions that had only fully matured in the light of the new crisis: the problem of a mass revolutionary consciousness, and the related construction of the refugee as the revolutionary subject, the need for an organisation that could link the sphere of politics and that of action, and the complex web of relations that had, until then, tied the leadership of the national liberation movement to a set of specific class interests (a critique which took aim at Arab regimes and Palestinian factions alike).

'Who are our enemies?', the Popular Front asks in *Strategy for the Liberation of Palestine* (1969), a product of its second congress which effectively functioned as its manifesto and political programme (an abridged version of the 150-page document is reproduced in chapter 7 of the anthology). The answers it provides are basically those developed by the ANM over the previous decade, save for a small addition: Israel, the Zionist movement, world imperialism and 'Arab reaction', the last of which was, in a subtle yet critical development, no longer simply associated with the Arab monarchies, long identified as pillars of imperial rule in the region, but was extended to 'Arab capitalism, whose interests are represented and defended by reactionary regimes in the Arab world'.[15] The category remains a rather nebulous one in the text, and all the more interesting for its lack of specificity – setting the stage, perhaps, for a more overt collision with the debris of Arab nationalism that was to mature in the following years.

'Who are our friends – the forces of revolution?', the text continues; here too we find an implied expression of the Popular Front's predicament. On the one hand, it underlines the importance of 'Palestinian national unity as a basic factor for the mobilisation of the revolution to confront the enemy camp', yet the critique of the Palestinian bourgeoisie is unsparing, and preventing it from taking leadership of the revolution is identified as one of the movement's top priorities – of note, given the brewing disagreements between the Popular Front and Fateh over support for King Hussein of Jordan, is the text's explicit reference to the stratification that had developed since the *Nakba* amongst Palestinians in Amman: 'all these people' – those in wealthy suburbs, working class neighbourhoods, refugee camps – 'cannot have the same attitude towards the revolution'.[16]

The growing tensions between Fatah and the PFLP would soon develop into a full-blown crisis, one which forms the essential context to understanding what is arguably the anthology's most important text. *The Resistance and its Challenges: the View of the PFLP* was published by the Popular Front in August 1970. Its lengthy, almost laborious preamble serves to establish the necessity in theory of a strategy the organisation had already begun actualising in the previous two years. In July 1968, three militants hijacked an El Al flight bound for Tel Aviv shortly after it had taken off from Rome. This would be the first of several operations targeting El Al, Israel's national carrier, along with other airlines, a tactic which would rapidly (and intentionally) bring the PFLP into the international spotlight.

The primary target of these operations was not Israel per se, but the developing negotiations – the 'Rogers Plan', as they came to be known, named after Nixon's first Secretary of State – between Jordan and Egypt on the one hand, and the US and Israel on the other, around a final peace settlement to the June War, one which included no commitments to Palestinian ambitions. The Revolution, in short, was besieged; its former guarantor on the verge of surrender. Relations between Arafat and the Jordanian monarchy were far from cordial by 1970, but since Fatah ultimately proved unwilling to remove King Hussein from power – a feat it could have probably pulled off by the end of the 1960s – the PFLP had no choice but to escalate the confrontation, 'one of the many ways', in Kanafani's own words, 'in which we tried to break out of the circle'.[17]

A month after the text was published, between September 6th and September 9th 1970, five planes were hijacked by Popular Front cadres, four of which were rerouted to an airstrip in northern Jordan (Leila Khaled, who had successfully rerouted a 707 the previous year, this time was intercepted at Amsterdam airport before her plane could take off). The ensuing hostage crisis provoked a final confrontation between the Jordanian army and Palestinian factions that would result in the latter's expulsion from the kingdom. Within the month – Black September, as it would be remembered in the annals of the revolution – the PLO had largely been cleared from the camps around Amman and Irbid, with the Jordanian army claiming the lives of over 5000 Palestinians.

The restraint that had characterised the ANM's approach to the struggle had been definitively jettisoned; the terms of the equation between Palestinian and Arab freedom finally reversed. 'Whether the revolutionary Palestinian intifada is the gateway to the Arab revolution, or whether it is, indeed, necessary for the cause of Palestinian liberation to become this revolutionary Arab gateway' the Popular Front claimed, presaging the confrontation, '*will be imposed through actions*, as such an assumption cannot be realised arbitrarily or by chance, and continual critical perspectives are required to find the most effective formula.'[18] Could one even still speak of a coherent Arab revolution? In an apposite moment of historical closure, Nasser would suffer a fatal heart attack at the end of September, immediately after chairing a summit of the Arab League with the aim of brokering a ceasefire between Jordan and the Palestinians. A year later, Kanafani would not shy away from attributing to Nasser his share of the blame, in an interview given to Fred Halliday in the *New Left Review* under his own name. 'The Egyptian regime', he notes, 'was one step removed from direct participation in this liquidation, since it had no direct contact with the Palestinians. The only way Nasser could help Hussein was by keeping silent: and that he did.'[19]

A people's war

It isn't clear whether Kanafani ever went to Jordan personally, or whether he witnessed the activities of the *feda'iyyin* there first-hand. In those years we almost always encounter him in Beirut, where the Popular Front kept an important foothold, and where it would ultimately relocate to in the early 1970s along with the rest of the Palestinian factions exiled by Hussien. In 1967, Kanafani had been offered a position on the editorial board of the well-respected daily *al-Anwar*, and was handed the editorship of its magazine. Far from slowing down, his literary output actually intensified. The preceding year he had published *All That's Left for You*, a novel about two siblings living in one of Gaza's refugee camps (which Kanafani would dedicate to Khaled al-Haj, who fell as ANM's first martyr of the armed struggle in November 1965) and his first study of Palestinian literature, *Resistance Literature in Occupied Palestine*. That same year came his landmark study *On Zionist Literature* (recently translated into English by Mahmoud Najib), a collection of short stories (*Of Men and Guns*) and the sequel to *Resistance Literature* in 1968. 'Among his 1969 works', Breony and Hamdi write in their introduction to the anthology, 'were: the novel *Returning to Haifa*, the play script *The Hat and the Prophet*; a critical editorial series of the post-1967 "settlement" promoted by Israel and its backers; a selection of literary reviews for *al-Anwar*, under the pseudonym Fares Fares; writing towards the epochal *Strategy for Liberation*; and an iconic, yellow poster proclaiming that: "the path of armed struggle is the path to liberate Palestine".'[20]

Kanafani worked incessantly. The breadth of his oeuvre is already hard to grasp, let alone the fact that he

simultaneously sat on the PFLP's Politburo and served as its official spokesperson to the international media (sure enough, Kanafani would soon resign from *al-Anwar* to direct the PFLP's new publication, *al-Hadaf*). Although it is difficult to establish the influence of individual authors on the Popular Front's collective texts, there is every indication that Kanafani's role in crafting them was central. Stylistically dense and acute, the texts are clearly shaped by an encounter with Maoism: the search for enemies and friends in *Strategy for the Liberation of Palestine* is a direct reference to Mao's thought (in 'Analysis of the Classes in Chinese Society', 1926), as is the characterisation of the 'organisational question' in *The Resistance and its Challenges*, as the bridge or boat necessary to cross 'from the shore of theory to the shore of practice'.[21]

Upon receiving his Lebanese citizenship in the mid-1960s the first trips Kanafani chose to take were to China, first in 1965 and then again in 1966 to speak at the Afro-Asian Writers' Conference (his account of these trips, published in Arabic as part of his collected works, are fascinating documents which await a good translation). One did not need to go to Beijing to become a Maoist in 1960s Beirut, but the experience of the Chinese Revolution on the PFLP's output is difficult to overstate, as was that of Viet Cong, which the Popular Front learned about through research conducted by the Pentagon itself, tracts of which they even republished, in the 1969 pamphlet *The Underlying Synthesis of the Revolution*.[22] An oft-repeated slogan of the late sixties called for Amman to be transformed into an 'Arab Hanoi' – an idea immortalised in the PFLP's iconography. A talented designer, Kanafani frequently drew the covers for his novels himself, and was known to have personally contributed to a number of the PFLP's political posters, which he sometimes worked on with the help of his two children, Fayez and Laila.[23]

Translated experiences of mass struggle in East Asia had a profound effect on the revolution's mental world, in no way perhaps more significantly than in the emergence, in theory and art, of the refugee camp as the primary site and cradle of struggle. At stake with the agreement reached in Cairo in 1969 for the PLO to take effective control of Lebanon's camps was far more than an influx of ready recruits for the revolution ('Launching bases or detention camps?', Kanafani would ask in *al-Hadaf* in the aftermath of the accords). Just as important were the organic ties this new connection could foster between the revolution's leadership and the revolutionary subjectivity produced by the camp itself. *Umm Saad*, the novella centred around Kanafani's elderly friend from one of Beirut's urban camps, is the great literary expression of this pursuit of a mass line: *ash-sha'b al-madrasa* ('the people [as] school'), as Kanafani would characterise the protagonist in the work's opening pages.[24]

To the extent that we can speak of Kanafani's late thought, it was virtually indistinguishable from that of the Popular Front. The individual author disappears into a collective elaboration of political struggle, two instances of a single movement whose distinction becomes increasingly difficult to make out. Theory here is less an attempt to stand outside of history, but a moment in its very unfolding. Originally commissioned in late 1971 by the Palestine Research Center, *The Revolution of 1936-39 in Palestine: Background, Details and Analysis* is a full-length study in its own right, the object of a recent retranslation – lucid, and of considerable stylistic merit – by Hazem Jamjoum. The work surveys the eruption of the Palestinian national movement into full-blown revolt against the British Mandate and its colonial client, Zionist settlement – the largest anti-colonial rebellion of the interwar period.

In probing the revolt's outcome the text also provides an immediate historical backdrop to the *Nakba*. Having suffered considerable losses – some estimates cite the death of one in ten men of fighting age – Palestinians entered the 1940s beleaguered from three years of costly struggle, whilst Jewish paramilitaries had benefited from their development as an auxiliary police force to the British counterinsurgency. The main theme of the text, however, is still arguably the same as that which animates the documents Kanafani had drafted with the PFLP in the preceding years: the organisational question (as he would call it), or more specifically that of revolutionary leadership. Kanafani's revolt is one that is always ahead of itself: a rising of the countryside, fatefully reined in by a vacillating urban leadership whose structural function and mode of self-preservation was ultimately to come to terms with the colonial authorities, rather than defeat them outright. 'At no point in the entire history of the Palestinian struggle', Kanafani writes, 'was the armed popular revolution as close to victory as it was in those months stretching from the end of 1937 to the beginning of 1939', the period, that is to say, in which the hold of the traditional leadership (Hajj Amin al-Husseini and the Arab Higher Committee) over the *fellahin* was weakest; the former at this point in exile in Damascus, just as the latter advanced over the course of 1938, managing to seize and occupy major urban centres: Hebron, parts of Jerusalem, Bir as-Saba'a, Tiberias and Nablus.[25]

To be clear, what Kanafani identifies here is not a spontaneous self-organisation of the masses, but rather the ability of an organic leadership to spring from its ranks: 'Abd al-Rahim al-Hajj Muhammad, for instance, a local commander from Tulkarm whose death in battle in March 1939 was one of the factors that contributed to the rebellion's defeat, or, more important still for the text, Sheikh 'Izz al-Din al-Qassam, the Syrian preacher and nationalist veteran whose foiled insurrection and martyrdom in late 1935 represented for Kanafani its truest point of origin. al-Qassam's death did not provoke the revolt as such, but somehow managed to synthesise all its political significance before it had even taken place. Present at his funeral are all the essential elements that would shape the subsequent three years of struggle (and, one could say, the many decades since):

> ... masses of people came to walk in the ten-kilometer burial procession to the village of Yajur. What is most significant about this moment is that it exposed the traditional leaders to the challenge of everything Sheikh al-Qassam represented, a challenge that leadership felt just as acutely as the British Mandate authorities. According to one Qassamist, al-Qassam had delivered a message through Musa al-Azrawi to the Mufti, Hajj Amin al-Husseini. In it, the Sheikh asked the Mufti to coordinate the declaration of a country-wide revolt. Al-Husseini refused, claiming that the conditions were not yet ripe for such action. The only people who marched in al-Qassam's funeral procession were poor people. The leaders' reaction, by contrast, was one of indifference.[26]

Kanafani's revisionism was, at a fundamental level, a recommitment to what he saw as the revolt's essential content: the growing chasm between an insurgent popular consciousness and an accommodationist bourgeois leadership. If his early nationalism can be summarised as primarily concerned with the strategic question of revolutionary unity, then making sense of his later Marxism must grapple with what can only be termed an overwhelming concern with democracy, as both the means and end of the mass popular struggle – 'the circulation of blood', as he would term it in the organicist vein of his youth, 'in our political body'. His greatest political tract was in fact his last, an exercise at once new and plainly familiar. The turn to historical inquiry emerged from and intensified his theoretical work of prior years, a continuation of his efforts to parse social reality from its laws of motion. But in this case the diagnostic, prescriptive register of the Popular Front's manifestos is absent; in its place, the relative certainty of causation, emplotted within a discrete historical narrative. The past, it turns out, remains as persuasive as any analysis of the present in pointing to the way out of the revolution's predicaments.

Letter from Gaza

Kanafani himself would be assassinated just months after penning his elegy for al-Qassam, on July 8th, 1972. That morning, he had left his house with his seventeen year-old niece Lamis, who was visiting from Kuwait. Her uncle had offered to drop her off in town on the way to his office. The explosives that Israeli agents had planted under his car detonated as they approached the vehicle. Kanafani's funeral was the biggest Beirut had witnessed in years: 'workers and farmers, intellectuals, refugees from the camps', his wife recalls, 'members of the different groups of the Palestinian resistance movement, representatives of most political parties and public life' accompanied his body through the streets of the city and on to its final resting place, amidst the pines of the Palestine Martyrs' Cemetery in the city's southeast.

It is said that on account of the chronic illnesses he developed over the course of his early adulthood, Kanafani was deeply aware of his mortality. Some have attributed his voluminous body of work to this sense of urgency, though his tirelessness was clearly overdetermined. Snapshots of his extraordinary range captured by the recent anthology of his writings include the satirist who mocks the vacuity of the bourgeois intellectual; the media strategist and spokesperson who reflects on the state of discourse around the Palestinian question in the European public sphere; the military theorist who synthesises the lessons of the global anti-colonial struggle for an escalating battle against Zionism. Out of view are yet more guises – the editor, the critic, the artist – known already to Arab audiences, and only now beginning to be appreciated abroad, thanks to the steadily increasing availability of his non-fiction in English (a trend not likely to subside given the extent of noteworthy work which remains untranslated).

Even then, any attempt to fully assess Kanafani's legacy requires us to step outside the prism of the individual genius. The organisation that he helped found, whose programme he honed, and which he led until his death survives to this day, playing no small part in the continuation of the Palestinian Revolution after Kanafani's martyrdom. Over the course of the 1970s, the PFLP remained in Lebanon, controlling large parts of its South until Beirut fell to Israeli forces in the summer of 1982. Inside Palestine, it contributed to reigniting popular resistance through grassroots organisations such as the Union of Palestinian Women's Committees, part of the web of associations that sustained and gave shape to the First Intifada. Its presence also grew massively amongst prisoners' movement as more and more Palestinians began to fill Israeli jails following the occupation's expanded policing over the course of the 1980s (Ahmad Sa'adat, the PFLP's current Secretary-General, has spent the last twenty three years in prison). *al-Hadaf*, now headquartered in Gaza City, continues to publish articles to this day (through the genocide) and has striven to preserve the Popular Front's intellectual heritage. Two texts included in the anthology were themselves reprinted by the journal in recent years for the anniversary of their publication.

When Kanafani spoke of Gaza – the Strip features prominently in his literary oeuvre – his words were almost always accompanied by a sense of awe and admiration. The work commonly identified as his first, dating from the mid-50s, is a 'Letter from Gaza', in which an unnamed author refuses to join his friend Mustafa to study in the United States after his young niece loses a leg in an Israeli bombardment ('come back', the writer urges Mustafa, 'to learn from Nadia's leg, amputated from the top of the thigh, what life is and what existence is worth').[27] When Israel occupied Gaza in 1967 the PFLP had been amongst the most powerful groups in the Strip, on account of years of freedom afforded to ANM activity under Egyptian administration. Kanafani would make repeated, excited reference in his writings to Gaza's resistance to the occupation in the late 1960s. His hope was that its unity and resolve could serve as a model for the *feda'iyyin* in Jordan and Lebanon. The rebellion there, along with the PFLP leadership, was ultimately quelled in 1971, and though the Popular Front never fully regained the place it had once occupied, it is difficult to imagine Kanafani greeting subsequent transformations of the resistance in Gaza with anything other than enthusiasm.[28] This in part, of course, relates to Habash's definitive break with with Arafat over the Oslo Accords – 'an act', in his words, 'of humiliation and betrayal' – but perhaps more fundamentally to the historical processes that underpinned the emergence of the leading political force the PFLP would join in its rejection of the accords. One might rightly object to an overly earnest reading of modern Islamism as a form of spontaneous mass consciousness, but it is impossible not to note the transformation in the Palestinian Revolution represented by the social character of Hamas, especially its leadership, one largely drawn from the sons of Gaza's refugee camps. Alongside them, shoulder to shoulder with those who claim 'Izz al-Din al-Qassam as the forefather of their struggle, the PFLP continues to mobilise, prodigiously, against an entire world bent on the annihilation of its people.

How might a people in revolt become conscious of itself and its latent power, and reflect this self-consciousness in its leaders, representatives and organisations? 'The enduring revolutionary effect – novel, rupture, transformative – of what we know and insist on as the Palestinian Revolution', Nasser Abourahme writes, is nothing other than 'the historical production of a collective subjectivity.'[29] This is the underlying preoccupation of Kanafani's later thought – a binding of the national and social question, yes, but one in which the latter emerges, under historically determinate conditions, as a radicalisation of the former. The agent of liberation could no longer be assumed as a force external to the revolution, or otherwise standing at its helm, a transformation which could not but reshape the entire structure of the struggle – its assumptions, its ambitions and the very parameters by which its fortunes are measured.

In the strict sense, then, Kanafani cannot be termed an organic intellectual. At stake here is more than just definitional accuracy. Acutely aware of his class position after experiencing its fragility after the *Nakba* – his father, a well-to-do lawyer, had in his early exile resorted to selling fruit from a cart in the streets of Damascus – he was profoundly aware of the distance that separated the revolution's leadership from its popular cradle. The problem posed an array of challenges, the most crucial of which was strategic. Revolutionary Arab nationalism proved itself unable to transcend the class character of the regimes it produced, leaving the Arab nation fatally fragmented and exposed to the co-option of its constituent parts. The mass organisation the PFLP began to theorise after 1967 is a direct response to this problem of failed state militarism. The question here was less one of representation and leadership as such, but, more profoundly, 'organicity' itself per Gramsci: the very need for a revolutionary consciousness proximate to the social reality mobilising for a very different kind of war – a people's war. The vernacular poetry and songs of the *fellahin* during the Great Revolt of the 1930s, which Kanafani includes in the section on 'the Intellectuals' in his study, and, perhaps most emblematically, the figure of Umm Saad and her son: these are the mental worlds Kanafani seeks to excavate, 'the only possible weapon', he says, 'in the face of the technologically more advanced imperialist countries – the weapon of the masses themselves'.[30] If the revolution stands undefeated half a century on, it is thanks to its astounding capacity, through its daily assertions of life, to transform this disparity into equation.

Francesco Anselmetti is a PhD candidate in History and Middle Eastern Studies at Harvard University.

Notes

1. Partial biographies can be found in Anni Kanafani, *Ghassan Kanafani* (Beirut: Palestine Research Center, 1974); George Hajjar, Kanafani: Symbol of Palestine (Beirut: Karoun, 1974); Stefan Wild, *Ghassan Kanafani: The Life of a Palestinian* (Weisbaden, Otto Harrassowitz, 1975); Mouin Rabbani, 'Ghassan Kanafani' in *Encyclopedia of the Palestinians*, ed. Philip Mattar (New York: Facts on File, 2000).
2. See Anis Sayegh, *Palestine and Arab Nationalism* (Beirut: Palestine Research Center, 1970).
3. Constantine Zurayk, *Ma'na an-Nakba* (Beirut: Dar al-

Ilm al-Malayin, 1948), 37.

4. A brief but exhaustive history of the ANM can be found in Arabic in Bassil Kubaissi, *Harakat al-Qawmiyyin al-'Arab* (Beirut: Mu'assasat al-Abhaath al-'Arabiyya, 1973), originally written in English and submitted as Kubaissi's doctoral thesis at the American University (DC) in 1971. The work is practically a first-hand account of the movement: Kubaissi, who had met Habash, Haddad and al-Hindi at AUB, was a member first of the ANM, then the PFLP. He was assassinated by Mossad in Paris in April 1973.

5. Ghassan Kanafani, 'On Childhood, Literature, Marxism, the Front and *al-Hadaf* (1972)' in *Ghassan Kanafani: Selected Political Writings*, eds, Louis Brehony and Tahrir Hamdy (London: Pluto Press, 2024).

6. Reproduced in translation in Walid Kazziha, *Revolutionary Transformation in the Arab World: Habash and His Comrades from Nationalism to Marxism* (New York: St Martin's Press), 65.

7. Barbari's account can be found in English in Sahbaa' al-Barbari, *Light the Road of Freedom*, eds, Ghada Ageel and Barbara Bill (Edmonton: University of Alberta Press, 2021). Bseiso's testimony is in Mu'in Bseiso, *Dafater Falastiniyya* (Beirut: Dar al-Farabi, 1978).

8. Kanafani, *Ghassan Kanafani*, 13.

9. The classic account of revolution and counterrevolution in the twentieth century Gulf remains Fred Halliday, *Arabia without Sultans* (London: Penguin, 1974).

10. Kanafani, 'Yemen and Iraq: One Story or Two?' in *Selected Political Writings*, 46.

11. The term in English is quite apt, and attributable to George Hajjar, Kanafani's biographer and PFLP militant. Hajjar transcribed and edited Leila Khaled's memoirs – one also finds similar turns of phrase there. See Leila Khaled, *My People Shall Live: The Autobiography of a Revolutionary* (London: Hodder and Stoughton, 1973).

12. Cited in Hajjar, *Kanafani*, 66–67.

13. Yezid Sayigh, *Armed Struggle and the Search for a State: The Palestinian National Movement, 1949-1993* (Washington DC: Institute for Palestine Studies, 1997), 111.

14. Ramzy Baroud and Romana Rubeo, 'The Arab Cause during the Era of the United Arab Republic: Seismic Changes and Shifts' in *Selected Political Writings*, 290–294.

15. 'Excerpts from PFLP: Strategy for the Liberation of Palestine (1969)' in *Selected Political Writings*, 97. A full translation of the pamphlet was recently republished by Foreign Languages Press.

16. 'Strategy', 104.

17. Kanafani, 'On the PFLP and the September Crisis (1971)' in *Selected Political Writings*, 182.

18. 'The Resistance and its Challenges: The View of the PFLP (1970)' in *Selected Political Writings*, 138.

19. Kanafani, 'On the PFLP and the September Crisis (1971)' in *Selected Political Writings*, 180.

20. Louis Breony and Tahrir Hamdy, 'Introduction' in *Selected Political Writings*, 7.

21. 'The Resistance and its Challenges: The View of the PFLP (1970)' in *Selected Political Writings*, 145–152.

22. The anthology presents the pamphlet's introduction, but not its additional materials. Kanafani, 'The Underlying Synthesis of the Revolution: Theses on the Organisational Weapon (1971)' in *Selected Political Writings*, 165–176.

23. Kanafani, *Ghassan Kanafani*, 21.

24. For a discussion of *Umm Saad*, the camp, and the problem of revolutionary subjectivity, see Nasser Abourahme, *The Time Beneath the Concrete* (Durham, NC: Duke University Press, 2025) 93–125.

25. Ghassan Kanafani, *The Revolution of 1936-39 in Palestine: Background, Details and Analysis*, trans. Hazem Jamjoum (New York: 1804 Books, 2023) 56.

26. Kanafani, *The Revolution of 1936-39 in Palestine*, 41.

27. Ghassan Kanafani, 'Letter from Gaza' in *The 1936-39 Revolt in Palestine* (London: Tricontinental Society of London, 1980).

28. An excellent overview of the struggle in Gaza between 1967 and 1987 can be found in Ann M. Lesch, 'Prelude to the Uprising in the Gaza Strip' in *Journal of Palestine Studies* 20/1 (Autumn, 1990), 1–23.

29. Abourahme, *The Time Beneath the Concrete*, 124.

30. Kanafani, 'The Underlying Synthesis of the Revolution: Theses on the Organisational Weapon (1971)' in *Selected Political Writings*, 170.

Reviews

Marketplace of dull ideas

Christoph Schuringa, *A Social History of Analytic Philosophy: How Politics Has Shaped an Apolitical Philosophy* (London: Verso, 2025). 336pp., £25.00 hb., 978 1 80429 209 9

The opening pages of the inaugural issue of this journal in 1972 begin with these words in the article 'Professional Philosophers' by Jonathan Ree: 'People who don't know anything about philosophy courses are likely to be astonished and dismayed by their effects.' In a trenchant critique of the dominant mode of Oxford philosophy of the day, Ree describes how students 'acquire a very mannered way of speaking and a knack of shrugging off serious ideas with half frivolous complaints about the words in which they are expressed' and he documents curious initiation rituals by which a student 'will acquire the superficial facility in argument.' Armed with this superficial facility, 'the philosopher has made a profession of amateurishness' and this philosopher 'has thought of himself as an intellectual lone ranger, who travels light, righting the wrongs in various intellectual areas.' After sketching this peculiar academic figure, Ree inquires with consternation: 'But what exactly is the intellectual tradition which has these sad results?' Christoph Schuringa's *A Social History of Analytic Philosophy: How Politics has Shaped an Apolitical Philosophy* provides a timely and detailed answer to that question. Written with wit, rigour and a deep concern about the future of an intellectual tradition harbouring colonial ambitions, Schuringa's book is essential reading for both contemporary practitioners of philosophy and anyone interested in engaging with contemporary academic philosophy. More than just a history of the analytic tradition, Schuringa depicts a bleak present of a discipline caught in 'methodological free fall'.

Balancing nuance, a sweeping overview of over a century of philosophical texts, and a knack for pithy summaries of works across 'a tradition that manages to think of itself as no tradition at all', Schuringa produces a persuasive case for analytic philosophy's fundamental role as a powerful intellectual tool of 'bourgeois liberal ideology'. The book is poised to serve two divergent purposes. First, for those of us trained outside of the analytic hegemon who are obligated to continually reassert our active professional distance from analytic assumptions and methodologies, Schuringa provides an invaluable diagnostic tool aimed at identifying the common ideological underpinnings of a broad and expanding tradition. Second, for those rooted in the analytic tradition, a tradition marked by a 'remarkable lack of methodological self-scrutiny', it will hopefully provoke professional self-analysis into the ideological entanglements of their own philosophical practice. The book ought to spark the very kinds of questions that analytic philosophy is – according to Schuringa's own analysis – professionally incapable of asking about itself. As Schuringa concludes: 'The tradition that is none cannot be touched.'

Schuringa is not content leaving this tradition untouched and the book aims to debunk analytic philosophy's 'retrospective fictionalized histories'. According to this dominant narrative, analytic philosophy traces its origins to the German logician Gottlob Frege in the 1880s. Through Frege, the analytic tradition developed its dedication to precision and logical rigour. This 'Myth of Frege', which Schuringa dates to Michael Dummett's work in the 1970s, 'has turned out to be little more than a means of validation of a conception of philosophy that seems highly technical and rigorous but serves no purpose at all.' Schuringa relegates this myth to a 'late stage' of the book in Chapter 7 and dedicates the preceding chapters to meticulously tracing the origins of analytic philosophy to a handful of distinct institutional spaces in the early twentieth century: the Cambridge of Betrand Russell, G.E. Moore and Ludwig Wittgenstein (Chapter 2); the Red Vienna of the Vienna Circle (Chapter 3), the 'home of dullness' in pre-World War Two Oxford (Chapter 4), and campuses of elite universities in the early coldwar United States (Chapter 6). Specialists will no doubt quibble with details in this sweeping intellectual history, however I want to focus on the overarching project of the book as an ideology critique written in the form of what Schuringa calls a social history. Schuringa's description of analytic philosophy as 'apolitical' is merely a restatement of the tradition's own self-understanding. The book is dedicated to translating a set of political commitments which analytic philosophy is professionally incapable of articulating about itself – even while forcefully solidifying and reproducing those commitments.

Schuringa describes his social history project as a history of 'what has sustained analytic philosophy in particular, rather than with the social reproduction of institutional academic formations in general.' In referring to 'what has sustained analytic philosophy in particular', he ultimately means the liberal political and economic order. Early in the book he describes how 'analytic philosophy, like its cousins behaviourism and neoclassical economics, serves to perpetuate a picture that is central to bourgeois liberal ideology.' With the waning of the British empire, analytic philosophy found a new home in academic halls of the US American empire. As John McCumber has shown in his books *The Philosophy Scare* and *Time in the Ditch*, analytic philosophy benefitted immensely from the anti-communist purges of the McCarthy era and played a pivotal role in, in Schuringa's words, 'shoring up the neoliberal project.' Schuringa excels at tracing that history. Given the tight links between analytic philosophy and the dominate economic logics of the day, I would suggest that the fundamental intervention of the book could be distilled down to a powerful basic claim: analytic philosophy is the court philosophy of neoliberalism. Schuringa never formulates his own project in that way, but he does hint at this possibility at various points. 'The ideology of analytic philosophy is that of liberalism', Schuringa writes, but he avoids explicitly drawing a more radical conclusion about analytic philosophy's role in shoring up the projects of neoliberalism. I would suggest that Schuringa gives us reason to conclude that analytic philosophy is in fact a tool of neoliberal governmentality. That is to say, neoliberalism both demands the sort of atomistic analysis which is central to analytic philosophy, while analytic philosophy has also served to solidify the cultural hegemony of neoliberal assumptions.

It is worthwhile to tease out more closely how Schuringa uses a social history of analytic philosophy to support this claim. The book is expressly not an institutional history, though it does provide rich fodder for institutional histories yet to be written. At times the book reads like a straightforward intellectual history and Schuringa demonstrates a subtle alacrity for getting to the core of his chosen subjects' thinking. He is intellectually at home in texts which might not be familiar ground for non-analytic philosophers. His choice of material skews by his own admission towards great thinkers (Russel, Moore, Wittgenstein, Frege as the canon of the classics; Sally Haslanger, Charles Mills, Robert Brandom, John McDowell as the stalwarts of the contemporary canon), but Schuringa attributes that to the way analytic philosophy 'promotes a cult of personality'. His intellectual-biographical sketches provide invaluable insights into the training in analytic philosophy as a form of *socialisation*.

The social aspect of this social history is brought out most persuasively in his evocation of the stuffy, homosocial atmosphere of pre-Second World War Oxford and Cambridge. A fair coterie of aristocratic types shuffle through these homogenous institutional spaces dominated by men trained at elite schools. Elizabeth Anscombe, Philippa Foot and Iris Murdoch do receive their due and Schuringa describes the misogyny that hampered their careers at various stages. Empire looms in the background of these academic spaces in a diffuse way that remains unexplored. To what extent, for example, do the connections to empire in the Oxford and Cambridge of the early twentieth century extend or relate to the nineteenth-century story told by Uday Singh Mehta's *Liberalism and Empire: A Study in Nineteenth-Century British Liberal Thought*? Yet by 1940 the links between analytic philosophy and the military-industrial complex are more explicit. The experience of WWII looms large in this period and Schuringa describes J.L. Austin's 'quasi-military operations' and documents the contributions to defence research at RAND by Hans Reichenbach, W.V. Quine, Donald Davidson and Nicholas Rescher.

If social history involves describing the social practice of analytic philosophy as embodied in its professional mores, then the book excels in that regard. Schuringa displays a knack for a clever turn of phrase and the occasional sly – but never gratuitous – zinger. He depicts a discipline 'remarkably stuck in the past' and 'a continuation of a basically eighteenth-century mindset.' Feminists, philosophers of colour, and diverse practitioners have long documented the marginalising power of analytic philosophy's 'highly combative' professional style in which 'all comers were welcome to participate', though ultimately 'a certain pushy, too-clever-by-half type predominates.' Schuringa persuasively shows how these combative elements are not merely professional tics which could be unlearned to make for a more inclusive analytic philosophy, but instead demonstrates how such combativeness constitutes the core of analytic practice. Schuringa's description of the Oxford tutorial of the 1940s is especially informative in this regard:

> Students were subjected to the iterated deployment against them of the question, 'What exactly does this mean?', to gloomy silences, and to other techniques of intellectual intimidation supposed to engender a self-critical attitude and cultivate the crafting of suitably precise statements of the expected kind.

This socialisation is shaped by 'a fantasy of consummate ease.' This fantasy is rooted in analytic philosophy's essential confirmation of hegemonic power structures and the self-assured comfort of indulging in thought experiments whose rigour is precisely guaranteed by their uselessness. This practice encourages and rewards those who feel at ease with the status quo and then 'pumps' their intuition for further philosophical justification of that very state of ease.

As Schuringa's description approaches the analytic philosophy of the present, he describes a '[r]eliance on intuitions' that 'is heavy, widespread and astonishingly casual', despite the 'discipline's own fetishization of "rigour".' Intuition pumping as a method is purportedly the guarantor for that rigour, which is not undercut, but is somehow reinforced by a number of professional practices which might raise the eyebrows of people accustomed to different standards of inquiry. First, there is 'the analytic philosopher's trope of not being fussed about historical details.' Second, Schuringa identifies an even more maddening defensive posture grounded tautologically in the purported rigour of the analytic philosopher's

uniquely trained and scrutinising eye: 'The profession [sic] "I do not understand this", if aimed by the right person at the right target, counts a powerful objection in analytic philosophy.' One very clear conclusion emerges: analytic philosophy is not in the first instance a practice of *reading*. This realisation alone has proven critical in articulating my own intellectual distance from the investments of analytic practice. What Schuringa shows – and this could be thought through more closely – is that reading is at most secondary and it is secondary not to thinking in the mode of, say, Hannah Arendt, but to *arguing*. Analytic philosophy's imagination of this arguing is predicated on an imagined neutral space – a featureless marketplace – bereft of power structures where, without any regard for hierarchy or the social production of power, the best argument wins in a clean and fair competition. A listener privy to such discussions might be treated to interventions such as: 'I've got the knock-down argument against that!'. Analytic philosophers might find it difficult to comprehend that not all philosophers, and certainly not all thinkers, find such modes of engagement intellectually productive.

In his 2008 defence-cum-history of analytic philosophy *What is Analytic Philosophy?*, Hans-Johann Glock describes what he calls the 'piecemeal approach' of analytic philosophy. This involves segmenting down a question to its smallest identifiable discrete unit – a practice applied fruitfully by Aristotle. Having segmented the question in that way, the analytic philosopher then pursues a hyper-local analysis of a highly specialised question. This results in the curious phenomenon of authors frequently citing their own earlier essays on a topic such as just deserts, while responding to another philosopher's recent critique of the author's own earlier argument about just deserts. This process continues *ad nauseum* with each incremental step filing down positions and counter-positions. Schuringa cites Ernest Gellner's description of this process as 'conspicuous triviality'. In this practice of triviality, the author is expressly discouraged from integrating their niche question into a larger whole or into a broader social or political reality, for the very refinement of the piecemeal stance away from an integrated whole is precisely the guarantee of scientific rigour. In this regard, there is a distinct break from Aristotelian practice, which both segments and synthesises. The logic of production built into this process is clear and it leads to essays of characteristic brevity within a field that eschews the production of books as the flipside to the aversion to reading. Here conspicuous triviality merges neatly with conspicuous consumption and gratuitous production.

The piecemeal treatment of discrete units neatly aligns with neoliberalism's reduction of all political analysis to the discrete unit of the individual. If, as Wendy Brown writes in her 2015 book *Undoing the Demos: Neoliberalism's Stealth Revolution*, '[n]eoliberalism governs as sophisticated common sense', then perhaps analytic philosophy is another name for that sophisticated common sense. In its characteristic style and in its content (and in the neat equation of style with content), analytic philosophy thinks in a neoliberal manner. Stated in this way, Schuringa does not so much write an intellectual or social history of a cohesive intellectual tradition, but instead a sort of intellectual etiquette manual for being congenial to the neoliberal order. Philip Mirowski and Dieter Plehwe described the diffuse intellectual agents of this movement as the 'neoliberal thought collective'. Analogously, Schuringa writes a history not of a unified intellectual project, but of a diffuse thought collective's congeniality to the neoliberal order through a particular mode of intellectual practice.

If analytic philosophy is at the very least ineluctably neoliberal, then that accounts for the palpable shift in tone in the final chapter 'Colonizing Philosophy'. Here Schuringa continues with the sober analysis of texts combined with a more urgent polemical tone in his description of analytic philosophy's tendency to 'neutralize and defang' whatever it touches. The chapter documents how analytic philosophers 'have been effective in subjecting a series of successive radical, non-liberal currents of thought to liberal marketization.' In particular, he analyses analytic feminism, critical theory, Marxism and the philosophy of race. It would be wrong to say that these radical traditions undergo a depoliticisation in analytic hands, for that would endorse analytic philosophy's foundational myth of being apolitical. Instead, these traditions undergo a distinct political translation into the neoliberal assumptions of discretion, production and the valorisation of the individual in a practice of segmented analysis concerned with discrete units. Here, according to Schuringa, something more sinister than conspicuous triviality is at work.

This chapter is sure to spark the most controversy, not least because it directs an ideology critique toward contemporary philosophers who present their work as the vanguard of progressivism. For example, Schuringa identifies the work of Charles Mills as a threshold figure who at once, 'struck at the core of the liberal project', but was nonetheless ultimately 'amenable to a reconstruction of liberalism.' Unfortunately, Schuringa does not take Mills' 2005 essay '"Ideal Theory" as Ideology' into consideration, which not only strikes at the heart of Rawlsian liberalism, but ultimately shows that the entire application of such ideal practice and, by extension, the entire reliance on thought experiments are a tool for defending a white-supremacist status quo. An alternative account of Mills' philosophical evolution might show that he could only think philosophically about race once he had departed from analytic philosophy. Yet Mills' defence of Kantian universalism in his late essay 'Black Radical Kantianism' may ultimately confirm Schuringa's description of Mills' liberalism – is it an entirely moot question whether he perpetuates that liberal project as an analytic philosopher or as something else?

Schuringa's fundamental thesis already projects the potential reception of the book. 'There is', as Schuringa writes, 'from within analytic philosophy, no means to secure a critical vantage point on this sorry situation.' If his critique is, to use the language of analytic philosophy, *taken on board*, then the very process of onboarding will repoliticise and appropriate Schuringa's radical critique of the entire analytic edifice. Perhaps, too, Schuringa's analyses might be mined by thinkers within the tradition to provide fuel for petty grievance politics against rival thinkers within the tradition. One could imagine various bad-faith appropriations of Schuringa's critique of analytic feminism and philosophy of race mobilised to debunk feminism and philosophy of race as a whole. Yet Schuringa's book is decidedly not a work of naïve flag-waiving. A critique of analytic philosophy does not necessarily amount to a defence of continental philosophy. Schuringa does not attempt the latter, though Chapter 6 does defend the existence of continental philosophy as a distinct tradition. Continental philosophy has certainly been apt to lapse into its own unproductive personality cults and there were doubtless members of its canon who were proper card-carrying fascists. Moreover, works such as Mariana Ortega's *In-Between: Latina Feminist Phenomenology, Multiplicity, and the Self* show how certain portions of the continental canon labour under their own assumptions of 'consummate ease'.

Although written as a social history, I would suggest that non-analytic readers will benefit from Schuringa's book as a diagnostic manual documenting a dazzling symptomology. Schuringa diagnoses a curious situation in the professional philosophy of the present. He speaks at once of analytic philosophy's 'methodological decrepitude', yet the entire book testifies to analytic philosophy's fecundity. Analytic philosophy thrives in the marketplace of ideas and not the least because it does not question the fundamental mechanisms of the market. Schuringa's depiction of a tradition marked by 'high levels of studied historical ignorance' and his detailed analyses of the tradition are an invaluable resource for those puzzled by that professional ignorance.

Lastly, it is worth noting how the book is also written in the mode of mourning. As J.M. Cohen writes in 1972 in the second issue of *Radical Philosophy*: 'These academics deserve the students they breed; but the students do not always deserve such academics: caveat emptor.' Schuringa's work will perhaps serve a valuable third function as a tool for orienting students perplexed and ultimately disappointed by the analytic style they encounter in their university classrooms. Readers of this journal have likely repeatedly had some version of a conversation with puzzled students or colleagues seeking to account for the social practices of analytic colleagues. We now all have a valuable resource to supplement those explanations.

For those who fight to keep institutional spaces for non-analytic philosophy alive, Schuringa writes to a bleak present. He speaks to an institutional setting in which critical philosophers are forced to market themselves as experts in a limpid form of critical thinking that is supposedly equally at home in the corporate board room, court of law, and in the fight for some corporatised form of social justice. Increasingly, we find ourselves as professional philosophers reduced to peddling a form of critical thinking purportedly bereft of content – as if critical thinking were not always critical thinking about something. Analytic philosophy effaces that very possibility and thrives in an imagined power-free space of neutrality. Our institutional survival means selling our wares as a neutral vessel of thought and thus involves a silent capitulation to analytic creep. Analytic philosophy thrives in that space because it labours under the assumption 'that a training in logic makes people better able to think in other domains', which Schuringa describes as 'a plausible sounding idea for which there nevertheless appears to be no evidence.' The realisation is a powerful one which we should wield in the university planning meeting instead of dusting off platitudes about the power of critical thinking.

Perhaps many of us carve out our institutional niche while touting this form of dogmatism and placating ourselves into thinking that we create spaces for different forms of thinking within the classroom. Schuringa provides a clear diagnosis of that tendency: 'It is not difficult to see that reliance on intuitions is a symptom of philosophical degeneracy. It is a form of dogmatism, and thus the antithesis of philosophy.' Schuringa's conclusion is a bleak one: if philosophy survives in institutions at all it is as the antithesis of philosophy. Should we be dedicated to promoting the survival of this moribund assemblage? Is Schuringa's book ultimately a critique of analytic philosophy, or of the institutions that sustain it?

Adam Knowles

Full-spectrum philosophy

Victoria Browne, *Pregnancy Without Birth: A Feminist Philosophy of Miscarriage* (London: Bloomsbury, 2022). 232pp., £21.99 pb., 978 1 35027 969 8

For some people, to disclose a pregnancy is to be assigned a place in the future almost immediately. It might start innocuously enough. If you are pregnant in Britain, a health professional might call you 'mum' when you least expect it. If you're in London, you might order one of Transport for London's 'Baby on Board' badges to let other passengers know you need a seat. One of the many issues with this badge is its rhetorical erasure: if the baby is already on board, the pregnant person might as well not be. For those with a lower tolerance for cutesy alliteration, or anyone unsure about disclosing their pregnancy to a carriage of strangers, TfL offers another option: the 'Please offer me a seat' badge. This is pitched at commuters with 'invisible' disabilities or health conditions, but it also caters to anyone not ready or willing to reveal their pregnancy. They might be considering termination. They might be worried about work. They might want to protect a pregnancy someone else wants them to terminate. They might not know how they feel about it. For wanted pregnancies, the standard account of the 'first trimester silence' hinges on the statistical likelihood of miscarriage in the first trimester. Nobody wants to have to 'un-announce' a pregnancy, the thinking goes. Personally, I'm not sure the process is always as rational as all that. I ordered the 'Please offer me a seat' badge in my first trimester because I was sick and clinging instinctually to the care I needed *now*, in the present tense.

Since reading Victoria Browne's *Pregnancy Without Birth: A Feminist Philosophy of Miscarriage*, I have a new term for what I was dodging with my niche taste in TfL badges: 'proleptic pregnancy', the normative pregnancy culture where, as Browne puts it, 'two imagined figures of the future – the mother and baby – are superimposed on to the present, such that they come to stand in for pregnant embodiment as such'. The culture of proleptic pregnancy 'leaves us ill-equipped to deal with the conceptual complexities and messy materialities of miscarriage', says Browne. Of course, the problems with proleptic pregnancy don't start and end with miscarriage. As the book notes, the superimposition of the mother-baby dyad onto the pregnant subject is one of the favoured rhetorical contortions of anti-abortion discourse. Even beyond abortion and miscarriage, Browne makes a powerful argument that the subsumption of pregnancy into the maternal future does a disservice to all pregnant people, however their pregnancies end. She writes:

> [R]eflection on the nonchosen nature of miscarriage brings into view the fundamental contingency of *all* pregnancies, whatever choices have been possible, even when

the choices made align with the eventual outcome. After all, aborted pregnancies, just like child-producing pregnancies, could always have ended otherwise.

This expansive approach initially made me wonder whether the subtitle of *Pregnancy Without Birth* might be too reticent. 'A philosophy of miscarriage' seemed too particular a term for Browne's exciting and radical intervention here, which takes miscarriage as a starting point for a new approach to the philosophy of pregnancy itself. Towards the end of the book, the language becomes bolder as Browne writes that the 'ultimate aim of this book has been to make a philosophical contribution to the full-spectrum model of pregnancy'. This model, inspired by the full-spectrum doula movement in the US, addresses experiences of birth, abortion, miscarriage and stillbirth on a level plain, breaking down the conceptual oppositions that divide them. From this perspective, the title *Pregnancy Without Birth* refers not primarily to the empirical fact of such pregnancies, but to the book's methods, which involve a 'conceptual suspension or "bracketing" of the presumption of birth and postnatal relations' in the theorisation of pregnancy.

Still, I came to understand why the foregrounding of miscarriage is crucial to Browne's project. It is partly because miscarriage has been so neglected in philosophies of pregnancy, even feminist ones. The book's engagements with canonical feminist philosophical treatments of pregnancy, from Simone de Beauvoir and Iris Marion Young to Julia Kristeva and Luce Irigaray, are no less generous for pointing out that many of these thinkers tend to assume that pregnancy ends in childbirth. Challenging this tendency, Browne argues that 'miscarriage should not be treated as a sub-category in the philosophy of pregnancy'. Rather, it should be the necessary starting point for any theory of pregnancy, which must reckon first of all with its contingency.

Time plays an important role in Browne's argument. She reveals how, even in a medical system that professes to have moved beyond the Aristotelean concept of biological telos, a notion of 'womb teleology' endures in causal-mechanistic accounts of the uterus as being 'for' birth. Alongside these 'womb teleologies' and cultures of proleptic pregnancy, Browne identifies another powerful temporal trope: the linear model of pregnancy as a liminal state that mediates the passage to maternity. The book suggests that the time of pregnancy might alternatively be framed as a 'multi-layered, multi-directional, polytemporal lived present, rather than a transitional stage of "middle passage" on the way towards something else'. This approach means that 'if pregnant time is not represented in exclusively future-oriented terms as being-towards-birth, or a means to an end, then miscarriage need not be understood as pregnancy's undoing'.

This conceptual reframing of pregnancy has significant implications for common ways of narrating and understanding miscarriage. The book engages throughout with what Browne terms 'miscarriage stories', largely from the US and the UK, which take diverse forms including memoirs, blog posts and interviews conducted through social research. The book takes its chapter titles from five themes that arise continually in these narratives: failure, control, ambiguity, suspension and solidarity. Organised around these themes, the narratives are explicitly not positioned as transparent lenses on experience; rather, they provide conceptually rich material that clarifies the stakes of the full-spectrum approach to pregnancy. Miscarriage, as these stories show, is often trivialised as 'normal' and 'natural'. While it is perhaps intended as a comforting reminder of the statistical frequency of miscarriage, Browne notes that the insistence on the normality of miscarriage is hard to disentangle from normative notions of the 'successful' or 'failed' pregnancy. In one of the narratives, the idea that miscarriage is 'natural' makes its medical management seem like a failure ('I couldn't even get miscarriage right'). Meanwhile, the flip-side of the insistence on the naturalness of miscarriage is a prescriptive culture of grief that, while meaningful for some, fails to register the full diversity of needs and experiences.

This terrain is fraught and entangled with both ideological weight and histories of trauma. The book devotes a fair amount of space to anticipating possible misunderstandings and sensitively framing its conceptual interventions so their affordances are not compromised. In the second chapter, 'Control', Browne takes up feminist theories of intercorporeality developed by Lisa Guenther, Rosalyn Diprose and Ann Cahill. The intercorporeal model posits that our individuality is constituted through our openness to others; as such, Browne argues, it can help forge common ground across divergent pregnant experiences and trajectories. There is a delicate balancing act at work here: Browne acknowledges that the language of 'corporeal generosity' is likely to be jarring to many feminists, and that the proposed de-individualisation of pregnancy is risky in contexts of oppressive state control. But she reminds us that these terms can be adapted: in place of 'corporeal generosity', we can emphasise 'interdependence, co-constitution, and affectivity'.

Politically, as well as in the realms of philosophy and daily life, miscarriage has occupied a marginal position. The predominance of 'choice' as an organising concept for feminist reproductive politics is difficult to reconcile with the un-chosen nature of the miscarriage. The structure of the political demand often presumes a choosing subject whose freedom is curtailed by external forces. How to craft a political demand around miscarriage? *Pregnancy Without Birth* inherits its critical approach to pro-choice models of reproductive freedom from the reproductive justice movement and the theoretical work of thinkers including Loretta J. Ross, Dorothy E. Roberts and Jennifer Nelson, as well as Shellee Colen's concept of stratified reproduction. The reproductive justice perspective is alert to the fact that the anecdotal passages with which I opened this review – of being addressed as 'mum' by healthcare professionals and invited to hail one's foetus as a 'baby on board' – are not shared by everyone, and the texture of these experiences will vary across different forms of raced, gendered and classed oppression. Underpinning *Pregnancy Without Birth* is a conviction that solidarity can be forged across radically different encounters with reproductive oppression.

Miscarriage might seem a counter-intuitive place to start – after all, as Browne observes, the treatment of miscarriage as a politicised issue often involves disturbing overlaps with anti-abortion politics and ideologies of foetal personhood. On the other hand, the criminalisation of miscarriage makes vivid the common ground shared by all pregnant people, and the necessity of solidarity across pregnancy's many possible ends. *Pregnancy Without Birth* was completed as the US Supreme Court heard arguments in the *Dobbs v. Jackson Women's Health Organisation* case. Since the book's completion, the Court concluded the case by overturning constitutional protections for abortion. In the wake of the 2022 *Dobbs* decision, nineteen states have imposed either outright abortion bans or highly restrictive time limits that can function as *de facto* bans. While the post-*Dobbs* landscape is readily framed as a criminalisation of abortion, it increasingly makes sense to understand it as a criminalisation of pregnancy altogether. In West Virginia, which has imposed a total abortion ban, prosecutor Tom Truman advises that anyone experiencing a miscarriage should get in touch with law enforcement. A CNN report quotes a response from the legal academic Kim Mutcherson who makes the point that 'it's always a mistake to invite law enforcement into your reproductive life'. This defence of the freedom of reproductive life, considered in all its variability, seems in tune with Browne's intervention here.

Britain is not immune from these currents. As I write this review, MPs have recently voted to decriminalise abortion in England and Wales for those who terminate pregnancies; others, including medical professionals, still face prosecution for assisting abortions outside the 24-week time limit. An expert review group is considering whether to review the law in Scotland and will report to the Scottish Government next year. The decision follows highly publicised cases of women who were arrested and even jailed after being accused of illegally ending a pregnancy, and new guidance that suggests police in England and Wales are entitled to examine menstrual tracking apps following stillbirths for signs that the pregnancy was aborted. One possible approach to these developments would be to decry the criminalisation of miscarriage and stillbirth as cases apart from the criminalisation of abortion. *Pregnancy Without Birth* demonstrates what we miss with this kind of approach. Browne never underplays the difference between experiences of abortion, childbirth, miscarriage and stillbirth, but insists that difference can be the grounds for solidarity. If contingency is a starting point for the philosophy of pregnancy, as Browne suggests it should be, then it becomes a lot easier to address the control, criminalisation and surveillance of pregnancy, which particularly impact the pregnancies of low-income and racialised people. This full-spectrum model of pregnancy reminds us that, in Browne's words, 'when we pay attention to miscarriage, we are not just learning things about miscarriage – we are learning things about pregnancy, and the imaginaries, temporalities, and power structures that shape it as symbol and as lived experience.'

Sophie A. Jones

Educational crisis

Walter Benjamin, *On Goethe*, ed. and trans. by Susan Bernstein, Peter Fenves and Kevin McLaughlin (Stanford, CA: Stanford University Press, 2025). 382pp., £103.00 hb., £23.99 pb., 978 1 50363 096 3 hb., 978 1 50364 222 5 pb.

'Goethe saw it coming: the crisis in bourgeois education', remarks Walter Benjamin in Convolute N, the most famous section of the mass of material gathered together as the *Arcades Project*. Although this comment is not reproduced in *On Goethe*, a new selection of Benjamin's writings about the German writer he engaged with more than any other, the crisis it alludes to casts a shadow over this relatively compact stand-alone volume, edited and translated by Susan Bernstein, Peter Fenves and Kevin McLaughlin, with additional translations by Jan Cao and Jonas Rosenbrück.

Benjamin was well acquainted with educational and academic crisis. His hopes of a conventional academic career were forestalled by the rejection of his *Habilitationsschrift*, the second dissertation needed to secure a German university position, in the context of scholarly closedmindedness, eventual plagiarism and an institutional antisemitism whose intensifications in the later 1920s and 1930s reverberate throughout the material here. *On Goethe* catalogues what Fenves – the author of the book's introduction – calls an equally 'dismal affair'. The event, or nonevent, in question is the rejection by the Insel-Verlag publishing house of a proposed monograph whose publication would have coincided with the 1932 celebrations marking the centenary of Goethe's death, and on which Benjamin had apparently pinned many hopes. News of the rejection seemingly inspired a journal with the morbid title: 'Diary of the Seventeenth of August, Nineteen-Thirty, until the Day of My Death'.

For the most part, the entries comprising the second part of *On Goethe* document Benjamin's critical responses, eventually under pseudonyms, to what *was* published, by other authors, for the 1932 *Goethe-Jahr*. Goethe's presence in German literary life in the early 1930s was so overbearing that one review is titled 'Books on Goethe – but Welcome Ones'. (First sentence: 'Every word not spent on speaking about Goethe this year is a blessing, and so nothing is more welcome than laconic anniversary books.') What Benjamin appears to welcome about the two books under discussion, besides their 'laconic' natures, is their factual rather than interpretive modes. One is a picture book that yields 'more solid instruction' for general readers than do most literary histories; the other a chronicle whose austerity (offering nothing but names and dates) is, not unlike the *Arcades Project* itself, paradoxically capable of inspiring 'fantasy', even among those readers most knowledgable about Goethe.

There are two things about this review that – in terms of both Benjaminian content and editorial form – typify what is going on in the volume as a whole. Regarding content, the cheery review of 'welcome' books stands out in the context of Benjamin's lifelong, often quarrelsome relation to the Goethe literature. His early sketch of a highly critical review of Friedrich Gundolf's wildly successful *Goethe* (1916) is reproduced here, as is an idiomatically-organised bibliography (sample headings: 'Concerning Goethe's Physiognomy', 'A Few Monographs') and a review of a 1000-page, two-volume book by Eugen Kühnemann, also called *Goethe* (1930), which, the editors guess, sought to emulate the sales of Gundolf's. Benjamin's review of the later *Goethe* unfavourably compares its international marketing of a sanctimonious 'human sciences' – the author travels around the world to present an idea that consciously minimises knowledge of Goethe's life or work, hence the review's title: 'Faust in the Sample Case' – with the far more modest 'philological method' practiced by one the university colleagues whose labours Kühnemann treats 'condescendingly'. The opposition of a minute philology, in which the researcher, like Goethe's natural scientist, 'makes himself intensely identical' to the thing studied, to the monumentalising but ultimately facile work of the Goethe cult, is at the heart of the material presented in the latter parts of *On Goethe*.

Insofar as Kühnemann also opposes philology (practiced by workaday scholars) to philosophy (the task of great men), clear links can be drawn to the earlier texts reproduced in Part 1, which more obviously capture the book's stated intention of opening up the 'laboratory' of Benjamin's thinking. It would be hard to summarise the many procedures by which Benjamin uses Goethe's 'nonphilosophical' ideal of the artwork as a means by which to probe how singular truths can register, without systematising, the otherwise unthinkable 'unity of philosophy'. (Cantor's set theory, which Benjamin knew about through his great-uncle, is hinted at as another possibility.) A relatively well-known image for this situation is that looking at an artwork, as a method of philosophical thinking, is a bit like speaking to the sibling of a secretive person: you might learn something about your interest indirectly, but you're still encountering another person entirely. Another staging of this problem, whose published English translation comes as very welcome, finds Benjamin addressing the assumption that 'ontology' could capture this higher unity. Not so, he says. Ontology doesn't concern the truth, as we might suppose, but rather 'cognitions'. Its insights can only have the 'dimensions' of individual paintings. This means that 'ontology is not the palace' of philosophy that it wishes to be (the higher unity); nevertheless, we can still 'fill out the walls of the palace with images, until the images appear to be the walls'. Art's truth-y nature, its modest dimensions, offers a better idea of how philosophical knowledge actually stands in relation to the thing – truth – that it's after, the fragment suggests.

All of this comes to a head in 'Goethe's Elective Affinities' (1924-25), whose scope and ambition still seem miraculous a century after its publication. Benjamin's account of the 'expressionless' – developed from his studies into the nature of lying; and naming a sublime, critical force that refuses the 'mixing' of semblance and truth in art – is probably where he departs most from Goethe's own writing, and where another through line to the work of Part 2 is established. In the context of *On Goethe* as a whole, it's as if the expressionless's 'moral word' is brought to bear on the liars who could not stop talking, certainly not when presented with the many publication opportunities offered up by an anniversary. He clearly wishes Goethe's celebrated readers would just shut up.

As for editorial form? The form-content dichotomy is a bad joke, of course, since Goethe's work regularly complicates the distinction, as most of his interlocutors recognise. Nevertheless, a strange economy governs the selection of sources here. The book is structured in two parts according to a Goethean 'polarity', though we are also told that it might in fact be a *Steigerung*: an intensification or elevation, as Benjamin's youthful literary-philosophical studies give over to materialist analysis. Yet these terms, Goethe's 'two great driving forces in all nature', are also polar opposites, we read, so we can't really escape polarity after all. Other Goethean models are at play. Only the main text of Part 1, 'Goethe's Elective Affinities', was actually published; the other texts are unpublished fragments, notes and so on. But in Part 2, the major text, the article Benjamin wrote for the *Great Soviet Encyclopedia*, is the only thing that *wasn't* published (at least not in the form Benjamin submitted it). This is just one moment in *On Goethe* where the chemical phenomenon giving its name to Goethe's novel *Elective Affinities* is happily invoked: A and B are bonded together, as are C and D; but, like a married couple whose remote estate is interrupted by newcomers, A can get together with C, B with D. For example, when Florens Christian Rang aids Benjamin in placing his essay in the journal edited by Hugo von Hofmannsthal, Fenves phrases the situation, being sure to confirm the comparison, as 'a delicate interplay among the four parties: Rang, Hofmannsthal, Benjamin, and the essay.'

Elsewhere, the editors invoke Gershom Scholem's report that Benjamin himself was involved in a romantic entanglement similar to that animating Goethe's novel: while still married to Dora Kellner-Benjamin, he was attracted to Jula Cohn, while Dora was drawn to another mutual friend, Ernst Schoen. Scholem insisted that Benjamin's one-time dedication of 'Goethe's Elective Affinities' to Jula Cohn ought to be foregrounded in the text's presentation in the *Gesammelte Schriften* (the standard 7-volume German language edition of Benjamin, now being superseded by a projected 22-volume set). But in the introduction, and again in a lengthy footnote, the editors take issue with this, claiming that its gossipy 'presumption of sentimental proximity' in fact 'obstructs access to [the] subject-matter' of Benjamin's essay. Here is one instance of a remarkable but truly curious – or even 'queer', as Goethe's *wunderlich* is newly translated – attempt of the collection to follow the difficult coordinates, outlined in Benjamin's Gundolf review, for respecting biographical detail without having it unduly influence how a work is read. Other instances abound: Fenves guesses that Benjamin deliberately misnames the Goethe book he is reading in a letter to Scholem because the latter, a student of mathematics, would be distracted by its scientific claims, while Benjamin wanted to keep his friend focused on more spiritual matters. Elsewhere, we can read speculations about why Benjamin would have omitted certain information from an essay about Goethe he wrote when he was leaving high school. Even if one doesn't know the names under discussion, the following gives some insight into the editorial method, equally odd and brilliant:

> By acknowledging Rotten's dissertation in the first footnote of the 'esoteric afterword' to the published version of his own doctoral dissertation, Benjamin may have been sending something akin to a secret signal, on the one hand, to 'the universal genius' and, on the other, to the siblings whose surname is contained in the suppressed name 'Noeggerath', that is Grete Radt and Fritz Radt, the latter of whom, as noted earlier, would later marry Jula Cohn, whose first name punctuates a poem Benjamin wrote around the time he was completing his dissertation, 'Sonnet in the Night'.

As all this might suggest, *On Goethe* as a whole calls out to be read as a narrative in itself, or, more accurately, as a series of narratives. In this sense, the effect of the book is not unlike that inspired by those stories Goethe enjoyed inserting into his novels, and which (like 'The Queer Childhood Neighbours', told in *Elective Affinities*) were often at the core of Benjamin's readings. Like the embedded tales, *On Goethe* draws attention to the unreliable act of narrativising itself, with all the baggage that goes along with it. (Benjamin's readings of another such tale, the story of 'The New Melusine' that Goethe placed in his final novel, *Wilhelm Meister's Journeyman Years*, are unfortunately missing from the volume, largely owing to the editorial decision not to include correspondence. Though understandable, this is a shame since much of Fenves and McLaughlin's recent work has pivoted around how Benjamin developed an undoubtedly queer philology out of Goethe's even queerer story.) This sense of competing narratives owes less to the multiplicity of translators and editors, who share what to me is an entirely accurate and enticing approach to Benjamin's work, than to the enjoyably combative attitude that's taken with regard to other, mostly long-dead interlocutors.

A final example of the book's strangeness resonates

with some of today's educational crises. It is again told in the form of a story (a 'curious coincidence' followed by 'still more coincidences', as the introduction has it). It's February 1923, a time of despair for Benjamin. He has just left a sanatorium on the Austrian border, cast aside plans for editing his own journal, begun 'something like a tour of Germany' during the nadir of hyperinflation, and has met Erich Rothacker, who teaches philosophy at Heidelberg. Seeking a home for the essay, Benjamin has passed his 'Goethe's Elective Affinities' onto Rothacker, who enters into a correspondence with Paul Kluckhohn, a professor at Münster. The two, equivalents of an 'adjunct' and 'assistant professor' respectively, have recently begun their own scholarly journal. They feel compelled to support the work of emerging 'would-be' scholars (a young Heidegger was in talks about submitting something too), but Benjamin's essay is of an awkward length, and he is unwilling to entertain the thought of cutting it. Besides, a more senior scholar, in fact Benjamin and Heidegger's former teacher, Heinrich Rickert, has submitted something which, though 'forgettable', needs to be published. Antisemitism also, again, inflects the mix of admiration and scorn: 'Strange, these altogether rigorous moral Jews (including Cohen quotes!) who have gone through Goethe and Hölderlin', Rothacker writes.

Ultimately the decision is a polite no, or rather a 're-vise and resubmit': 'Benjamin is accused', we read, 'of making a mistake typical of young scholars, who are always trying to cram everything they want to say into a single piece of writing.' This summary might give us pause. Is the judgment Fenves' or that of the journal's editors? Might it apply to today's young scholars too, as the interpolation of contemporary academic jargon suggests? The use of free indirect speech makes it hard to be sure, but it's suggested that, rather than trying to say everything, there are still opportunities for the kind of 'philological rigour' that Benjamin himself admired in others, which might help to curb such tendencies. Half of Rothacker's correspondence with Heidegger is now lost '(or is perhaps still in the Heidegger archive, waiting to be found)', for example. Fenves later asks a good question about how Benjamin, just about eking out a living, might have related to Kühnemann's overlong book, which happened to come out with the same publishing house that rejected his own: 'But is this separation of good from bad philology enough to generate the energy required to go through a thousand-page nullity?' It's very hard to say.

Christopher Law

Communist encounters

Robert Linhart, *The Sugar and The Hunger: An Inquiry into the Sugar Regions of Northeastern Brazil* (Helsinki: Rab-Rab Press, 2023). 177pp., €16.00 pb., 978 9 52651 834 3

In September 1979 Robert Linhart, former *établi* and militant of the *Union des jeunesses communistes marxistes-léninistes* and *Gauche prolétarienne*, undertook a two-week investigation into the condition of sugarcane workers in Pernambuco, Northeast Brazil. Following an amnesty after fifteen years of military dictatorship, Linhart travelled as a 'French journalist' to the *zona da mata*, the historic centre of the sugarcane plantations. There he made wide-ranging inquiries with landless agricultural workers, small peasants, trade unionists, government supporters, mill owners, scholars and old revolutionaries, documenting a new and deadly capital-intensive transition towards the production of ethanol fuel.

What he found there 'shattered' him: an escalating situation of 'elaborate hunger, advanced hunger, a hunger to be booming, in one word, a modern hunger', driven by a new wave of dispossession and mechanisation that eliminated whatever precarious access to land remained on the margins of the estates. Families were pushed to the slums from where they still travelled to work in the fields for less pay. Stuck between the urban and the rural (as one worker put it, 'lost in the middle of the world'), this intensified regime of real subsumption generated a crisis in the reproduction of labour-power: extreme malnutrition and alimentary monotony, widespread disease and high childhood mortality. For Linhart it was a 'systematic production of subaltern humanity, reduced to an almost vegetative existence, but one from which capitalism draws a workforce'. Francisco Julião, the exiled leader of the *Ligas Camponesas* (Peasant Leagues) likewise described the region in 1968 as 'a concentration camp where twenty million starving human creatures are suffering'.

The Sugar and the Hunger, now translated forty-three years after its publication in French in 1980, is an exposition of the bloody origins of neoliberalism in the repressive laboratory of Latin America, and its operation as a movement to re-coup the super-profits of imperialism in the face of anti-colonial and agrarian revolutions. This short and vivid book deals with this transitionary moment as it occurred in Brazil. Prior to the coup of 1964, Pernambuco was the site of intense class struggle and international interest over the so-called 'Northeastern Question'. Peasant Leagues awakened the spectre of agrarian revolution as the left popular regional government of Miguel Arraes struggled to implement reforms in tension with US interference under the guise of aid relief. Paulo Freire experimented with literacy programs in Recife. Ted Kennedy even visited Eugenho Galileia – the expropriated mill from which the peasant movement originated – promising a generator. In the end the US gave the green light for the military takeover.

In his encounters fifteen years later, Linhart can still detect amidst the fear and destitution a legacy of resistance carried on from the Peasant Leagues, and in a poignant final scene, the survival of Eugenho Galileia. Witness to the stirrings of a strike that is eventually settled, his account of this political re-awakening also prefigures the *Movimento dos Trabalhadores Rurais Sem Terra* (MST). Founded in 1984, the MST has revived the occupations of the huge *latifundios* and now has approximately 900 encampments with 150,000 families living in them across Brazil.

More broadly this book also speaks to a wide range of recent debates over primitive accumulation and super-exploitation, the relationship between the market and violence, necro-politics, unequal ecological exchange, extractivism and critiques of green capitalism and developmentalism. It shares much with Mike Davis' work on slums and late-Victorian holocausts. Linhart's main conceptualisation of 'modern hunger', builds on the anti-Malthusian work of Recife-born Josué de Castro whose pioneering *Geography of Hunger* (1946) first brought global attention to the crisis in the Northeast.

Linhart account of the thanatotic force of capital in the slow destruction of human bodies, his detailing of foetal brain damage and dwarfism from malnourishment, can only now remind the reader of what is being inflicted on Gaza's population by Israel's relentless campaign of genocide. Zionism's operation as a system of apartheid and now outright extermination, raises the question of capital's ambivalent interest in the reproduction of human life in settler colonial contexts, just as the same question is posed by the transition from chattel slavery to a kind of wage slavery in Brazil.

Linhart's investigative outrage is also in the same vein of Engels' prototypical communist encounter with the proletarian world of 1840s Manchester in *The Condition of the Working Class in England* (1845). Where Linhart speaks of an 'immense rotting' without end, Engels excoriated the 'social murder' of early industrial England. This book serves as a latter part of that long and largely neglected genealogy of communist ethnography which begins with the young Engels, whose immersion in the diversity of working class life was the pre-condition for historical materialism's reading of political potential in an otherwise immiserated proletarian condition.

More provincially it also serves as an alternative ending to the adventure of French Maoism, one which counters the renegade teleology of the *nouveaux philosophes*. As former comrades sank quietly back into civilian life or turned to the right, and other *établissements* and *enquêtes* like those of Badiou's *Union des communistes de France marxiste-léniniste* and *Le groupe d'information sur les prisons* ended, Linhart continued to experiment with investigative forms in the 1970s. Focused on revealing the hidden and changing world of production and the concrete reality of situated class struggle, he wrote reports on technology transfer in Algeria (1977) and the petrochemical complex near Marseille (1978), as well as a series of sociological inquiries in the 1980s with his sister Danièle Linhart on a neoliberalising industrial France.

Yet he is perhaps best known through his other ethnographic memoir *L'établi* (1978), later published in English as *The Assembly Line* in 1980. A first-person account of his year-long *établissement* in a Citroën factory in Choisy directly after the unsettling experiences of May '68, during which he led the UJCml to oppose the events as a petty bourgeois ploy, Linhart focuses on the racialised division of labour within the factory. Passed from job to job as incompetent, but still judged more skilled than his Algerian, Yugoslavian or West African co-workers because he was French, the story unfolds through a series of sustained encounters at different points of the assembly line. Character profiles of immigrant histories and strategies towards work build a focus on the coloniality of the division of labour, and the plurality of proletarian experience. The book counters the idealisation (or demonisation) of the working class as a homogenous bloc, railing against the illusion that the middle class 'have a monopoly on personal histories'.

Inspired by Mao's famous 1930 dictum 'no investigation, no right to speak', *établissement* was a movement to re-educate intellectuals in the school of the masses, and through working and militating in factories and fields build a new kind of party rooted in actual working class struggles and aspirations. An *enquête* (investigation) was a short-term inquiry, not necessarily focused solely on the working class nor immersed in a space of labour. In Brazil Linhart relied on two guides, a young student Reynaldo and union activist Antonio, and spoke to people across a spectrum of classes. In the metaphoric typology of Mao's 1957 speech, it involved 'dismounting the horse to look at the flowers' as opposed to 'settling down'.

If in *L'établi* Linhart works solidly through a more ethnographic narrative fixed to the mise-en-scène of the factory floor, *The Sugar and the Hunger*'s visually fleeting style expresses its mobile and aleatory investigative form. Its 131 pages are split into 26 short, punctuated chapters which visually register a stream of different characters and scenes, building a momentum that integrates various scales of historical context, facts, worker and peasant testimonies and expert opinions, just as it is animated and undercut by a frequent descriptive zooming in and out of the cleaved social reality, an aesthetic that matches the uncertain political situation. This disjointed yet fluid style acts out the disjuncture of the encounter itself, of First World meeting its preconditions of violence and immiseration hidden away in the Third World.

This is aptly introduced in the prologue with the scene of driving in a car. Beatles songs and disco hits play as movie posters and golf club lawns pass by, whilst malnourished families set off to work. 'You pose questions about their living conditions. They give you short answers, disjointed phrases. And you understand, as they speak, that they are hungry, their women are hungry, their children are hungry'. Yet you carry on, 'the road, again, that takes you far away. For you, life continues'. As one interlocutor puts it: 'The hunger in the North-East will make the cars go around in the whole country'.

The explication of starvation as a constitutive pillar of imperial living elsewhere exposes the reader to formerly repressed and excluded zones of capital's violent operation, generating an expanded sense of the totality of capitalism through which a new solidarity can be developed. *L'établi* identified how Citroën extended globally to 'skim off the poverty of the most remote villages', both preserving and re-making it in the fine hierarchies and complex technical composition of the factory. *The Sugar and the Hunger* follows the commodity to its origin point of destitution and traces its entanglement in historical legacies of colonial chattel slavery and *latifundismo*, now dynamised by multinational capital and innovations in the internal combustion engine.

Through this abiding preoccupation with revolutionary and capitalist transitions, Linhart developed a sophisticated account of inter- and intra-class formations in their relation to technical changes in the production process, and ensuing divisions of labour, all within the neo-imperial realities of combined and uneven development. Early in his trip he is confronted with the complexity of agrarian class positions, registered in the proliferation of different terminology. Day labourers are colloquially referred to as *boias frias* (cold lunches) or more technically *clandestinos* for their lack of papers in comparison to *fichados* (contracted). *Caboclo* is a racialised term, originally meaning a mixed-race indigenous person. It now 'denotes a miserable peasant'. The Peasant Leagues chose the term *camponesa*, even if in Pernambuco their inter-class alliance was largely formed of landless workers, as well as small *posseiros* who held precarious land rights, and *corvée*-style sharecroppers too.

Steeped in the history of post-revolutionary Russia – his 1976 *Lénine, les paysans, Taylor* remains untranslated – Linhart developed a concept of class as above all a political process of shifting formations. Linhart suggests in his work that class struggle can only be understood concretely: fought out through particular lives, from particular positions and conditions of living, in decisions, places, historical conjunctures and mobile situations. This revolutionary imagination seemed only to have survived the 1970s through a committed experimentation with the method of investigation, which kept him in contact with the dynamics of different political movements. It was also the outcome of working through his early Althusserian theoreticism and Maoist immediation, whilst critiquing the disillusioned workerism that re-wrote the *établi* experience as bourgeois *Bildung*.

Importantly, compared to many of his contemporaries, since his early days at the *École normale supérieure* Linhart was an active participant and observer of revolutionary struggles outside of metropolitan France. As he put in an interview in 1977, 'I don't see myself as a child of 1968. I made my choice several years earlier, in the Algerian self-managed farms, then in the French and immigrant working class. I find justification for my adherence to Marxism in all that I have seen and lived over fifteen years, not in a supposed moment of unrest'.

In 1964 he visited Algeria, bringing back the Maoism that would lead him to the people's communes in China in 1967 alongside other UJCml militants. He again went to Algeria in 1974, and it was his direct involvement in the land reform process in southern Portugal after the Carnation Revolution in 1975 that led him to Brazil over the winter of 1976-77 and again in September of 1979. Rather than being forever tied to the drama of May '68 and the legend of French Maoism, Linhart's work might instead be seen in terms of his sustained commitment to communist encounter and concrete struggles – both urban and agrarian, often centred on transitions, and often to do with the 'Third World' as both place and project.

In 1980, in an interview included in the book, Linhart critiqued the 'wooden language, ideological simplifications, media hypes and abrupt amnesias' of French intellectual culture. He spoke about the need 'to invent a style, ways of functioning, a kind of credibility' – outside the pseudo-survival of Marxism in the university – that could produce 'a living culture of social analysis'. Yet this cultural emphasis avoids in a certain sense a more diffi-

cult question: what kind of organisational form might mediate this analysis as part of political struggle? Despite his engagements, by the late 1970s Linhart cuts a rather lonely figure. Working as an academic and economist, he individually continued with investigation but was unmoored from a party-form that was supposed to be constructed through such praxis and occupy an obstetric or editorial role vis a vis the working class.

The work of American anthropologist Nancy Scheper-Hughes, who conducted fieldwork in Pernambuco throughout the 1980s, also raises this issue of organisation. Focusing on the everyday violence of rampant childhood mortality and the 'death without weeping' that came with it, Scheper-Hughes was forced to rethink her assumed neutrality in response to interlocutors' outrage at her lack of participation and seeming indifference to their political struggles. In 1995 she called for a 'politically committed and morally engaged' 'militant anthropology', animated by the 'primacy of the ethical' through which individual ethnographers could act less like friends or colonial patrons, and more like comrades. If Linhart never shared this notion of anthropological or academic neutrality and viewed the problem of the traditional intellectual within firmly communist terms, both figures are nevertheless united by a concern to act in fidelity to the struggles of their interlocutors and the vicissitudes of the encounter. Both likewise leave open the question of a possible third *organisational* accountability, one that could house their commitment and put their inquiries to use beyond either the academy or public culture.

The Sugar and the Hunger represents the fruits of a long, difficult and patient course, or what Linhart referred to as the often 'circuitous path' of inquiry. In our moment of techno hype and fascist spectacle, and when left theory all too easily reproduces capital's own omnipotent self-image, this book is a timely methodological call to inquire into the concrete realities of working class experiences and struggles, as a political strategy. In an oblique way it also raises a question which can only be answered in practice: what organisational form might politically mediate and use such a method, and how might this form – of the party for instance – rescue a Marxism barely surviving in a now crumbling university system.

Jacob Seagrave

Years of lead, years of hope

Michael Hardt, *The Subversive Seventies* (New York: Oxford University Press, 2023). 312pp., £21.99 hb., 978 0 19767 467 3

Michael Hardt's latest book, *The Subversive Seventies*, is first and foremost an exercise in reclamation. 'Many of the progressive and revolutionary projects of the seventies today remain relatively unknown', he writes in the introduction, 'obscured or discounted in relation to the conventional images of the 60s.' Dominant interpretations of the decade tend to oscillate between the contention that nothing much happened, representing little more than the settling of the radical tides that crested in '68; or proffer a variation of what Hardt christens the 'good sixties/bad seventies' thesis, reflected in the titling of influential histories of the era, such as Todd Gitlin's shift from the 'years of hope' to the 'days of rage'. Whether ripped apart by the internal torsions of identity politics, crushed by overwhelming state repression, or trapped by the *cul-de-sac* of clandestine activity, such accounts present the movements of the era as cautionary tales.

Hardt's approach departs decisively from this *doxa*. Marshalling an impressive range of material with an emphatically internationalist orientation – from Angola and Nicaragua to South Korea and Germany – he renders a survey of the decade as a 'history of the present', positioning it as a 'vantage point from which to see more clearly what liberation movements can be and do today.' Licencing this is a contention that such movements are, fundamentally, our *contemporaries*, both in the theoretical questions their practices evoked – principally, how to coordinate across multiple struggles or axes of antagonism, and how to generate autonomous modes of organisation beyond the recuperative forces of parties and trade unions – and the context in which they did so. Unlike the sixties, which figures in this narrative as the culmination of a prior regime of accumulation and attendant cycles of struggles (civil rights, anticolonialism, industrial organising), the global recomposition of labour set in train in the 1970s produced the political and social space in which we operate today. What Hardt terms the 'end of mediation' – in which the institutionalised means of interest aggregation characteristic of the post-war settlement gave way to intensified exploitation, state repression, and political cartelisation – establishes an integral continuity between the two conjunctures, a shared baseline from which to interpret the efficacy of the tactics and strategies inventoried across the text.

In doing so, *The Subversive Seventies* constitutes an implicit contribution to the burgeoning literature concerned with the problem of organisation following the failure of both the 'horizontalist' and 'left-populist' currents of the 2000s and 2010s (works like Vincent Bevins' *If We Burn*, Jasper Bernes' *The Future of Revolution* and Isabelle Garo's *Communism and Strategy*). More specifically, there's a sense Hardt's restoration of the seventies is an attempt to interrupt what Rodrigo Nunes, in *Neither Horizontal Nor Vertical*, diagnosed as the double-melancholia of 1917 and 1968. Treating Wendy Brown and Jodi Dean's earlier theorisations of 'left-wing melancholia' as symptomatic mirror-images, Nunes considers the mutual recrimination between the pantomime roles of 'Stalinist' or 'anarchist' as prohibiting clear thinking about the limits of each organisational modality, with failure always externalised as the fault of the other's insufficient fidelity to one's preferred position. Hardt's selection of case studies confound any such simplistic organisational disjunction: we learn, for instance, of what he calls the 'double-organisation' or 'dual-strategy' of the Black Panthers, Autonomia and Turkey's Fatsa Commune, in which the centralising tendencies characteristic of quasi-militarised organs of self-defence existed alongside the democratic base-building of popular assemblies and community institutions. Such cases exemplify Nunes' injunction to cease thinking about organisation as the search for a discrete *form* appropriate to every and all situations, but instead as a balance of relative *forces* – centralisation/dispersal, coordination/autonomy, coherence/plurality – appropriate to a variable set of relations and problems.

Key to this is Hardt's adoption of an ecumenical approach, reflected in one of his central methodological principles, namely to 'analyse and appreciate revolutionary movements ... relatively independently from the resulting outcomes'. This generosity is most visible in his reconstruction of the rationale behind the pivot to armed struggle and terrorism, from the Weather Underground in the US and the East Asian Anti-Japan Armed Front, to the notorious Red Army Faction and Red Brigades of Germany and Italy. While Hardt is under no illusions as to the limits of these tactics – beyond the obvious ethical objections, he is astute on the isolationism engendered by their fugitivity, divorcing underground units from the pulse of the mass movement, and the unwinnable arms race of counter-repression it provokes – he is nevertheless able to illuminate them as a response to 'increased state and fascist violence in the late 1960s and early 1970s', epitomised by the shocking 'state massacres' carried out with impunity as part of the Italian government's 'strategy of tension' against the extra-parliamentary left.

Nevertheless, Hardt's analytical demarcation of a movements' potential from its resultant, and his correlative intention to distinguish (internal) failure from (external) defeat, sometimes truncates the discussions. This is evident in the chapters dedicated to encampments which sprung up against destructive infrastructural projects. For instance, opposition to the construction of Narita airport in Sanrizuka, Japan, provoked local residents into action; the arrival of student radicals and party militants shortly thereafter, intent on digging in for a long fight against 'militarist expansion', deepened their resistance and inaugurated a powerful alliance. It's clear that Hardt sees in their collaboration an exemplar of a call made in his 2017 work *Assembly* (co-written with Antonio Negri) for an inversion of the usual distribution of strategy and tactics in a movement, which sees the former the preserve of a prudent leadership, the latter appropriate to the instinctiveness of the base. At Narita, on the contrary, the tactical inclination toward nonviolence on the part of the locals gradually gave way to the 'students repertoire of confrontational practices', their vanguard-function operating only to distribute the technical knowledges developed through prior collisions with the state, preferring to defer to the residents when it came to strategy. Such originality notwithstanding, Hardt notes soberly a few pages later that 'the airport definitely opened in May 1978', the protesters turfed out by security forces. Thus the encampments failed to meet their goal, and failed in a predictable way, unable to extend beyond the immediate logic of defence and exceed their own half-life in a manner repeated by its descendents (the Standing Rock protests against the construction of the Dakota Access Pipeline, steamrolled by a Trump executive order in 2017, are instructive). One wonders whether that aforementioned distinction between failure and defeat is so easy to uphold, not least because defeat is rarely intelligible outside of the internal dynamics of the project to which it pertains. The question of how to negotiate the asymmetrical coercive capacity of the state is, of course, one that animates the logic of the vanguard, of Party, of centralising and generalising modes of organisation, and we do not have to fetishise such forms in order to recognise their attentiveness to this problem. Strategies and tactics, in other words, are not formulated in a vacuum, but ought to involve an attempt to anticipate the types of obstacles or counterforces thrown up in the course of a specific confrontation, especially when such obstacles are intelligible as structural features of the terrain itself. By side-stepping such questions, Hardt's generosity can come hand-in-hand with equivocation.

Hardt analyses these movements through the concepts actualised in their practices, thereby advancing an implicit model of theoretical production that elides the conventional division of labour between intellectual and militant, theorist and mass, and renders it as a product of the complex metabolism of movements themselves. In a pivotal chapter concerning the crisis of governability in industrial production we find the 'other' workers' movement, whose demands extended beyond that of conditions and wages 'to transform power relations within the factory and, at times, in society as a whole.' Disillusioned with the corruption of union bosses, itself derivative of their organisation's function in the reproduction of capital, a new generation of workers, horns sharpened by the struggles of the 60s, consistently challenged the corporatism of the established institutions, reacting against the discipline and hierarchisation which cohered the nexus of capital, state and union. Deprived of their ability to placate through conventional means, this political crisis precipitated capital's attempt to eliminate the workforce's structural leverage through 'the closure of factories, increased automation, the shift of industrial labor to subordinated parts of the world', and so on. Hardt draws on Grégoire Chayamou's work to index the panicked awareness of labour indiscipline in the political and management literature of the time, whilst sidelining other potential drivers of the reconstruction ('impending economic crises', creative destruction, etc). His reliance on workerist premises here is self-evident – specifically Mario Tronti's Copernican turn, which denied capital its principal status as motor of antagonism in favour of labour – but never explicitly argued for; the effect being that those already unconvinced by the framework have little reason to change their mind.

Nevertheless, this is not always the case. Hardt is at his most incisive in analysing the instituent creativity of many of these movements, for whom an antagonism toward the established modalities of struggle was not tantamount to a rejection of organisation as such, but an imperative to generate new forms adequate to their horizons. Hardt tracks the prevalence of various participatory structures – for instance in Portugal's Carnation Revolution of 1974, whereby a latticework of direct-democratic residents, workers and peasants councils portended the arrival of a 'Lisbon Commune' large enough to seize power – capable of interlocking and scaling across spatial or thematic differences; as well as the administration of counter-institutions, capable of fulfilling state-functions from welfare to education to housing. This implies an effective retort to the Italian philosopher Roberto Esposito's somewhat limp rendition of 'instituent praxis', often counterposed to Negri's work. For Esposito, the reduction of institutions to a static and dominatory function, rigid operators of sovereign command on the model of Hobbes or Hegel, effaces their potential dynamism and emancipatory generativity. But this correction comes wrapped in a post-Marxist social ontology derived from Claude Lefort and Maurice Merleau-Ponty, amongst others, which tends to divorce institutions from the antagonistic rhythm of class struggle and the conditions imposed by the problem of material reproduction. The inadequacy of this framework is clarified when pitched against that of Hardt's protagonists, for whom radical democratic institutional forms are almost always constructed as a means to address collective material needs during the convulsions of a determinate struggle, an improvisational project which rapidly becomes hitched to revolutionary horizons. In this respect Hardt's argument once again dovetails with his and Negri's earlier *Assembly*, in which the problem of constructing 'nonsovereign institutions' is integral to surpass the ephemerality of horizontalism. The gestural elision of the distinction between theory and practice enables Hardt to escape the reformist pull of Esposito's work, restoring to these debates a proximity to revolutionary movements.

The strength of *The Subversive Seventies* lies in this proximity. As the centre continues its death-spiral and the right consolidates hegemony over the articulation of various late capitalist dislocations, a pivot towards a previous era of political possibility, one whose basic structure overlaps with our own, is much-needed. The chapter on the liberation movements against Portuguese colonialism in Mozambique, Angola and Guinea-Bissau is exemplary here. In the absence of established mechanisms of mediation under the comparatively thin conditions of Portuguese domination, less able to establish effective incorporative structures and more willing to rely upon sheer might, Amilcar Cabral and other revolutionary leaders confronted this institutional abyss as an opportunity. Hence the emergence of a theory of 'revolutionary democracy' and 'popular power' as leapfrogging 'European liberal democratic society', whose institutional expression took the form of participatory village action committees which expanded via delegation along both lateral and vertical axes. It is interesting to note here the importance of a vanguard-form to this process, in which revolutionary parties had to take the near universal 'poverty and illiteracy as its point of departure and build from there a capacity for self-government.'

Whatever the fate of these sequences (Hardt brackets a consideration of the regimes to which they gave rise), the basic problem they faced – how to institute forms of antagonistic collective life without the affordances of prior modalities – thus mirrors our own moment more accurately than, say, the analyses of autonomous workers movements at the acme of Fordism. Such forms had the luxury of a dialectical relation to constituted power; they were versed in traditions of association and habits of struggle on which they could draw, an inheritance preserved (and consequently reified) by the bureaucratised mass institutions against which they could launch. It was this context that forged many of these radical instituent experiments, as revolutions within the revolution; and as the process of disintermediation that Hardt narrates has intensified, the 'hollowing out' of representative institutions catalysed by the anti-social tendencies of communicative capital, we now have no choice but to circumvent this first stage, to massify from the bottom upwards in an attempt to maintain some semblance of the front-foot against the encirclement of reaction. If the political scientist Peter Mair once characterised the empty carapace of contemporary bourgeois democracy as 'ruling the void', it is perhaps in this that we find Hardt's enduring lesson: that the 'void here, in other words, implies potential autonomy and opportunity for invention', a space to 'transform the meaning of democracy, build it from the ground up, and give it a profoundly revolutionary direction.'

Trey Taylor

Abolition as method

David Gordon Scott, ed., *Abolitionist Voices* (Bristol: Bristol University Press, 2025). 324pp., £90.99 hb., 978 1 52922 403 0

David Gordon Scott and Emma Bell, eds., *Envisioning Abolition* (Bristol: Bristol University Press, 2025). 360pp., £90.99 hb., 987 1 52923 477 0

In May 2025, Lord Chancellor Shabana Mahmood announced that the UK was facing 'a total breakdown of law and order'. The cause? In Mahmood's analysis, a prison estate that has failed to grow at the rate of the incarcerated population, which has nearly doubled since 1990. Her solution? The most significant programme of prison building and expansion since the Victorian era.

For some arms of the state, the size of a population clearly determines the scale of infrastructure required to serve it. In this, Mahmood riffs on an intuitive theme: just as young people need places in nurseries and classrooms and the elderly need access to healthcare, in her account, the incarcerated need spaces in prisons. But ageing is different from criminality. One is an inevitable process; the other is just a very effective idea. The category of crime is a moveable one, and the responses it prompts are similarly unfixed. Yet when Mahmood projects growth in the prison population – to some 100,000 by 2029 – she does so in the register of the inevitable. The timely publication of *Abolitionist Voices* and *Envisioning Abolition* invites us instead to think in the register of the provisional.

These texts are a welcome addition to the fast-growing literature on prison abolition. Though released together, each volume has a distinct aim. *Abolitionist Voices*, edited by David Scott, is the more general of the two. Through theoretical and practical chapters that cover figures from Friedrich Nietzsche to Angela Davis, geographies from Argentina to Canada, and methods from phenomenology to eco-criticism, its contributors offer access to abolitionist perspectives both established and emergent. The key structuring idea for this volume is, in Scott's terms, the 'abolitionist rhizome' – a decentralised, horizontal network of interplay, independence and exchange. While *Abolitionist Voices* takes on this expansive view, *Envisioning Abolition*, co-edited by Scott with Emma Bell, homes in on a single nodular cluster: libertarian socialist thought between the late eighteenth and early twentieth centuries. Though thematically targeted, the expertise collected in the volume is, once again, vast. Focussed on Europe and the United States, its contributors re-examine activist-theorists of socialism, communism and anarchism, bringing historical writings and case studies into conversation with contemporary analysis. Both volumes have much to offer us at this moment.

Where Shabana Mahmood so confidently deploys the category of the incarcerated criminal, *Envisioning Abolition* operates in a historical context where large-scale imprisonment was still in a primordial state of strangeness. It offers the reader access to a time before crime and punishment had solidified in the imagination. This defamiliarisation is, I feel, the volume's greatest achievement. Take, for instance, Ruby Tuke's excellent chapter on William Godwin, a contemporary of two more high-profile figures in the history of British incarceration, Jeremy Bentham and John Howard. Tuke's chapter shows us that, at a point remembered for that divide between punitive and reformative models of the prison, Godwin was forming a wider critique: first, that legal and political institutions not only define crime, but produce it, and second, that punishment is not a resolution to harm, but a recapitulation of it. On the prison specifically, Tuke describes how Godwin 'finds it almost impossible to imagine how offenders could be improved by removing the care and positive influence of others'. This remains a striking critique, further explored in the contemporary feminist literature by figures like Gwenola Ricordeau and Mariame Kaba. A compelling guide through Godwin's thought, Tuke leaves the reader with a sense of the criminal justice system as made rather than simply received.

While those interested in contemporary abolitionist work may have encountered the shapes of Godwin's critiques elsewhere, *Envisioning Abolition* will also introduce such readers to new lines of inquiry. The impressive chapter from Federico Testa, on nineteenth-century philosopher Jean-Marie Guyau's critique of sanction, is especially interesting in this regard. With clear and effectively structured writing, Testa introduces us to Guyau's moral critique of punishment, a welcome addition to abolitionist studies which tend to be, for good reason, sociological and contextual. Central to Guyau's thought, Testa describes, is a division between *will* and *sensibility*. While it's tempting to link together chains of vice and suffering, goodness and pleasure, Guyau argues that moral conduct and bodily or emotional feeling are separate. As Testa explains, Guyau understands legal punishment, being directed towards the body, as affecting only a tool rather than the will of the subject who controls it. Legal sanctions, then, do not reach their necessary target: an individual's centre of moral deliberation. Ineffective, punishment of this kind can only be gratuitously cruel. Testa's analysis of Guyau's moral vocabulary stands out among the many excellent chapters as a particularly incisive contribution.

The goals of *Envisioning Abolition* seem aimed in two directions. The first are historical; the second, coalitional. Let's consider each in turn. There is a certain energy to be drawn from the longstanding (or forgotten) abolitionist critiques of the past. And yet, these historical examples leave us with a vexing question: if abolitionist critiques have persisted and resisted for centuries, why, then, do prison systems continue to expand? Penny A. Weiss' chapter on Emma Goldman makes this frustration clear:

> We know what oppression does to some and what privilege does to others. We know what capitalism wants from its workers, as we know what patriarchy demands of each sex. We do not know what we might become if such things, including prisons, were to disappear as our commitments grow to human rights, freedom, individuality, equality, and the satisfaction of basic human needs. Yet, this is what Goldman dared to imagine.

Chapters like Weiss' show us that critics have long known the prison to be a failure, whether measured against either its own aims, or those of an equitable and flourishing community. While the volume offers many moving calls to action, critique and connection, I feel it could have been enhanced by engaging the question of why abolitionist thought has not – in neither these historical contexts, nor today – acquired more widespread political traction. In fairness, one answer to this problem is suggested by the volume's second, coalitional aim. In Scott and Bell's words, this collection advances the idea of 'libertarian socialism' by presenting 'visions of freedom and justice that reach across the divide between anarchists, Marxists and democratic socialists'. While perhaps a factor, division on the left does not seem to me a fulsome explanation for abolitionism's lack of widespread popularity. This aside, the collection's 'abolition in red and black' has its own internal rifts. Its unity is most convincing when undertaking abolition's critical tasks, and less so for its constructive ones. In other words, the volume effectively critiques incarceration but is less persuasive when imagining ways forward without it. While many chapters offer compelling (yet also sensitive and thoughtful) treatments of their material, some interventions may come across to the reader as combative and ideologically heavy-handed. That both *Envisioning Abolition* and *Abolitionist Voices* include chapters on the life and writings of anarcho-communist Pyotyr Kropotkin is an interesting editorial quirk. But more interesting still are these chapters' distinct approaches. While I found Ruth Kinna's contribution on Kropotkin constructive and enriching, Robert D. Weide's framing of contemporary abolitionism – as suffering variably from the 'myopia' of foregrounding chattel slavery in the American context, the 'glaring deficiency' of not referencing Kropotkin in general, and the possibility of Marxist scholars 'intentionally excluding Kropotkin's work' – came across as unnecessarily hostile. This somewhat antagonistic approach seemed out of step with the 'rhizomic' ideals of the volume.

In aiming to bring together a scattered political cluster, there is more than one point of tension in the project. A key disagreement within 'libertarian socialism' as gathered here is over the role of government, with the anarchist contributions tending to be quite absolute: prison abolition entails state abolition. This argument runs through much of the volume, but it would perhaps need to be more clearly developed to sway a reader not already committed to anarchist thought. Those chapters advocating for an abolitionism aimed at both state and prison did not convincingly connect the two ideas, nor flesh out how they might be made material. Though Scott and Bell offer some commentary on this disagreement over the state in their opening chapter, I remain unconvinced that the difference can be, as they suggest, transcended. The volume would have been enhanced by a fuller treatment – perhaps by building further on Davide Turcato's illuminating description of Errico Malatesta's 'anarchy as method' – as to how 'libertarian socialism' can proceed in the constructive tasks of abolition without consensus on this issue.

The diverse contributions to *Abolitionist Voices* provide a satisfying counterpoint to the focus of *Envisioning Abolition*. Again, there are a number of excellent chapters to digest. Lisa Guenther's chapter on phenomenology is an extremely sophisticated methodological piece, and Joy James reflects compellingly on the contradictions and challenges of movement-building. Other chapters offer valuable points of entry into specific critical lenses, with Hannah Bowman's chapter on Christianity and Thalia Anthony and Harry Blagg's on colonial carcerality both providing a thought-provoking balance of breadth and depth. Nathan Stephens-Griffin and Andrew Brock's chapter on eco-abolition is a welcome inclusion alongside Valeria Wegh Weis' grounded analysis of Southern abolitionist feminism. Though rich with ideas, *Abolitionist Voices* is not without its peculiarities. In its selection and interpretation of sources, unusual definitions of key terms, and lack of examples pertinent to the abolitionist context, I felt that Michael Dellwing's chapter could have benefitted from further methodological and argumentative scrutiny in the editorial process. At times, Dellwing's text veers into the conspiratorial (see discussion of the Uyghurs' persecution in China as an American 'invention'), and its argument is unevenly applied (as in its discussion of a programme screened on the state outlet *Russia Today*, despite arguing throughout against state media in general). I would encourage the reader to approach the sources and debates Dellwing invokes with a critical eye.

Where contributions to *Envisioning Abolition* tended to place high faith in the ability of anti-capitalist structures to dramatically reduce social harm, *Abolitionist Voices* reminds us that anti-capitalism, while important, will not solve everything. Sexual, racial, gender-based and anti-queer violence, for instance, could well endure in a world without capitalism. As Viviane Saleh-Hanna's chapter emphasises, profit fuels violence but

does not fully explain it. Both our capacities to hurt and the reach of state punishment exceed the logics we use to understand them. Having breadth of analysis is, then, imperative. Though containing many excellent and highly developed chapters, I wonder if *Abolitionist Voices*, as a general text, might have benefited from some further contributions to give the reader a wider sense of the 'rhizome' it addresses. For those interested in exploring further, the *Routledge International Handbook of Penal Abolition*, edited by Michael J. Coyle and David Scott (2021), has a broad geographic reach and some highly instructive, if shorter, contributions from approaches less represented in *Abolitionist Voices*, including from critical disability, incarcerated and queer theorists.

At a moment in which the powers of state punishment are expanding through both familiar and newfound techniques, *Envisioning Abolition* and *Abolitionist Voices* make timely and thought-provoking interventions. Effectively countering the politics of punishment while offering their readers numerous avenues to explore further, these volumes promise to enliven many an abolitionist imagination.

Isabella Gregory

Minor premises

Andrés Saenz de Sicilia, *Subsumption in Kant, Hegel and Marx: From the Critique of Reason to the Critique of Society* (Leiden: Brill, 2025) 260pp., £120.00 hb., 978 9 00471 382 6

The term 'subsumption', literally meaning 'taking under', first emerged in thirteenth-century scholastic philosophy to describe the logical subordination of a particular to a universal. In the syllogism, *All human beings are mortal; I am a human being; therefore, I am mortal*, the minor premise, 'I am a human being', thus represents the 'subsumption' of a particular term (me) under a general one (humanity). How, then, did 'subsumption' also come to describe the processes whereby a peasant family agrees to spin consignments of wool for a local merchant, or a team of graphic designers gets laid off when their firm invests in image-generating software? Moreover, what are the stakes of grasping the connection between this logical operation and such economic processes as more than some baroque metaphor or etymological coincidence?

As Andrés Saenz de Sicilia argues in his new book *Subsumption in Kant, Hegel and Marx*, Karl Marx's appropriation of the term 'subsumption' to describe capital's control and transformation of commodity production was premised on the profound reconfiguration of this concept within post-Kantian philosophy. What is ultimately at stake for Saenz de Sicilia in this conceptual history is a deeper understanding of the 'logic' of capital and a clearer sense of how it might be overcome. The book accordingly has a double aim: first, to retrace subsumption's theorisation and problematisation within Immanuel Kant's and Georg Wilhelm Friedrich Hegel's systems in order to contextualise Marx's deployment of the concept; and second, to elaborate a more comprehensive theory of subsumption as a dynamic of social reproduction, going beyond Marx's narrower account of capital's subsumption of the labour process. For Saenz de Sicilia, Marx's account has continually led to reductive interpretations of capital's logic as being or having become non-contradictory and self-identical, which in turn have occasioned various 'moralisms of the abstract/concrete' that repudiate the very terms of dialectical thought as oppressively all-subsuming. He therefore seeks both to address misunderstandings of the concept and to redress the limitations of Marx's account that inspire such forms of dogmatic speculative closure and naïvely terminological resistance.

The first chapter traces the development of the notion of subsumption in Kant and Hegel's thought. Kant takes the structure of judgment in a syllogism's minor premise as 'the model for [his] entire theory of rational cognition', yet crucially, subsumption here also becomes a process of 'form-determination' that actively shapes the representations and concepts that it connects. Even the universal categories of experience do not pre-exist this process but are only actualised through it. Accordingly, the totality of an individual's experience must be understood as something they themselves produce, or as what Saenz de Sicilia terms a 'compositional totality'. Hegel's subsequent critique of Kant then shows how the subject of judgment is itself processual and social. Hegel thus demotes subsumption from the model of cognition in general to merely one moment of the derivation and development of the compositional totality of the universal collective structures that subsume and actualise individuals. Although neither Kant's nor Hegel's philosophical treatment of subsumption was immediately the model for Marx's account of the subsumption of labour under capital, Hegel's notion of subsumption under objective social forms was a foundational insight, while subsequent debates over the speculative closure of Hegel's system were the matrix for Marx's development of historical materialism.

This development is then traced in the second chapter, which documents how, from the early 1840s, Marx 'adopts a series of increasingly coherent and comprehensive conceptual frameworks ... moving from *praxis* to *production/consumption* and finally to *social reproduction*'. For Saenz de Sicilia, these frameworks nonetheless remain essentially consistent in their materialism. He quickly skates over the significance of the theorisation of 'modes of production', much debated as *the* key critical break in Marx's thought, turning instead to Bolívar Echeverría's reinterpretation of Marx's thought as a unified philosophical anthropology of 'social reproduction'. Admittedly, amidst this rich genealogy, the thread of subsumption is sometimes entirely lost, yet one payoff of rehearsing Marx's theoretical career is the bold argument that historical materialism requires something like a general theory of human nature, and that Marx's critique of capital furnishes us with 'transhistorical' yet 'open' concepts of social being – such as 'social reproduction', but also, more controversially, 'use-value' and 'concrete labour' – which are necessary for historicising capitalist social forms and, by the same token, making non-capitalist and post-capitalist societies conceivable.

Following this exhaustive conceptual-historical groundwork, the latter two chapters then constitute the book's theoretical core, clarifying and extending Marx's account of capitalist subsumption. The detailed exposition of this account in the third chapter is unequivocally the book's strongest section. For readers without the patience to parse through the dense philosophical excursus of the book's first hundred-odd pages, it is also, gratefully, quite portable. After briefly discussing commodification as a more elementary subsumption of the 'socio-natural' category of use value under the value-form, Saenz de Sicilia surveys the three forms of the subsumption of labour under capital described by Marx: *formal*, *real* and *hybrid*. Throughout, he emphasises that 'the distinction between these forms of subsumption is neither an empirical typology nor a historical periodization of different forms of capitalist production'. This criticism of periodising interpretations of subsumption will be familiar to any reader of the journal *Endnotes*. More illuminating is Saenz de Sicilia's framing of its different forms as 'strategies' of capital accumulation that coexist, often in competition or combination. Formal subsumption entails a capitalist's direct ownership of a previously non-capitalist production process and the supervision of waged workers. Here, capital extracts absolute surplus-value by extending working hours, increasing the pace of production, or expanding its scale, though 'the specific material-practical content of the activity undertaken by the worker remains unchanged from its pre-capitalist form'. Real subsumption is then 'the transformation of the material content and technical structure of the labour process in order to increase productivity ... through the implementation of co-operation, divisions of labour, [and] machinery'. Such tactics for extracting both relative surplus-value and greater absolute surplus-value are widespread even before extensive mechanisation. Lastly, with hybrid forms of subsumption, 'surplus-value is 'extorted' by capitalists without the production process being even formally subsumed to their command' and 'without the mediation of a direct wage', generally operating instead through relations of debt or bondage. As Saenz de Sicilia emphasises, drawing on Jairus Banaji's work, 'hybrid forms must be grasped not simply as residual forms of exploitation but as a permanently present strategy of exclusion and outsourcing that is functional for capital as a response to both cost-cutting imperatives and class resistance'. Hence, if it is ultimately more profitable, a branch of production will remain only formally subsumed or may even revert to a hybrid form.

As incisive as this survey of Marx's account of subsumption is, Saenz de Sicilia's tendency to avoid robustly engaging with other commentators and broader debates in favour of pursuing his own theoretical reconstruction becomes somewhat frustrating here. Major interpretive claims about Marx's account and its place within the broader structure of his critique of political economy, as well as key divergences of interpretation among scholars, are too often only mentioned in passing or relegated to footnotes. For instance, Saenz de Sicilia does not delve into why Marx 'almost completely eradicated' his discussion of subsumption from the published version of *Capital* and instead concluded with the section on primitive accumulation. Yet whether Marx did this for conceptual, structural or logistical reasons strongly determines whether we should understand the relationship between these two accounts as contradictory, duplicative or complementary. Saenz de Sicilia has only a cursory and eclectic discussion of primitive accumulation, and the thorny questions of capitalism's origins and primitive accumulation's 'ongoingness' remain bracketed by abstract pronouncements against periodising schemas. This is particularly disappointing because his own discussion of hybrid forms of labour's subsumption under capital might have equipped him to wade into these debates and help clarify some important theoretical and historiographical questions. Indeed, one crucial affordance of theorising hybrid subsumption is the ability to then specify the *capitalist* character of patterns of production beyond heavily industrialised regions and outside formally waged sectors, such as colonial uses of indentured or enslaved labour, both during and after any singular 'transition'.

In the book's fourth chapter, Saenz de Sicilia turns to developing his own theory of subsumption as a dynamic of social reproduction. For him, Marx's account is limited insofar as it is only expounded at the level of individual capital rather than total social capital, and it reflects a 'discursive tension' between Marx's revolutionary orientation and his 'capital-centric' systematicity, which 'lends itself to functionalist reductions of class struggle and social reproduction'. A less economistic, more politicised theory of subsumption thus requires 'undoing the "tendential" or "provisional" closure' of Marx's account and developing a more dynamic one beyond the immediate process of production. Saenz de Sicilia also finally offers some robust engagement with other theorists of subsumption here, critiquing several for likewise succumbing to either 'diachronic' or 'synchronic' forms of speculative closure. Reproducing an argument popularised by *Endnotes*, he debunks the crudely stageist notion of 'total subsumption' – that is, of 'the historical completion or totalization of capitalist subsumption ... across the full compass of human life' – exemplified by Theodor Adorno and Antonio Negri; although, as he sharply observes, this notion remains the 'regulative idea' of most discussions of late capitalism. He then considers the synchronic closure of Chris Arthur's 'systematic dialectics', where the 'hyper-idealized' presentation of capitalist society as a 'closed logical totality' precludes 'theoretical comprehension of concrete development ... and systemic change'. Although this critique of synchronic closure is rather telegraphic – and notably, the discussion of Moishe Postone promised in the introduction never appears – it is worth recalling his earlier recuperation of Marx's philosophical anthropology, according to which capitalist forms subsume transhistorical features of social reproduction and therefore retain an immanently antagonistic and transformable character. The logical functionalism characteristic of 'value-form theory' more generally is thus rooted in a one-sided conception of capitalist society and its categories as absolutely subsumed, severing any ability to effectively historicise and resulting either in fatalistic depoliticisation or in a compensatory fetishisation of capitalism's 'outside'.

But what, in the end, is Saenz de Sicilia's theory of subsumption? He distinguishes three levels of subsumption operative in capitalist society: first, the elementary subsumption of 'socio-natural' objects through commodification; second, the three forms of the capitalist subsumption of labour in production; and third, the subsumption of social reproduction *tout court* under capital's relentless drive towards accumulation. Insofar as the dynamic of subsumption thus traverses every level of capitalist society, it must be recognised as '*the* concept of capitalist domination as such'. Beyond positing this new schema, however, it would be more accurate to say that he merely stipulates the criteria of an 'open' and 'dynamic' theory of subsumption that would resist diachronic or synchronic closure. This speculative project also bears a strong family resemblance to Søren Mau's *Mute Compulsion* (2023), which likewise offers a more expansive account of subsumption, critiques the abstract formalism of many value-form theorists from the perspective of a Marxian philosophical anthropology, and attempts to develop a new concept for capital's total – yet, crucially, not absolute – domination of our life-world through its stranglehold on social reproduction.

Yet the affinity between Saenz de Sicilia's and Mau's projects also prompts the question of whether it is really necessary to rethink Marx's critique of capital through this one particular Marxian concept rather than another, such as Mau's 'economic power'. Indeed, while it may make logical sense to speak of capital's subsumption of objects other than the labour process, doing so may also sacrifice much of the term's analytical precision – especially as Saenz de Sicilia himself admits that 'the classification of the forms of subsumption loses its explanatory power beyond the immediate process of production'. Moreover, his condemnation of 'speculative closure' at times verges into its own 'moralism of the abstract/concrete', and in emphasising the non-teleological character of the dynamic of subsumption, he arguably underrates its path-dependency, notably omitting any discussion of the rising organic composition of capital and the profit-rate's tendency to fall, as well as any engagement with crisis theory. Another significant omission here is any serious engagement with Marxist feminism, all the more surprising given that 'social reproduction' is the cornerstone of his rethinking of subsumption. Ultimately, however, such frustrations and disappointments index the fruitfulness of Saenz de Sicilia's intervention as both a definitive clarification and a provocative challenge for contemporary Marxist theorists. To embrace a more utopian form of speculative closure, then, perhaps this work may one day prove to have been a minor premise in a more practical syllogism: the revolutionary deduction that capital – as a logic, as a mode of social reproduction, as the tyrannical accumulation of humanity's own dead labour – is also mortal.

Christopher Geary

It's all in the landing

Melyana Kay Lamb, *Philosophical History of Police Power* (London, Bloomsbury Academic, 2024). 220pp., £85.00 hb., 28.99 pb., 978 1 35020 404 1 hb., 978 1 35020 408 9 pb.

In the aftermath of a series of large pro-Palestine protests in the UK in 2024, the Metropolitan Police spokesperson responsible for protests, Matt Twist, gave an interview to the right-wing think tank the Policy Exchange, where he admitted that the police had not got everything right, but rejected that there were double standards when it came to policing certain groups over others. Much criticism of the police from the right has argued that there is a two-tier system. Leftist causes like BLM, environmental issues or Palestine protests are allowed to disrupt the general public, they claim, while patriotic causes are harshly policed. Twist rejected this, arguing that, in fact, there were infinite tiers of policing.

This phrase has stuck with me. It might be dismissed

as the vacuous ramblings of a bureaucrat who excels in saying absolutely nothing, but in attempting to say nothing Twist has accidentally arrived at a cogent description of the reality of policing. The received wisdom about police power is that the democratic organs of the state make laws, and the dutiful public servants of the police merely enforce them, in a value neutral manner. Yet even the most ardent cheerleaders of state violence cannot feasibly claim that there is only one, unified form of policing. Policing instead is something so dispersed and omnipresent that it is infinite in form and appearance. In order to understand the infinity of policing, we must try, as Goethe argued, to approach the finite from all sides.

Lamb's *Philosophical History of Police Power* is such an attempt. She argues that despite the presence of police power in our lives, policing has been incorrectly theorised. Consequently, political philosophy inevitably finds itself in a quagmire of aporia and contradiction without a theorisation of police power, which she adeptly demonstrates with readings of Hobbes and Foucault, Hegel and Fichte, Schmitt, Benjamin and Agamben, and da Silva.

Serious critique of the police is frequently cast as an extremist position, but I would argue that the police are the most universally repudiated of institutions, maybe only matched by border guards. Yet you will find few introductions to political theory that fail to mention policing at all, aside from reading Hegel's *Philosophy of Right*, accompanied by an explanation that policing (*Polizei*) and police are very different, with policing referring to ordering and police the formal institution of police. One important rejoinder that Lamb makes early on is that this reading, which is heavily influenced by Foucault, diffuses an analysis of the police, so that the locus and power of the discrete institution itself is lost, and we move further, rather than closer, to a critique of police violence and power.

Lamb argues that theories of the police often historicise moments of rupture. Foucault is the most egregious of these, but Lamb artfully shows that Hobbes makes the same, widely accepted, claim despite the shaky ground that such a supposition rests on. Hobbes saw himself as making a fundamental break with the Aristotelian anthropology, which saw humans as political animals (*zoon politkon*) that mediates conflict through collective discussion. For Aristotle, order is the natural state. 'It is supposedly in Hobbes we find the transition from a natural/divine order to one that is "produced" – a transition, moreover, which has been widely understood as inaugurating the modern phenomenon of police.' For Hobbes, the Leviathan figure restrains the barbaric state of nature. The connection to the police is ingenious. Reading Hobbes against himself, Lamb rejects this typical reading, and shows that Hobbes' Leviathan does not abolish the violence of the state of nature, but rather subsumed it into his power. Hobbes' state appears historically after the state of nature, creating a fission between order and nature. Crucially, Hobbesian order 'becomes an incessant activity, and indeed the proof and product of a sovereign will.' The sovereign cannot, constitutionally, be condemned by the law, even for murder, and this is itself the foundational power of the police.

The chapter discussing Hegel and Fichte makes a similar move. In Hegel's *Philosophy of Right* the state and civil society emerge as opposites. For Hegel, this is a split between 'the sphere of the universal, that is the state, and the sphere of the particular, which is comprised of atomistic individuals in civil society.' The state can no longer be thought of as the point of discussion and action, but instead is extrinsic to the body politic, a point of mediation between factions that cannot feasibly directly communicate over every challenge, necessitating a mediating police power.

Hegel's notions of the police become clearest, for Lamb, in contrast to Fichte. Hegel, in *Philosophy of Right* sees *Polizei* as a 'union of security and welfare, an administration of civil society that raises it from the level of particularity to universality.' Fichte, on the other hand, sees '*Polizei* as a securitarian power designed to prevent the possibility of crime occurring.' Fichte's police force would be one that must always exert itself in protecting the rights of citizens, and they must command obedience. Fichte argued that for this to happen, citizens would have to be always transparent to the police, for example, by carrying a light with them in the dark or carrying identification.

Hegel fiercely rejects this, arguing it would produce 'a world of galley slaves' but Lamb argues that the authoritarian and totalising elements that Hegel strongly reacts to in Fichte's analysis are also present in his own. For Lamb, Hegel and Fichte are both concerned with the mediation of the universal state and the individual, and she shows that their thinking around the state of exception is closer than either thinker might like to admit. Police power, for Hegel, must also be unrestrained and omnipresent, especially in the state of emergency.

Lamb's argument is laid out with the precision of a lawyer. Every chapter is clearly signposted giving the text a tight flow. Few readers can expect to have Lamb's granular knowledge of each of these thinkers, so it is a welcome, if slightly unrelenting, structure. In just over 200 pages Lamb blasts through some of the most troublesome thinkers in the canon, and this can produce moments where this leads to conclusions that feel overly abstract, if not downright prosaic. Theoretical abstraction is an important method, but a work that remains at this register for too long can seem divorced from the life-denying violence it is discussing.

The chapter on Agamben is the most gnomic of these. I find Lamb's aim compelling. Trying to find a line between Schmitt and Agamben, who both theorise the state of exception, she charges Schmitt with a totalising notion of the emergency, such that it cannot exist in a meaningful, everyday way even under totalitarianism. Agamben attempts to redress the balance, but cannot escape the categories of law, meaning that attributes of normal law like the prison or the police do not fall within the state of exception at all. The most prevailing question of political philosophy is how can legitimate power be justified, and in Lamb's view Agamben effectively normalises the exceptional racist violence of the state that deviant racialised minorities live under.

Early on she explains her method, writing that she is not interested in a genealogical search for origins, or an etymological analysis of the police, but rather, qua Agamben's method, a philosophical analysis of the 'metaphysical grounds operative within political structures.' She terms this a philosophical history, clearly thinking with Agamben's historico-philosophical method in *Homo Sacer*, although it is unclear what the difference is. Both attempt to disrupt a historical narrative of mechanistic cause and effect, and complexify political sovereignty through an understanding of continuities that are as

much disrupted as they are continuous, showing how 'what is usually presented as secondary or derivative is in fact a founding power itself' so that we can think 'differently about the ontologies of power.' Unlike, for example, Mark Neocleous' work on the police, she is not so much interested in the 'historical specificities of *the police as institution* in different geographical and temporal contexts', but rather the metaphysical heritage of state violence.

This strikes me as a more limited, and less novel, approach than she makes it sound. Are the historical specificities so separable from the metaphysical heritage of state violence? Is this even a meaningful distinction? Agamben's historical method has been heavily criticised, in part because it can feel like his philosophy leaves little room for nuance or incompleteness, but also because he seems to tend towards passivity over action. We live in a time where police power has become a central topic of concern – in part evidenced by the many works dealing with this question, including Lamb's, as well as events outside the academy.

I welcome an approach that tries to understand the 'specificity of police as a concept and as an institution', rather than devolving in to the undifferentiated theory of power that Foucault theorised. However, in adopting Agamben's approach, some of the original criticisms that Foucault articulated in his own analysis of the police seem to return. Policing *does* seem to happen through various institutions, some of which are not clearly identifiable as police. Take for example, the case of teachers in the UK. Educators have a legal duty to report extremist views, which has included support for environmental movements, legally protected criticism on Israel, and, perhaps most importantly, ensnared many Muslim students in the bureaucracy and secrecy of anti-terrorism. Migrant students are surveilled through registers, which are submitted to the Home Office. The abolitionist Ruth Wilson Gilmore, certainly no Foucauldian, calls this process deputisation, and points out that in fulfilling these duties, an expanding group of people have effectively been made to carry out the function of the police, even if they don't carry a badge. What is their role in the mediation between transcendence and immanence? How do these non-cop cops project the mythos of sovereignty and government? These questions are left unresolved by Lamb's relatively sparse definition of the police.

The concluding section of the book takes the phrase 'no drugs were found', which for Lamb becomes 'an excuse invoked in a process of ritual myth making.' For me, this misses something substantial and reproduces the Agamben's messianism and passivity. For Lamb, the claim that no drugs were found takes on the reverence of a prayer, absolving the police and assuaging the public that violent and invasive searches were justified because there *could* have been drugs, even when there were not. Couldn't we have another reading, one which motivates a praxis of resistance against the police? The statement could remain an expression of foundational sovereign power, but less a homily and more an insult – a lie so naked that it dares you to object, a fuck you. Wouldn't this be a more accurate understanding? It would also explain other justifications for police violence: resisting arrest; in fear for my life, etc. In this way, the same expressions of foundational sovereign power are outside the law but can be radicalised into an inducement. The more power is used the greater the resistance. Blackness, especially in the Black Radical Tradition, took on a revolutionary power because of the injustices that black people were subject to. The injustice of society, which necessitate police violence, is negated by a subject formation that emerges against police violence. Placing the illocutionary acts of the police as part of a transcendence obscures the immanence of their power, taking the speech act to be primary to the act itself.

Despite my scepticism of the Agambenian approach, there remains much to take away from Lamb's text. The interpretations are extremely sharp, and the analysis of police power in relation to sovereignty is advanced through her work. Her critique of the colonial boomerang explanation of racist police violence convincingly shows its insufficiency. Using da Silva's work, Lamb shows that thinking of colonial power as a 'frontier of new technologies of subjugation that eventually find their way back into the metropole', as Foucault and Marx did, falsely creates a prehistorical outside that reifies a false European exceptionalism. Once again, for Lamb, the genealogical approach fails to explain police power. Police violence becomes something that emerged 'back then', 'over there', an artifact of a more violent and unfair time, rather than a central component of contemporary police power. However, there are ample examples of precisely this sort of interplay, which few people would see as unidirectional.

Other works of police critique, such as Mark Neocleous' recent *Pacification*, Anna Feigenbaum's *Tear Gas* or Leah Cowan's *Why Would Feminists Trust the Police?* show a level of sophistication in discussing this question that cannot be wholly rejected by Lamb's account. What is more, these accounts often include the corollary, and show how resistance also exists within a dialectical relationship between the spaces of the colony and the metropole, something that is largely absent in Lamb's analysis.

Oscar Talbot

The consequences of infinity

Mohammad Reza Naderi, *Badiou, Infinity, and Subjectivity* (Lanham: Lexington Books, 2023). 350pp., $125 hb., 978 1 66693 104 4

It is likely that we have only seen the beginning of English-language scholarship on the work of French philosopher Alain Badiou. Though his work has been in circulation in the Anglophone world for close to thirty years, the third volume of his imposing systematic philosophy *Being and Event (The Immanence of Truths)* was only translated into English in 2022, and translations of his seminars continue to trickle in from Columbia University Press every couple of years. We are only just beginning to grasp the full picture of Badiou's thought.

Mohammad Reza Naderi's book, *Badiou, Infinity, and Subjectivity*, is a singular contribution to this project. It goes far beyond mere exposition – it unearths the at-times submerged coherence and the necessity of the various stages of Badiou's intellectual development, revealing the reasoning behind some of the claims and positions he stakes out in his mature philosophy that could otherwise appear arbitrary. But, as he does this, a new concept emerges as itself necessary for holding together Badiou's project – and not only that, but for understanding what thinking calls for now, as a consequence of Badiou's philosophy. This is the concept of *discipline*. Disciplines are areas of being – such as Badiou's four conditions for philosophy (love, science, art and politics) – marked out for thought through the use of axioms. They are underwritten ontologically by the axiom of infinity, meaning they can be infinitely stratified to both account for new 'events' in their thinking and overcome their own ideological impasses 'in interiority'. Axioms give disciplines their 'productive constraints' that allow them to think novelty while remaining within their disciplinary boundaries – and, if being is infinite according to the axiom, there is no 'natural' end to the thinking of a discipline; the resources in being for new thinking are properly endless. But this also means there is no proper beginning to thinking (or philosophy). Thus, with his theory of discipline, Naderi is making a strong claim about what form, in the wake of the event of the axiom of infinity and significantly informed by Badiou's theory, thinking must take.

Naderi's book has three parts. Part I addresses the debate between Badiou and Jacques-Alain Miller in the pages of *Cahiers pour L'Analyse* in the 1960s. Part II is an illuminating but extremely dense analysis of the early work *Theory of the Subject*, which entails a creative reworking of Hegel and Lacan that lays the groundwork for Badiou's mature understanding of the subject. Part III is focused on the consequences of infinity and axiomatic thinking for Badiou's conception of the subject, touching on *Being and Event*. This is also the section where Naderi coheres much of the previous work of excavation into his own constructive concept of discipline.

Naderi is untangling a knot of questions that Badiou's work addresses, the answers to which ultimately make up his mature philosophy. These include the question of the 'beginning' of philosophy, the relation between being and thought, and the possibility of thinking the new. But I want to say that, at the core of Badiou's system, there is a basic *political* question, which Naderi articulates as the stakes of even the seemingly arcane debate between Badiou and Miller that opens the book: 'What was at stake was a theory that could show how ordinary people could leave their places in society and form a collective agency together with a new, common objective'. This seems right to me, and it points to the fact that so much of what Badiou is doing through his 'red years' and into *Being and Event* is navigating between two poles: that of the metaphysical tradition of Plato, Descartes and Hegel, on the one hand, and that of structuralism, particularly the Lacanian variety, on the other. Naderi helpfully articulates the position Badiou feels the need to stake out as 'beyond metaphysics and *prior* to the concept of structure'. This is what so occupies him in *Theory of the Subject*, the analysis of which makes up the heart of Naderi's book. Badiou, as a disciple of Jean-Paul Sartre but a student of Louis Althusser, had no interest in returning to the sort of humanism Sartre (for some time) advocated, but he also could not tolerate the totalising structure of Althusser, which left little room for subjective action. (And getting beyond the latter was ultimately what led Badiou away from that stodgy Marxist-Leninism characteristic of the Parti Communiste Français and toward the more practical and effective politics of Maoism.) He sees in Lacan a structuralism for which the subject is not only an important element but positively essential and does not fall back on the traditional subject of metaphysics. But Badiou still sees a problem in how Lacan formulates the relation between the structure, or symbolic order, and the real.

The important thing is that for Lacan, the real is thought primarily in terms of the *inaccessible* – the traumatic, unsymbolisable region that also is the source or 'cause' of the structure itself. Lacan is trying to do the same thing Badiou wants to do – think what cannot be thought by the structure into the structure itself – but Badiou cannot accept Lacan's conclusion. Naderi articulates the difference between them as the difference between the real as cause (Lacan) versus the real as consistency (Badiou); for the former, the real constitutes the subject's limit, while for the latter the real is the support for subjective construction within a discipline. Whereas Lacan will turn that which is inaccessible to the structure retroactively into what causes it in the first place and establishes its dominance, Badiou (through Hegel) reads the structure and the real as mutually 'contaminating' forces, such that the real splits the structure – in a sense, converting the real as inaccessible into the real as indiscernible, a later Badiouan term. The real becomes a part of the structure as that which the structure does not already have a place for, and establishes a new role for the subject that is different from Lacan's. These indiscernible regions of the structure require decisions, which are the work of a subject. In the first part of the book, Naderi explains how Badiou established that disciplines are capable of being developed *in interiority* through subjective acts – the real that is the source of such acts is internal to the structure. In the second part, Naderi shows the historicity of structure means there is not one 'structure' and one 'real' – instead, there are many structures with reals local to them, with the real being that which has not yet been thought within the structure and the source of novelty internal to the structure.

Earlier, we pointed out three questions Naderi believes Badiou's philosophy is addressing, and which the theory of discipline becomes necessary to answer, before turning to the relation between structures and reals: the question of beginning in philosophy, the possibility of thinking the new, and the relation between being and thought. Badiou addresses the first question through axioms. Naderi believes Badiou's mature ontology is called forth by his implicit proof of the existence of at least two disciplines in his early work – science in the debate with Miller, and politics in *Theory of the Subject*. Ontology is the theory that can establish the condition and possibility of disciplines as such. But this necessarily entails questions of beginning – how does one begin a discipline? Axioms provide pragmatic tools for marking out existing regions of being for thought (disciplines) *and* give them a space within which to develop internally. It is similar to how rhyme and metre can be the very elements that enable the most interesting experiments in poetry. In this way, axioms allow Badiou to circumvent the problem of beginning – all thinking occurs *in medias res*, and axioms formalise that truth. While axioms establish how to begin, the axiom of infinity is what allows Badiou to address the thinking of novelty. If being is infinite, then each discipline is capable of infinitely stratifying itself in order to think new events that take place within it – including by coming up with new axioms. Finally, the subject is at the crux of the relation between being and thought. For Badiou, because he thinks of infinity mathematically rather than qualitatively, there is no region of being that is absolutely inaccessible to thinking – only provisionally so, until thinking gets 'big' enough to encompass a previously un-accessed region. The subject is precisely the operator that brings this previously unthought region of being to thought as the thought of the new. These three questions, and their answers, are all intertwined. The axiom of infinity retroactively makes axiomatic thinking itself a necessity, as there is nowhere to begin if being is infinite, and naturally, there are no consequences of the event of the axiom of infinity without the mathematical subject that thinks them. Behind the axiom of infinity and axiomatic thinking generally is Badiou's call, echoed by Naderi, to 'think maximally'. While it is at times difficult to tell if this is a normative or descriptive statement (do human beings naturally think maximally, or is thinking maximally an ethical imperative?) there is no doubt this impulse lies at the heart of Badiou's project.

Badiou, Infinity, and Subjectivity is a truly necessary work, the first since Peter Hallward's 2003 volume that attempts to articulate the internal logic of Badiou's thought. It is ultimately successful in showing the inner necessity of Badiou's at times shocking philosophical positions, and it convincingly argues for the necessity of a disciplinary mode of thinking if we are committed to thinking maximally. Though questions remain about the relation between discipline and philosophy – does discipline replace philosophy, or is it doing something different? – the more vexing aporias are those of Badiou's thought, and not Naderi's. For me, the primary one is the precise relation between the Ideas, including the axiom of infinity, and the local, earthy situations in which truths, according to Badiou, are actually created. In conversation with the author, we identified the unique challenge this poses in the context of the infinite. If infinity can only be posited axiomatically, 'from above', as it were, how is it that truths, which are a subjective work within a particular situation, through their universality in some sense 'touch' the infinite, as it seems there is no path to infinity from below? Naderi's conception of the composing and disposing of truths is an attempt at conceptualising this process. While there is no space to go into it here, more work needs to be done in this area. One can only hope Naderi's will be a prominent voice helping us to navigate Badiou's later work with the same rigour and inventiveness he exhibits in this book.

Joe Stapleton

Paulin Jidenu Hountondji, 1942–2024

Zeyad el Nabolsy

The history of African philosophy in the second half of the twentieth century cannot be told without invoking the spectre of ethnophilosophy and its nemesis, Paulin J. Hountondji.[1] Hountondji passed away in 2024, having left an indelible mark on the development of African philosophy as an academic field, both on the continent and beyond.

Hountondji was born in 1942 and was thus a teenager in 1960, the so-called 'year of Africa', during which seventeen African countries attained independence, including Hountondji's own country of Benin. As Hountondji tells us in his memoirs, *Combats Pour Le Sens: Un Itinéraire Africain*, his first encounter with philosophy was at the École Victor-Ballot in Porto-Novo, an educational institute for the future elite of Benin.[2] Hountondji's philosophy teacher, Hélène Marmotin, must have made an impression on the seventeen-year-old Hountondji for he still remembered the first lesson that she taught him: 'philosophy has to be learned'.[3] Philosophy, for Marmotin, was not a matter of innate talent or intellectual intuition, but hard work and scholarly earnestness: a lesson Hountondji would never forget. Hountondji went on to Paris and enrolled at the Lycée Henri-IV in 1960 to complete his *hypokhâgne-khâgne* – in preparation for entry to the École Normale Supérieure in Paris. The subject of his doctoral dissertation, under the supervision of Paul Ricoeur, was Husserl's conception of science as laid out in the *Logische Untersuchungen*.[4]

Yet Hountondji, despite successfully defending his dissertation in 1970, never published the results of his work on Husserl, feeling he would not be justified in writing primarily for a foreign audience, especially given the political turbulence of the 1960s on the African continent. Hountondji in his 1970 article, 'Remarques sur la philosophie africaine contemporaine', had already posed the questions which would exercise him for the rest of his life: for whom does the African philosopher write? And for whom ought the African philosopher write?[5] Even as a student he was deeply involved in political debates through *Présence Africaine*, under the editorial leadership of Alioune Diop. From the perspective of African philosophers, there was a demand, and indeed an unbearable pressure, to relate philosophical disputes to pressing questions of national independence. In 1970, Hountondji returned to the African continent as a professor in Zaire, and then in 1972 he became a professor at the National University of Benin in Cotonou. He later held positions as a visiting professor and researcher in different universities across Europe, while always remaining based in Benin. He participated in the democratic movement in 1990 which inaugurated the Republic of Benin; and served as Benin's Minister of Education (1990-1991) and as Minister of Culture (1991-1993).

Even though Hountondji never published the results of his doctoral research on Husserl, his encounter with Husserl crucially informed the project for which he is most famous: his critique of ethnophilosophy. Building on a series of articles in the late 1960s and 1970s, it eventually culminated in *Sur la 'Philosophie Africaine': Critique de l'ethnophilosophie*.[6] In this book, Hountondji criticised attempts at reconstructing a philosophical system through the ethnographic study of the 'worldview' of a particular African people. The entire debate was launched by the publication of Placide Tempels' *Bantu Philosophy* in 1945. In this book, the Belgian missionary, based on his missionary work amongst the Luba people in the south-central region of the Congo, purported to have discovered an implicit philosophical system based on a vital force ontology which, according to Tempels, was adhered to by all Africans who speak Bantu languages. According to Tempels, the Bantus believe that being is essentially force and that there is a hierarchy of beings or forces, and that hierarchical interactions between these forces explain observable phenomena. Tempels' book was celebrated by the circle around *Présence Africaine* – it was republished by the journal's publishing house in 1949 – and eminent African philosopher-statesmen such as Léopold Sédar Senghor, and it came to be seen as providing a model for work in African philosophy.[7] The dominance of this ethnographic approach in African philosophy in the 1960s is not surprising, since, in Europe, the study of African philosophy was essentially the prerogative of missionaries and anthropologists until the 1960s.[8]

Hountondji argued that such ethnographic projects are ill-conceived for a variety of reasons. First, the researcher almost always projects a philosophical discourse upon material, such as myths, which does not present itself as having any philosophical pretensions. Second, this ethnographic approach to 'discovering' African philosophies presupposes what Hountondji called the 'myth of primitive unanimity',[9] according to which, in African societies, there is no dissent and everybody essentially agrees with everyone else. Third, this discourse involves implicitly, and sometimes explicitly, a search for an essential difference in kind between African peoples and 'Western' peoples. The positing of an essential difference in kind between Africans and non-Africans was the basis of justifications of colonial rule on the African continent.[10] We can therefore understand Hountondji's suspicion of any discourse that takes reified differences between Africans and non-Africans for granted.

The fourth criticism which Hountondji levelled at ethnophilosophy is perhaps the most important, since it constitutes a thread running through his life's work, starting from his anguish over having to write primarily for a foreign audience as a Husserl scholar. Hountondji argued that the most debilitating limitation of ethnophilosophy is that it is fundamentally directed towards a non-African audience. For Hountondji, ethnophilosophy is essentially a performance that is put on in order to satisfy an 'Other' who occupies a position of power vis-a-vis the performers. Hountondji thought that the other faults of ethnophilosophy essentially stem from this 'extraversion', i.e. the fact of being directed towards an external audience. Extraversion is what explains the overemphasis on African originality: 'the quest for originality is always bound up with a desire to show off. It has meaning only in relation to the Other [*l'Autre*], from whom one wishes to distinguish oneself at all costs. This is an ambiguous relationship, inasmuch as the assertion of one's difference goes hand in hand with a passionate urge to have it recognized by the Other".[11]

According to Hountondji, this assertion of difference was encouraged by the 'Other', former colonising powers, especially when the assertion of cultural difference and cultural authenticity was used to mask political and economic dependency. Hountondji's suspicion of any discourse of cultural authenticity was reinforced by his experiences in Mobutu's Zaire. Starting in 1971, Mobutu launched a discourse of authenticity. While engaging in anti-Western posturing, Mobutu supported US interventions in Angola, and established trade ties with apartheid South Africa.[12] It is no surprise, then, that Hountondji was very suspicious of culturalist discourses of authenticity, which, as experience had shown him, were quite compatible with subservience at the political and economic level.

There is indeed a Husserlian strain in Hountondji's critique of ethnophilosophy. It is clear that Husserl's distinction between philosophy proper as a strict science [*als strenge Wissenschaft*] and pseudo-philosophy, i.e. philosophy as mere wisdom or a worldview [*Weltanschauung*], influenced Hountondji's rejection of ethnophilosophy. One important feature of Husserl's account of philosophy *als strenge Wissenschaft* is that it must be explicitly presented in argumentative form with a clear distinction between premises and the conclusion which is taken to follow from them. There cannot be an implicit philosophy as a strict science, for its hallmark is conceptual clarity and a determinate logical organisation. Thus, on this view, a given people's worldview cannot, by definition, amount to philosophy proper, i.e. philosophy as a strict science. Moreover, Hountondji claimed that philosophy proper, insofar as it requires the clear and explicit presentation of arguments, requires literacy. Hence, there cannot be a philosophy, as a strict science, that is conveyed through oral traditions. It is worth remarking here that while Hountondji was primarily focused on African philosophy, his critique of ethnophilosophy remains relevant to contemporary discussions about Indigenous philosophy in the Americas.[13]

The ethnophilosophers, from Hountondji's Husserlian perspective, were guilty of equivocation regarding the word 'philosophy'. Not only that, but they were also guilty of another unforgivable sin in Hountondji's eyes; they were guilty of contempt for Africans. They wrote as if a mere worldview is good enough for Africans as far as philosophy goes. Hountondji thought that what appears as a gesture of generosity on the part of the likes of Tempels was really a gesture expressing contempt. The idea that one must lower one's standards when it comes to Africa was particularly loathsome to Hountondji, who would return to this problem in his later writings on scientific dependency.

It is also evident that Husserl's modernist attitude in relation to the relentless demand for rational justification, and the suspicion of whatever is inherited from the past, is carried forward towards an emancipatory project in Hountondji's own work. Hountondji would doubtless agree with Husserl that all received traditions and prejudices must be treated with suspicion by the philosopher.[14] In other words, philosophy proper presupposes individual autonomy. This Cartesian aspect of Husserl's project appealed to Hountondji, who was, above all, concerned with establishing the necessity of the individual autonomy of the thinker. That is, Hountondji sought to demonstrate that anybody who wishes to see African philosophy flourish must also work towards the institutionalisation of guarantees for individual autonomy. Only a fully autonomous subject can dare to attempt a project as bold as Descartes' or Husserl's. Hountondji was very clear about the political stakes in his critique of ethnophilosophy. He saw himself as defending the autonomy of the individual which he thought is a necessary condition for the development of a rigorous philosophical discourse. He would emphasise this point again in the 1980s in a series of articles, especially in his 1982 article 'Occidentalisme, élitisme: Réponse à deux critiques'.[15] In this article, he indicated that there was a political motivation behind his critique of ethnophilosophy insofar as he thought it was a cover for the ideology of group domination which sought to crush individual freedom.[16]

Hountondji's concern for the autonomy of the individual did not make him a liberal philosopher. In fact, Hountondji's work is deeply marked by his encounter with Marxism as articulated by Louis Althusser. Hountondji attended Althusser's seminar on *Capital* as well as Althusser's lectures on 'Philosophy for Scientists'. Hountondji, in his memoir, claims that he was deeply influenced by Althusser's contention that philosophy as a theory of science should cease to pretend to have a foundationalist project with respect to the sciences. Instead, philosophy should take as its task the retrospective description and systematisation of the real procedures of the sciences. Here we can see that the influence of Althusser and Husserl pulled Hountondji in opposite directions.[17] From Althusser, Hountondji also adopted a historical materialist approach to the history of philosophy and history of science which he would retain for the rest of his life.[18] According to this approach, the history of philosophy is parasitic on the history of science, which in turn is parasitic on the history of technology as well as economic and social history. Thus, the history of philosophy cannot be explained independently of wider socio-historical developments. In the parlance of contemporary discourse about the historiography of philosophy, we could say that Hountondji was an externalist.[19]

Hountondji applied this approach to the history of African philosophy. Aside from showing the limitations of ethnophilosophy as an approach to African philosophy, he also attempted to explain why so many African philosophers and leaders, such as Senghor, found it appealing at this particular historical juncture. Hountondji argued that ethnophilosophy was itself a by-product of underdevelopment and a weak post-colonial petty bourgeoisie that is incapable of carrying out an economic and political struggle for real independence, and which therefore seeks to transform the struggle for real independence into an exclusively cultural struggle centred on assertions of cultural authenticity and difference.

From Marxism, Hountondji also took on a deflationary view of philosophy. Hountondji in an important article published in 1981, 'Que Peut la Philosophie?',[20] would turn to Marx and Engels' critique of Left Hegelianism to criticise those who thought that Africa's salvation is to be had through philosophy. Doubtless, Hountondji thought that philosophy can play an important role in the transformation of African societies but only if it gives up on its delusions of autonomy vis-à-vis the first order sciences and social reality. Hountondji remarked that many look to philosophy 'for miracles. They require of philosophy to solve all problems: metaphysical problems of the existence of God, of the nature of man, of life after death, etc. Political problems, economic, social, of ways and means of national liberation, of the emancipation of the exploited masses, briefly, of revolution'.[21] Philosophy, according to Hountondji, cannot do any of these things. At most, philosophy can clarify to us certain key concepts, but it cannot do more. To do more we have to 'get out of philosophy'.[22] One also suspects that, in adopting this deflationary approach to philosophy, Hountondji was trying to protect the autonomy of African philosophy from incessant pressures to contribute directly to political and social movements. We could say that Hountondji was attempting to demonstrate that philosophy is not, in fact, too important to be left to the professional philosophers.

As a philosopher who believed that philosophy is parasitic on first-order scientific discourse, it is no surprise that Hountondji would concern himself with the fate of the empirical sciences on the African continent in the 1990s and the first two decades of the 2000s. It is unfortunate that this aspect of his work has not received the same level of attention as his more well-known critique of ethnophilosophy. For arguably it is in these writings that Hountondji really showed us what it means to 'get out of philosophy' without entirely abandoning philosophy. For example, in his 1990 article 'Scientific Dependency in Africa Today', Hountondji drew on philosophy of science, history, sociology of knowledge and dependency theory, as articulated by Samir Amin, to present an account of the nature and causes of scientific dependency on the African continent.[23] Among the indices of dependency that he discusses is the fact that African scientists write primarily for an audience situated in the Global North and they work in research paradigms that have been mostly developed in the Global North. Here we see the spectre of extraversion rearing its head again.

Hountondji never really developed a fully worked out account of how Africans can overcome scientific dependency. However, he did recognise that it would require a clarification of the relationship between what he called 'endogenous knowledge' on the one hand and modern science on the other hand. Hountondji's attitude towards endogenous knowledge was neither celebratory nor dismissive. Instead, he thought that what one must do is test the claims that are made by the practitioners of endogenous medicine, rainmakers, astronomers, and so on, using the methods of hypothesis testing that are deployed in the modern empirical sciences. It is only after having passed through these tests that these claims to knowledge can acquire the epistemic warrant that is necessary for becoming scientific knowledge properly so-called. Hountondji was quite hostile to purely descriptive approaches to the ethnosciences which sought to record endogenous claims to knowledge without testing them. Hountondji attempted to develop a different approach to the ethnosciences that would be concerned with questions of truth-value and justification as opposed to the discovery of mere intellectual curiosities. One important outcome was the volume he edited, *Les savoirs endogènes: Pistes pour une recherche*, where Hountondji lays out in the introduction some of the central concerns that animated his research agenda for the last two decades.[24]

Hountondji has been accused of both mindless servility towards the 'West' (a category that Hountondji himself was not keen on),[25] as well as adopting a dogmatic rejectionist stance towards modern science.[26] Some of his critics never quite understood that his concern for the development of an autonomous modern scientific discourse on the African continent was not the product of servility towards the Global North but rather was animated by the desire to overcome such servility which today, we must all admit, stands simply as a *fait accompli*. It is all very well to declaim against colonialism and neo-colonialism on the African continent, but these declamations ring hollow when one has to stand in line, hat in hand, waiting for crumbs. It makes little difference whether these crumbs take the form of vaccines, military equipment, loans or cash aid. Perhaps Hountondji's most valuable insight for us today is that any emancipative discourse in African philosophy must start out from the concrete material fact of dependency and domination and eschew any Left-Hegelian temptation to convert material subordination to a purely philosophical issue which is to be resolved, as if by magic, by decolonising the mind.

Zeyad el Nabolsy is Assistant Professor of Philosophy at York University.

Notes

1. Parts of this text draw upon and are informed by the author's recently published book, *Paulin Hountondji and the Science Question in Africa* (New York: Springer, 2025).
2. Paulin Hountondji, *Combats Pour Le Sens: Un Itinéraire Africain* (Cotonou: Editions du Flamboyant, 1997). English translation: *The Struggle for Meaning: Reflections on*

Philosophy, Culture, and Democracy in Africa, trans. John Conteh-Morgan (Athens, Ohio: Ohio University Press, 2002).

3. Hountondji, *The Struggle for Meaning*, 3.

4. Paulin Hountondji, 'Why Husserl in Africa? Autobiographical Reflections', in *Phenomenology in an African Context: Contributions and Challenges*, eds. Abraham Oliver, M. John Lamola and Justin Sands (Albany: SUNY Press, 2023), 63–77.

5. Paulin Hountondji, 'Remarques sur la philosophie africaine contemporaine', *Diogène* 71 (1970), 120–140. This article would later be republished as the first chapter of *Sur la 'Philosophie Africaine'*.

6. Paulin Hountondji, *Sur la 'Philosophie Africaine': Critique de l'ethnophilosophie* (Paris: François Maspero, 1977). English translation: *African Philosophy: Myth and Reality* (2nd Ed.), trans. Henri Evans with the Collaboration of Jonathan Rée (Bloomington: Indiana University Press, 1996).

7. Léopold Sédar Senghor, *Prose and Poetry*, trans. John Reed and Clive Wake (Ibadan: Oxford University Press, 1965), 36.

8. Valentin Y. Mudimbe, *The Invention of Africa: Gnosis, Philosophy, and the Order of Knowledge* (Bloomington: Indiana University Press, 1988), 154.

9. Hountondji, *African Philosophy*, 60.

10. See Mahmood Mamdani, *Define and Rule: Native as Political Identity* (Kampala: Makerere Institute of Social Research, 2013).

11. Hountondji, *African Philosophy*, 44.

12. Winsome J. Leslie, *Zaire: Continuity and Political Change in an Oppressive State* (London: Routledge, 2019 [1993]), 151–159.

13. See for example the discussion about the distinction between philosophical sources and philosophical texts in Jorge Sanchez-Perez, 'Beyond Gatekeeping: Philosophical Sources, Indigenous Philosophy, and the Huarochirí Manuscript', *Metaphilosophy* 55:3 (2024), 365–280, as well as the discussion about the seeming absence of explicit argumentation in Aztec philosophy in Robert Eli Sanchez Jr., 'Review of *Aztec Philosophy: A World in Motion* by James Maffie', *Notre Dame Philosophical Reviews* (2014), https://ndpr.nd.edu/reviews/aztec-philosophy-understanding-a-world-in-motion/

14. Among these traditions and prejudices is Eurocentrism, which Husserl himself fell victim to. For a compelling Hountondjian critique of Husserl on this point, see Carmen De Schryver, 'Philosophical Universality in Crisis: Hountondji's Interruption of Phenomenology', in *Phenomenology in an African Context: Contributions and Challenges*, eds. Abraham Oliver, M. John Lamola and Justin Sands (Albany: SUNY Press, 2023), 99–124.

15. Paulin Hountondji, 'Occidentalisme, élitisme: Réponse à deux critiques', *Recherche, pédagogie et culture* 56 (1982): 58–67. English translation: 'Occidentalism, Elitism: Answer to Two Critiques', *Quest: An African Journal of Philosophy* 3:2 (1989), 3–30.

16. For a helpful account of Hountondji's conception of pluralism, see Thomas McGlone, Jr., '"No Less Than a Complete Revolution": On Paulin J. Hountondji's Negative Pluralism', *Symposium* 26:1/2 (2022), 242–259.

17. For a detailed account of this problem, see Zeyad El Nabolsy, 'Paulin J. Hountondji on Philosophy, Science, and Technology: From Husserl and Althusser to a Synthesis of the Hessen-Grossmann Thesis and Dependency Theory', in *Africana Studies: Theoretical Futures*, ed. Grant Farred (Philadelphia: Temple University Press, 2022), 34–64.

18. Hountondji, *African Philosophy*, 97.

19. For an example of the externalist approach, see Joseph M. Bryant, *Moral Codes and Social Structures in Ancient Greece: A Sociology of Greek Ethics from Homer to the Epicureans and Stoics* (Albany: SUNY Press, 1996).

20. Paulin Hountondji, 'Que Peut la Philosophie?', *Présence Africaine* 119 (1981): 47–71. See also the English translation: 'What Philosophy Can Do', *Quest: An African Journal of Philosophy* 1:2 (1987): 2–29.

21. Hountondji, 'What Philosophy Can Do', 8.

22. Hountondji, 'What Philosophy Can Do', 13.

23. Paulin Hountondji, 'Scientific Dependence in Africa Today', *Research in African Literatures* 21:3 (1990), 5–15.

24. Paulin Hountondji, ed., *Les savoirs endogenes: Pistes pour une recherche* (Paris: Éditions Karthala, 1994). English translation: *Endogenous Knowledge: Research Trails* (Dakar: CODESRIA, 1997).

25. Samuel Oluoch Imbo. *An Introduction to African Philosophy* (Lanham, Maryland: Rowman & Littlefield, 1998), 88.

26. George L. Simpson Jr., 'Review of *Endogenous Knowledge: Research Trails*', *The International Journal of African Historical Studies* 32:2/3 (1999), 565–567.

www.ingramcontent.com/pod-product-compliance
Lightning Source LLC
Chambersburg PA
CBHW080239040426
42333CB00046BA/2470